ROBERT SERVICE

Robert Service ca. 1905.

ROBERT SERVICE

UNDER
the
Spell
of the
YUKON

Enid Mallory
FOREWORD BY JACK WHYTE

VICTORIA • VANCOUVER • CALGARY

Heritage House Publishing Company Ltd.
#108 – 17665 66A Avenue
Surrey, BC V3S 2A7
www.heritagehouse.ca

Heritage House Publishing Company Ltd.
PO Box 468
Custer, WA
98240-0468

Library and Archives Canada Cataloguing in Publication
Mallory, Enid, 1938–
    Robert Service: under the spell of the Yukon / Enid Mallory. — 1st ed.
Includes bibliographical references and index.

ISBN-13: 978-1-894384-95-7; ISBN-10: 1-894384-95-4
    1. Service, Robert W., 1874–1958. 2. Poets, Canadian (English)—20th century—Biography. I. Title.
PS8537.E78Z75 2006 C811'.52   C2006-905049-X

Library of Congress Control Number: 2006934920

Edited by Jonathan Dore
Proofread by Marial Shea
Cover design by Roberta Batchelor/r-House Design
Cover photo courtesy of Yukon Archives
Maps by Darlene Nickull

Printed in Canada

Heritage House acknowledges the financial support for its publishing program from the Government of Canada through the Book Publishing Industry Development Program (BPIDP), Canada Council for the Arts, and the province of British Columbia through the British Columbia Arts Council and the Book Publishing Tax Credit.

The Canada Council | Le Conseil des Arts
for the Arts | du Canada

BRITISH COLUMBIA
ARTS COUNCIL
Supported by the Province of British Columbia

This book has been produced on 100% post-consumer recycled paper, processed chlorine free and printed with vegetable-based inks.

contents

To Gord, who always shares the quest

acknowledgements

Among those who supplied facts or directed me to new material, who supplied pictures or led discovery trips, I am especially indebted to Marguerite Service and Beatrice Corbett. Others whose help is much appreciated include Elizabeth Rowley, Dorothy Sugden, Nicholas Sugden, Flo Whyard, Tracie Harris, Alvin McGee, Doreen Nelson, Beverly Gramms, Richard Egolf, Joyce Egolf, Ruth Fritz, Ellen Clutton, Alice Boyes, Frances MacLeod and Shelagh Wotherspoon.

A special thanks to editors Jonathan Dore and Vivian Sinclair for their diligence and sense of direction and to publisher Rodger Touchie for wanting to tell the story.

foreword

Robert W. Service first came into my life in my early boyhood in Scotland, in the approaching winter of 1946, when the local County Council finally got around to repairing the damage done by convoys of heavy tanks as they rattled and roared along the main road in front of our house at the end of the war. I lived in a garrison town, filled with Allied soldiers, but it was those tanks, and the damage their steel treads did to our road, that brought Mickey Canaa—and, through him, Service—into my life for a brief but unforgettable time.

Mickey, a veteran of the Irish Fusiliers in the First World War, was the night watchman set to guard the roadworks and prevent people from falling into the deep ditch dug to hold the new water mains. The start of his shift at nightfall was the signal for me and three or four of the other neighborhood kids to approach a kind of terrifying heaven, for Mickey was a master storyteller, specializing in tales of banshees and other supernatural Irish phenomena, and there was nothing he loved better, to while away the early hours of his shift, than to frighten the wits out of an appreciative audience of wide-eyed boys. We would crowd into his tiny hut, lit only by a single lantern and the radiant glow of his coal-burning brazier, and he would feed us sweet, strong tea brewed in an open can on top of the coals and tell us of things that howled and went *bump* in the night, so that we were frequently too frightened to go home alone, despite the fact that none of us lived more than a hundred yards from his hut.

On one magical night, however, and I have no idea what prompted the departure from his usual routine, he recited "The Shooting Of Dan McGrew" for us, and he was magnificent. His delivery was word-perfect and flawless and I had never heard anything like it, the proof of being the fact that I still have a rush of goose flesh every time I remember it. Mickey Canaa, whom my grandmother called an old reprobate, changed my life and taught me the power of the spoken word, kindling a passion in me that has never gone out. A few nights later, tickled by my insistence on hearing more and my obvious enjoyment of his earlier performance, he treated us to "The Cremation of Sam McGee" and several other Service poems, and I was never free, after that, of the spell of the Yukon.

I didn't grow any closer to old Mickey—he was a pensioner then and I was six years old—so I never discovered where he had learned those poems, but I can clearly remember him saying, "I met the fellow once, in France, during the Real War, and so I bought his book." He must have been referring to *Songs of a Sourdough*.

In school, in the years that followed, I found more of Service's poems, and those of his coequals, Rudyard Kipling and the Australian Banjo Paterson, and I devoured them all, relishing the driving narrative rhythms of their work and loving the way their words rolled off the tongue, demanding to be articulated with clarity, precision and passion. Those poems and others like them, the great narrative poems of empire and conquest, have fallen from favor and into oblivion nowadays, but they were the morality tales on which I cut my storytelling teeth. Each one of them had a lesson to teach and a message to impart, and each one made an indelible moral impression on the mind of everyone who heard it properly delivered. But I had no idea, back then, that the literary world was changing and that the days of teaching and learning and loving narrative poetry were numbered. T.S. Eliot had long since written "The Waste Land," and people like W.H. Auden, Ezra Pound and e.e. cummings had already changed the structure of English poetry forever. Narrative verse was about to fall into a limbo of indifference and sneering disdain, and literary pretentiousness would soon consign it to the garbage can of history. Thank God no one ever got around to telling me that back then, and thank Him, too, that I was educated in an old-fashioned, classics-oriented school for boys, because by the time I became aware that narrative verse had been excommunicated from the canon, I was far too dyed-in-the-wool to accept such an atrocious proposition.

Ever since I began to write, and long before I thought of writing novels, I have written and performed narrative verse, and the shade of Robert Service inhabits much of my work. For me and for countless others, he has always been a shining light, his work embodying the truth that there is no stronger vehicle for interpersonal communication than the commanding voice of a passionate storyteller who understands how the rhythm and tempo of life, and of life's most memorable events, can carry straight from his mind and voice to affect and influence the individual souls of his audience. Skilful rhyme is a potent persuader, and when it is reinforced by an instinctual understanding of classical rhetoric and the rhythms and cadences of the human voice, its influence increases dramatically, and therein lies the reason why narrative verse remains alive and well today among ordinary people everywhere. But how many North Americans, one wonders, have ever thought to regard Gordon Lightfoot or Bob Dylan as natural successors to Service? And how many older folk have ever stopped to consider that the despised and driving rap so prevalent today might arguably be presented as a natural extension of narrative verse? It is no accident that country music remains the broadest, fastest-growing and most successful form of popular music in North America today, just as it is no accident that Service's works continue to be published and sold in large numbers. Both are narrative verse, and both communicate clearly and succinctly at a level that ordinary people can identify with and understand.

That said, however, I have always felt slightly nonplused in reading the biographies and the literary commentaries on Service's work, because to me they have always seemed picayune, slightly carping and inelegantly ponderous in seeking resonances within his day-to-day life to explain the quality and the enduring popularity of his poetry. Who really needs to seek underlying and deep-running motivations for genius? It's either there or it isn't, and to my way of thinking, motivation has little to do with it. Genius, like murder, will out.

The reason for the biographers' fascination with Service becomes obvious, nevertheless, when one acknowledges the inexplicable and mysterious elements of the man and the poet, because although he was prolific when it came to his poetry and fictional writings, he was evasive to the point of opacity on matters relating to his personal life. Close to 40 years elapsed between the creation of the ballads featuring Dan McGrew and Sam McGee and his eventual, reluctant consent to write his memoirs.

In two separate volumes, *Ploughman of the Moon: An Adventure into Memory* (1945) and *Harper of Heaven: A Further Adventure into Memory* (1948), Service compiled a blend of lucid insights and mysterious vagaries that left fans, critics and scholars confused for the next half-century. Most curious were his omissions, minimal reference to family, aliases for many of his acquaintances over the years and stories of his Yukon years that sometimes defied the calendar. It is precisely this kind of inconsistency that causes moaning and wailing and gnashing of teeth among biographers, but among avid fans like me, such idiosyncrasy is to be tolerated and even expected from time to time.

My personal world would be a different and darker place had I never experienced the thrill of visualizing and imagining the spell of the Yukon, and for that I will remain eternally grateful to Mr. Service, and my cup runneth over each time I listen to his voice, transcribed onto a precious audiotape for me by a friend, reciting his own words on an old and broken glass-disc recording he made at a CBC station in B.C. some time in the late 1940s.

My hope is that this new book, in addition to illuminating the poet's life more clearly, will galvanize and inspire new readers to discover the magic that Service wrought, and wrote, so brilliantly, and that it will move even aficionados to go back and recapture the spell of the Yukon that transfixed them years ago.

Jack Whyte
Kelowna
August 2006

introduction

The purpose of any biography is to shed new light on a person who in some way has touched the lives of others. In Robert Service's case, his poetry has touched the lives of millions of North Americans in his and succeeding generations. Although it is 100 years since the would-be poet wrote "The Cremation of Sam McGee" in a bank building in Whitehorse, Yukon, almost every adult over the age of 40 in Canada and Alaska, and a large following of fans in the continental United States and Great Britain, carry the first lines of the ballad around in their heads:

> *There are strange things done in the midnight sun*
> *By the men who moil for gold;*
> *The Arctic trails have their secret tales*
> *That would make your blood run cold;*
> *The Northern Lights have seen queer sights,*
> *But the queerest they ever did see*
> *Was that night on the marge of Lake Lebarge*
> *I cremated Sam McGee.*

Robert Service arrived in Canada from Scotland in 1896 and spent seven years as a west-coast vagabond, wandering from British Columbia to California and Mexico, doing odd jobs en route to sustain himself. Back in B.C., he worked on Vancouver Island as a cowhand and country-store clerk before getting a job in Victoria with the Bank of Commerce, which eventually led to a posting at the Whitehorse branch in the Yukon. There, the publication of *Songs of a Sourdough* made him an overnight sensation and lifted him from poverty to riches.

Service was reticent about his personal life, but new light has been shed in recent years from several sides. From his younger brother Stanley, who wanted to publish a book himself "to set the record straight." From his brother Peter, who had the family Bible and Robert's tiny typewriter (returned to Dawson City in 2005 by Peter's daughter-in-law, Marguerite). From personal letters kept by the daughter of Vancouver's first mayor, which reveal the ecstasy and anguish of young love.

Service's sketchy autobiography *Ploughman of the Moon* is our primary source of information about his first, unsettled years in Canada. Few people knew him well in his wandering years; a rolling stone leaves only a faint imprint. We can, however, read between the lines of his self-told story to see a solitary young man who was sometimes very melancholy and sometimes incredibly happy.

As he explored Seattle and San Francisco and Los Angeles, he stored the color and vivacity of these cities in his mind to feed his imagination later. As he discovered the natural wonders of the deserts of the American southwest, he tasted complete freedom and complete solitude, and stored that knowledge too.

For his years in the Yukon, by contrast, we have a plethora of people who knew—or claimed to have known—Robert Service. A whole crowd of them claim to have shared a cabin with him; others, such as Judge Wickersham, reported meeting him in Dawson City several years before he went there. But there were others, like Laura Berton, Martha Black, T.V. Fleming and Hiram Cody, who really did know Service, and left anecdotes that help us understand him.

Whitehorse friends recalled seeing him wandering the trails above Miles Canyon, seemingly in a world of his own. Not until the publication of *Songs of a Sourdough* would they have some idea of what went on in his head on those solitary walks above the powerful, dramatic Yukon River. Dawson friends who remembered him on the A.C. Trail leading to the Midnight Dome already knew it was poetry that seethed in his head.

After the publication of *Ballads of a Cheechako* and *The Trail of '98,* Robert spent the early months of 1911 with his family, who had immigrated to Canada 10 years after him and settled in Alberta. His brother Stanley, a teenager on the farm, leaves us a picture of the famous and puzzling brother who appeared suddenly in their midst.

In the spring Robert headed to Dawson the hard way, via the Edmonton route. He traveled down the Mackenzie River with northern explorer George Douglas, whose book *Lands Forlorn* lets us see Robert en route. Meanwhile, in *Rhymes of a Rolling Stone,* Robert gives us glimpses of Douglas and the other memorable characters through whom he portrays the deadly attraction of the Mackenzie territory.

In 1912 Robert left the Yukon and the following year settled in France, where he married Germaine Bourgoin. All too soon we see him as a Red Cross driver in the awful scenes of the First World War. We glimpse him through other Canadians who met him there, we see him in the articles he wrote for the *Toronto Star Weekly,* and finally through his *Rhymes of a Red Cross Man,* acclaimed by some at the time as the best poetry of the war.

In the Second World War Robert and his family returned to North America to escape the German occupation of France. Canadians welcomed him with delight, and ex-Yukoners in Vancouver were thrilled to have him live among them again. In Los Angeles a writers' group discovered him spending his winters there and the media celebrated his presence, while Metro-Goldwyn Mayer put him in a movie and the U.S. Army made him an entertainer for their troops. And his publisher, Dodd Mead, talked him into writing his autobiography.

When the war was over he returned to France, but visited North America once more, when he attended the International Sourdough Convention in Vancouver in 1948. By now many of the stampeders were walking down the trail of old age. Robert entertained them with poetic memories that brought tears to their eyes.

He himself lived to the age of 84, wrote a thousand poems (and six novels) and made a million dollars. More than this, the youth who often portrayed himself a misfit and a failure achieved the freedom to write, as well as lifelong love and great happiness, and remained young at heart all the days of his life.

This new look at his life, with emphasis on his years of adventure in North America, follows him from early doubt and despair to "radiant living," a journey of inspiration for young and old.

Part 1

Toward the *Yukon*

"To see the ordinary with eyes of marvel may be a gift or it may be there is no ordinary and wonder is true vision."

Ploughman of the Moon

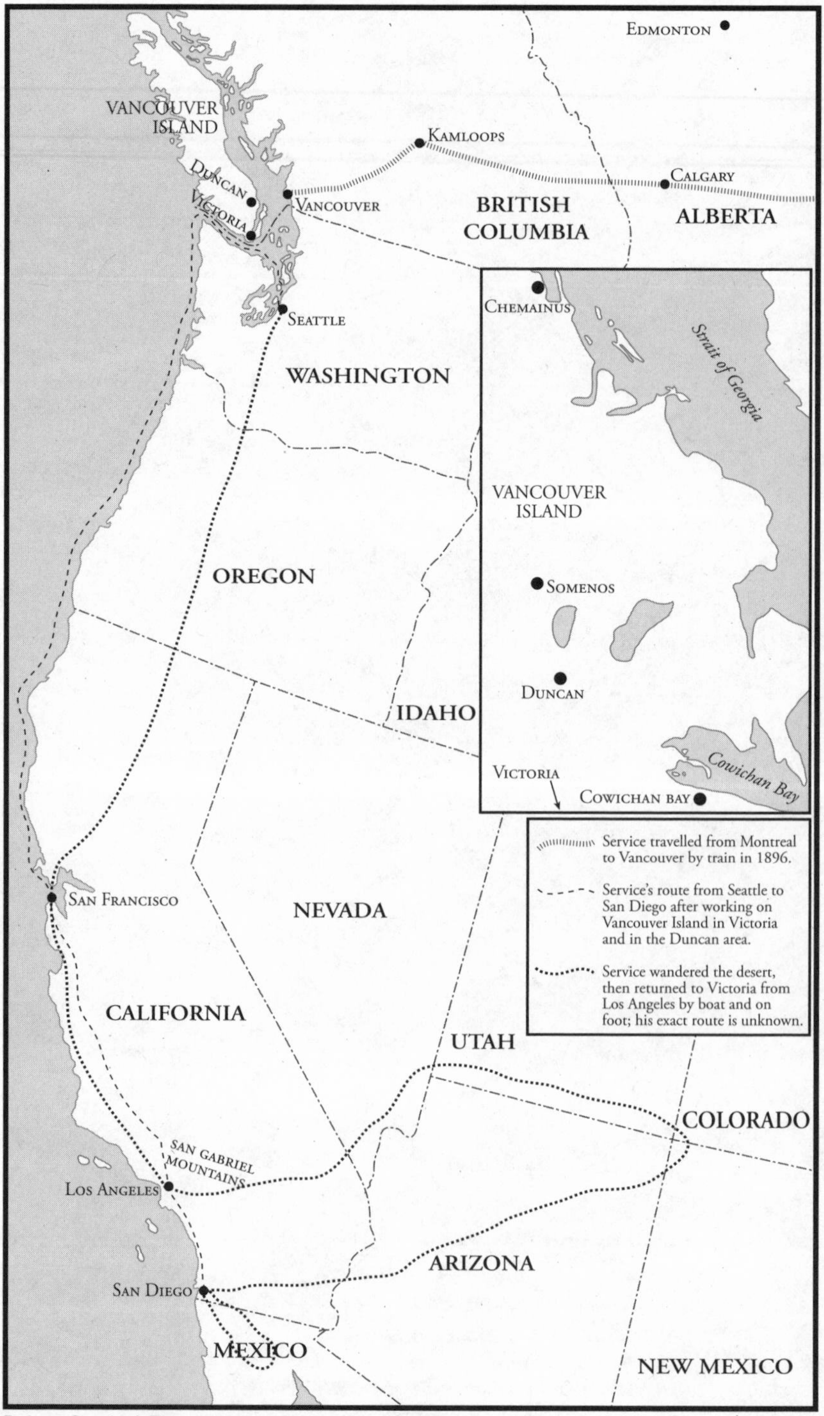

Edmonton
Vancouver Island
Kamloops
Calgary
Duncan
Vancouver
Victoria
British Columbia
Alberta
Seattle
Washington
Oregon
Idaho
Nevada
California
Utah
Colorado
San Francisco
San Gabriel Mountains
Los Angeles
Arizona
San Diego
Mexico
New Mexico
Chemainus
Strait of Georgia
Vancouver Island
Somenos
Duncan
Victoria
Cowichan Bay
Service travelled from Montreal to Vancouver by train in 1896.
Service's route from Seattle to San Diego after working on Vancouver Island in Victoria and in the Duncan area.
Service wandered the desert, then returned to Victoria from Los Angeles by boat and on foot; his exact route is unknown.

Robert Service's Travels in the West, 1896–1904

chapter 1

In the spring of 1896 a young man is riding in one of the "colonist" cars of a train traveling across Canada, not sure where he is heading. He is a small man with a sober face, high cheekbones, bright blue eyes and a ruddy complexion. He has sailed from Scotland on the SS Concordia, *a tramp steamer whose main cargo was sheep, cattle and horses. It brought him up the St. Lawrence to Montreal, where he hopped straight onto the train headed west.*

He is full of wonder and foolishness. After a night of sleeping on the luggage rack, reveling in the discomfort of it all, he has changed his costume in the toilet, emerging as Buffalo Bill, complete with high boots and a sombrero—an outfit his father bought at an auction in Glasgow. Now he feels equal to any occasion. Robert Service is alone on his adventure. He is 22 years old, in love with life and already in love with Canada, which he finds "gloriously empty."

In Scotland Robert had worked in a bank from the age of 14 until he set out on his grand adventure, armed with a pocket copy of Robert Louis Stevenson's *The Amateur Emigrant*. Getting to Canada took all the savings he had accumulated in his young life, so he headed across the continent with just five dollars in his pocket. Along the way he sold his Gladstone bag, his Harris tweed suit, his gun and his camera. To make money he needed to get himself off the train and find work, but he decided the prairie was too flat and the work looked too hard. In spite of his cowboy outfit he let Alberta slide past the train window too and, "in a spirit of irresponsibility," crossed the Rockies in a state of wonder and joy.

Canada seen by train is still a wonder today, still special in an era of airplanes and space travel. In 1896 the transcontinental was only 11 years old. No line of comparable grandeur or difficulty of construction existed anywhere in the world; the Canadian Pacific Railway's long thin line, which eventually stretched 3,630 miles from Halifax on the Atlantic to Vancouver on the Pacific, was literally creating a nation out of a wilderness.

The trip across the Dominion was a landmark experience for Robert, as it was for the thousands who would pioneer each year in the Canadian west. First came the settled farms along the St. Lawrence valley, then the long northern route around the immense lakes Huron and Superior. Limestone gave way to granite, colored now in pink and pale grey. And the trees! Immense pine at first (these had been used by the British navy for masts, thought Robert). Then the skinny conifers with a knob of branches on top, which a conductor told him were black spruce. Animals, briefly glimpsed, were all new to him—moose, bear and fox. Once, an eagle flew beside his window. He was up at the first light of dawn, watching the sinuous curve of the passenger cars as the engine pulled them around the edge of a lake or plunged into unbroken forest; he was hungry for more of this land, overwhelmed by its vastness, puzzled that his traveling companions did not share his ecstasy. Most of them were immigrants like himself, but unlike Robert, they were grumbling about the slow progress of the train. Mixed with exhilaration about their "promised" land was an undercurrent of dread. What lay ahead? What would appear around the bend? Robert tried to understand their mood, comparing it to his own and wondering who was right. Was he gifted to see with "eyes of marvel," or was nothing, in fact, ordinary—was seeing with eyes of wonder the "true vision"?

Blue lakes beckoned to him and he longed to live on one with a rod, a gun and a canoe. " ... Thoreau and Borrow fought in me, the one to make me live by a lake, the other to urge me to ramble on."[1]

After Winnipeg, the rocks were gone, the hills were flattened, and trees were wiped off the canvas. Robert saw mile after mile of emptiness, flat or rolling land reaching to sky—the Canadian prairie. Then, after more than 800 miles, the prairie quite suddenly ended, and now mountain rivers rushed along beside the train, ramparts crowding it on either side, and grand soaring snow-capped peaks stood high on all horizons. "Here was something greater than my imagination had ever conceived."[2]

As the train rolled on Robert knew that this was what he had always wanted: to be moving, to be swept along in a sensory perfection of changing scenes, to be a rolling stone, a person going somewhere—or perhaps a person running away. Maybe he would never be this happy again: alone, penniless and insecure, but excited almost to a state of worship, alert and aware far more than his fellow passengers were.

It was only when they left the mountains and sped through forest to reach the sea at Vancouver that reality began to kick in for Robert and fear began to rear its anxious head. What he feared most was work.

All his life Service would hate physical work. When his father had found him a place in the bank in Scotland, he had agreed because it seemed physically the easiest job that someone without a university education could hope to attain. Now here he was, alone, already divested of his few possessions, arriving at the end of the line, his taste of freedom and wanderlust too brief. If he wanted to eat, he would have to work.

The imposing bank buildings in Vancouver held out no invitation to him. His avowed purpose as he resigned from his Scottish bank was "to live an open-air life." Moreover, Robert would have assumed that he could not get back into a bank. In the paternalistic work environment of Britain at that time, company loyalty was unquestioned and it was assumed that jobs were for life—barring unforeseen economic upheavals. So if someone voluntarily left a job at a bank, it would be very difficult to get a job with another bank. Any prospective employer would assume such a person was flighty, unreliable or disloyal. Robert thought he had closed that door.

He had just enough money left to take the ferry across the Strait of Georgia to Vancouver Island, where he had a reference—to a farmer, a relative of a Glasgow friend. Major James Mutter's 200-acre farm was at Somenos, just north of Duncan in the Cowichan Valley. In the long days of June Service became what he called a "mud-pupil," picking stones, hacking down trees, milking cows, bringing in hay.

Robert would always tend to see the people around him as players on the stage of life. He was always a little off to one side, observing and analyzing without getting emotionally close. He could do that even to himself, and in this first exposure to unwelcome physical exertion he took a detached look at himself, deriding the "fat little bank clerk" who had set out to become a "dashing cowboy."

Even in his own family he had felt some emotional distance, as if he never quite belonged. He was born on January 16, 1874, in Preston, Lancashire, where his father, Robert Service Sr., a 35-year-old Scottish bank employee, had married 17-year-old Emily Parker, daughter of James Parker, a prosperous wholesaler, tea merchant and cotton miller. Robert and Emily christened their first child Robert William; he was called Willie by the family to avoid confusion with his father, but later chose to be known as Robert.

James Parker, on his death in 1876, left Emily a trust fund that, according to Robert in *Ploughman*, yielded an income of £200 a year. With this, Robert Sr. quit—or perhaps lost—his bank job and tried to make a living as an insurance agent, first in Preston, and then in Glasgow. By 1878, when they made the move to Scotland, Robert and Emily had three small sons. But there, as in Preston, Robert's business failed to prosper. He gradually gave it up and busied himself running the household as frugally as possible on his wife's income. He may have been ill at the time of the move because in that same year, he and Emily sent their two elder sons, Robert, four, and John Alexander, three, to Kilwinning, a small town near the coast some 20 miles southwest of Glasgow, to live with their Service grandparents and four maiden aunts, one of them dying of tuberculosis. Only their third son, baby Thomas (known as Harry), stayed with them.

Strangely, Robert's autobiography makes no mention of his grandmother or of his brother John. He seemed to remember himself in this period as a lone child overwhelmed by rather dour adults and already living very much in his imagination. Jennie, the eldest aunt, cared for Robert; it was she who introduced him to poetry and the magic to be found between the covers of a book.

When Robert was eight, he and John were suddenly retrieved by their parents, who took them back to Glasgow. But Robert's immediate family had become strangers to him. In his own account he tries to come to terms with his father, but scarcely mentions his mother or his siblings. While he and John had been away at Kilwinning, three more brothers—Joseph, Peter and Stanley—had been born; three girls—Agnes, Beatrice and Isobel—would follow, and then a boy, Albert.

Stanley, later in life, remembered how the family was always waiting for the next instalment of Emily's legacy and marveled at how his mother could bring up 10 children on $100 a month. Stanley put it bluntly:

> For papa never did another tap of work and he tried to break the will and get his hands on the capital many times, but Mr. Eastwood [the trustee] always stood in the way. I suppose this stayed with me because of the frustrations stirred up in papa by this very old man who refused to die. Even you must be long since gone, my dear Mr. Eastwood, but wherever you are, I thank you—and hope you never meet papa.[3]

In Glasgow, Robert soon discovered the nearby lending library, and read the novels of Jules Verne, R.M. Ballantyne and Captain Frederick Marryat late at night, soaking up the tales of dangerous adventure in exotic lands as the noisy, crowded house finally became quiet around him. He did not excel at school. When he was 13 (the school leaving age in Scotland at the time) his parents decreed that he must finish his formal education, but he misbehaved to the point where it was politely suggested by the school that he leave before the end of the year. His parents found themselves with a 14-year-old who wanted to join the Merchant Navy. To prevent this, Robert's father got him a job in the Commercial Bank and there, until he emigrated at the age of 22, Robert worked—while his heart and imagination roamed the seven seas, discovering new lands, living a life of vicarious adventure, his imagination fueled by his favorite authors, and the new ones he continued to discover. Burns was an early delight, then he added Tennyson and Browning. He loved the rhymes and wordplay of W.M. Thackeray, Thomas Hood and Edgar Allan Poe, and soon discovered the American west seen through the prose of Bret Harte and the verse of Eugene Field. By the age of 16 he was imitating them, and sending his verse to Glasgow papers. Seeing early efforts such as "The Song of the Social Failure," "It Must Be Done" and "Shun Not the Strife" in print gave him great satisfaction, but no cash.

By 17 he had discovered sports and put poetry on the back burner. Then, just as suddenly, he lost interest in sports and took up theater, attending every play he could and acting in minor roles. He left that enthusiasm in turn to become a part-time student at the University of Glasgow. Writers such as Stevenson, Kipling, George Borrow, Henry David Thoreau and Jack London, with their mixture of adventure narrative and nature observation, delighted him during his brief stint of student life, which came to an end in an argument with his professor over an essay in which Robert called Hamlet's would-be lover Ophelia "a bit of a slut," and threatened the professor with fisticuffs.

He bided his time at the bank, sometimes working on poetry in his mind while he tallied up figures. His friends were a bohemian crowd, many of them would-be writers, and together they produced a single issue of a literary magazine. At university a friend had introduced him to French literature, and he read Balzac and Hugo, Zola, Flaubert and Maupassant.

For a time, Paris was his mecca; then he read Morley Roberts's *The Western Avernus* (1887), a muscular memoir of travel and toil in western North America, and his focus shifted to that part of the world. About this time his brother Peter returned trim and healthy from work on a farm, and Robert began to see a rural future for himself. He read everything he could find on Canada, including pamphlets put out by the Canadian immigration department, which pictured western Canada as a golden land of glorious opportunity.

All he needed was the £6 for a ticket, steerage class. His chance came when his apprenticeship period at the bank ended and his salary increased. By the end of March 1896 he had the money he needed, and he gave the bank his resignation.

Now here he was on Vancouver Island, learning the hard facts of Canadian farming. The two sons on the farm were six-foot specimens of rural strength, and Robert was their "green mud-pupil" who couldn't keep up. The adults in the community were either Britons (mostly Englishmen) convinced they were a superior breed even though they were often idle remittance men (younger sons sent abroad with a small annual allowance by families who didn't know what else to do with them) or Canadians who referred to the former as "fool Englishmen." The "gospel of stern toil" was an ethic that grew out of the Canadian soil, but the British immigrants had to adopt it or be defeated by the Canadian landscape.

At first it was pride that made the young Scotsman try to keep up. Then it was a decision that if he had to clean out a pigsty, he might as well do it well. As Robert weeded turnips in terrific heat, his hands were worn raw and his back ached, but around him was unexplored forest, and the slopes of Prevost Mountain rose to a clear blue sky. The turnip row was the price he had to pay for all this beauty.

He chopped trees and sawed up the limbs. He liked the excitement of haying, but was slow to get the hang of milking cows. Digging potatoes was good, and picking apples almost fun. Best of all was the threshing bee, with its festive atmosphere and laughter, and the abundant harvest table at noon.

By the end of the summer Robert was strong and healthy, but aware also that he was getting nowhere. He had always hated hard work, and now, to his horror, he realized that nothing but that lay ahead of him. He had become a slave with freedom only to starve.

Thus began a pattern that would characterize Robert's life for the next seven years. Tired and disgusted at the grimy toil of one manual job after another, he would quit and stretch out his hoarded earnings to give himself as long a holiday as possible, then go back to work only when he had to.

The holiday venue this first winter was a shack owned by Harry "Hank" Evans. Hank was a gentle, patient "mossback," and the chore list was short for whoever helped stem the loneliness of a dreary winter, so Service moved into Hank's cabin farther up-island. Hank's 20 head of cattle roamed the mountain by summer and came down to the lowlands for the winter. All Service had to do was light the morning fire, sweep up, bake bread, keep the woodpile stocked with sawn wood and help feed the cattle. He felt joyously free.

The highlight of life with Hank was the discovery of a pile of old *Harper's Weekly* magazines. In his 1945 autobiography, *Ploughman of the Moon*, Service wrote: "We must be hungry to appreciate literary fare. In my case I was famished."[4] The tales of travel he found between the covers of *Harper's* rekindled the desire for adventure he had first felt reading library books as a boy. So as he built blazing fires and sat with the old dog on one side, the old cat on the other and old Hank yarning stories in front of him, Robert was formulating a new dream. In *Harper's* he read articles on southern California, a land he knew from the pen of Robert Louis Stevenson. The illustrations showed him groves of fruit trees, and Service vowed he would pick the oranges, grapefruit, olives and figs in that Garden of Eden. Hank had lived there—and could tell a good tale—so while the rain beat on the moss-covered roof of Hank's shack, California became Robert's golden, sunny dream.

When cabin fever threatened, there were neighbors to visit, mossbacks who had built log barns and carved stump fields out of the Douglas-fir forest. Robert felt closer to these folk than to the English settlers. In his leisure time he wore a black shirt, white tie and Stetson, in total contrast to the men with knee-breeches and stock ties who didn't accept him as one of their own. He suspected that the mossbacks didn't either, seeing him as a "specimen of the damphool English." Since he didn't fit with either crowd, he decided that his only route to social acceptance would be his ability to entertain. From boyhood Robert had always played some instrument, and that winter he played Hank's battered banjo and sang at gatherings in the log schoolhouse on the edge of the forest. Afterwards, in the wee small hours, he would walk the dark forest trail back to the shack.

Sometimes, sitting in the shack by the firelight, he would experience a longing to write, but he would be overwhelmed by conflicting emotions that left him unable to translate feelings into words. Frustrated, brooding—but intensely aware of the present and excited about the future—he would roll into his blanket on the floor.

When spring came in 1897 Robert had a plan. He headed for the largest ranch in the area, George Corfield's Eureka Farm on Cowichan Bay. His goal was to winter in southern California, some 1,000 miles to the south. Working for Corfield during the summer months would earn him enough to get there for the winter.

Meanwhile, almost 1,250 miles to the north, where the Klondike River flows into the Yukon at Dawson, some 1,500 people, mostly men and mostly miners, were camped on the mud flats under a scar-faced mountain known as the Midnight Dome. They were starting a quest that Robert Service's poems would one day immortalize. In the previous August, just before freeze-up, George Carmack had found thumb-sized nuggets of gold and staked a claim on Rabbit Creek (soon renamed Bonanza Creek). In early 1897, as the ice left the Yukon River, news of the find traveled via two small river steamers 1,700 miles down the Yukon River to the port at St. Michael, Alaska. There, prospectors with packs full of gold boarded two ocean-going ships: *Portland*, bound for Seattle, and *Excelsior*, headed to San Francisco.

Their news set off a frenzy greater even than that of the California gold rush of 1849. Hobos, heads of companies, photographers, reporters, lawyers, criminals, doctors, society women, prostitutes, judges, pastors and poets stopped what they were doing and headed for the Klondike. The clarion call of gold never rang louder than in did in 1897–98 in the United States and Canada, where men and women had been caught in the grip of a long economic depression. Here at last was hope. By the time the news spread it was already too late to reach Dawson that year before freeze-up, but that didn't stop the first wave of humanity from jumping on whatever boats they could find heading north. Thousands more would take the winter to prepare, to travel from Winnipeg, Toronto, Halifax, Chicago or New York to Seattle, Victoria or Vancouver, to outfit there and embark in the spring of 1898 on the vast flotilla moving up the Inside Passage to Skagway, Alaska. The exodus started before the ice was out of the Lynn Canal and intensified until an estimated 100,000 people were on the move, most of them by water but hundreds also trying to reach the Klondike overland.

If this excitement reached Service in his Cowichan Valley bunkhouse on Eureka Farm, he paid no attention to it. He was California bound, daily accepting the drudgery of farm work until the dark days of November became too cold for the clothes he owned. Rather than buy boots, woollen underwear and a heavy Cowichan sweater, he put his plan into action, and with $100 saved and the promise of his job back next spring, Robert headed south.

chapter 2

By December 1897 Robert Service was in Seattle, his $100 stake already dwindled to half. A musician who called himself The Great Zanzini offered him the job of being his assistant. Robert's naïveté made him slow to realize that Zanzini wanted him as a partner in bed as well as in business. Robert quickly made his escape when he saw a poster advertising passage to San Francisco for one dollar.

With a hundred nomads as fellow passengers, he embarked on a dreadful journey on SS *Mariposa,* trying to sleep in a cockroach-infested bunk, with the seasick around and above him. On his arrival, in spite of the hellish reputation of its Barbary Coast, San Francisco looked like heaven.

Service was soon sitting on a bench on the edge of Chinatown, in Portsmouth Square, where the first American flag in a future California had been raised six decades earlier. Nearby was a memorial to Robert Louis Stevenson that had been unveiled just two months before. "So I sat in a trance of happiness," he later wrote. "In the peace of the pale sunshine I was worshipping at the shrine of my favorite hero. Here, among strangers, in a strange land, was a bit of Scotland. The whaups were crying over the heather, and the dew was white on the peat … In this quiet square, amid the fever and tumult, I dreamed by the hour, and seemed to find my soul again."[1]

His hotel at the base of Telegraph Hill was expensive, costing him 50 cents a day, so he moved to the Latin Quarter, where he got a big room with a four-poster bed. In his travels Robert would sleep in all sorts of slums and hovels without complaint—unless there were bugs. Here he awoke to find the white bed curtains patterned with bedbugs. After that he slept on the floor.

From Nob Hill to the Mission, from the Barbary Coast to Chinatown, Robert explored San Francisco. The brothels and opium dens, the theaters, restaurants and joss houses, the Portuguese fishermen unloading their boats, the scum of the Seven Seas drinking in the bars. Soaking it all in, he was an artist painting and storing pictures in his mind.

The people Robert had worked with on Vancouver Island had become friends of a sort, but once he headed south there were no friends. Most people he met were like characters from a Dickens novel—shysters, criminals, down-and-outers, opium smokers, girls in the Kearney and Market Street dives who would woo a man to pick his pockets. The experience of being in a bustling seaport rekindled his teenage ambition to go to sea. He might have hopped on any southbound ship he could find, but as fate would have it, he just missed a vessel sailing for Tahiti. He was often accosted by men wanting crews for whalers, and narrowly avoided being pushed into a cab with a drunken captain out to shanghai a crew for the Bering Sea. Robert had no interest in going in such a chilly direction. After a confrontation with a pair of con artists, he bought himself a knuckle-duster, which he had to use in a dark alley when one of the men—pretending to be giving his money back—attacked him instead. He was beginning to see himself as a roughneck, willing to defend himself if need be.

San Francisco was the most exciting place Robert had ever been. The waterfront, with its worldly hustle-bustle and its spectrum of improbable humanity, ignited his imagination and filled it with characters. As they raced around in his head, he would sit in the square beneath his hero's monument and yearn to express himself as Stevenson had.

In a bookstore he met an author—someone who actually made a living from writing—and the longing came over him again "to write, to write, even if I starved."[2] Starving was a real possibility. On a day when he had been in San Francisco about a month, he awoke and stared at his last $10 bill. Suddenly frightened, he took to reading the want ads in the papers and haunting the employment agencies in an increasingly desperate search for work. A note appeared on the blackboard that laborers were wanted in the Los Angeles area at $2 a day. He took the job without knowing where he was going or what the work would be. Glued to the window of the Southern Pacific coach, he was delighted and excited to be going south again.

The work was to dig a tunnel through the San Gabriel Canyon to bring the waters of the San Gabriel River down to the valley. Unable to stand up in the tunnel, the men worked bent over and soaked by the continuous dripping of water from the low ceiling. Robert could hardly make it through the day. Light-headed from exhaustion, he was ashamed of his performance at the heavy work of loading gravel and cement into boxes, lifting them onto trucks, and pushing the heavy trucks out of the tunnel. On that first day he was without gloves, so his hands were raw and bleeding.

Ten days later, when a cable broke on the bucket that lifted men and supplies to the site, it killed two men, and Robert decided he had had enough: he asked to be transferred to the gravel pit. Here he worked longer hours—7:00 a.m. to 7:00 p.m.—but at least there was birdsong and blue sky.

On Christmas Eve morning he quit the job. Instead of being paid what he was owed in cash, he was given a time check—a record of hours worked that could only be exchanged for cash at the company's office in Oakland, 350 miles to the north. With understandable bitterness he later wrote in his autobiography that because he was penniless, he could be made to risk his life at dangerous work, then be kicked into the ditch when he was no longer needed.

Useless check in hand, he took the trail down the scenic canyon, the beauty of what he saw helping to revive his spirits. High up, the forests were pine and oak, but down in the canyon alongside the San Gabriel River there were cottonwood and willow; songbirds sang and coyotes and rabbits crossed his trail. Above him, red-tailed hawks and golden eagles soared, and his heart soared with them. He was free again.

Just when he was becoming ravenous with hunger, he came upon an orange grove. The oranges were still green and sour, but he was so hungry that he ate some anyway.

Along the trail he discovered an envelope containing blueprints for the canyon work and picked it up. When a rider passed and asked him if he had seen them, Robert was still so angry with the company that he said no. On arrival at the little valley town of Azuza, he could get no food or lodging without money. In the hotel barroom he overheard an engineer bemoaning

Robert Service in his wandering years. He commented later that his pockets were stuffed with books and papers and he was a "tough looking case."
PHOTO: QUEEN'S UNIVERSITY ARCHIVES

the loss of his blueprints. Service attempted to make a deal: if he could find the blueprints, would the engineer cash his time check?

The man gave him his word, and Service produced the blueprints. Then the engineer handed back the check and refused to cash it. "He turned his back on me with contempt. I was just another bum to be treated like a dog."[3] Robert was ready to fight and was about to call him a son-of-a-bitch when the stage driver offered him $10 in exchange for the $20 time check. It was a bitter moment, but Robert was desperate, and he took it.

There was no room left in the inn and he spent that Christmas Eve in a chicken coop infested with fleas. During the night he suffered the revenge of the green oranges: such severe stomach cramps that he thought he would pass out.

In the morning he bought a train ticket to Los Angeles. He would later recall that he viewed that city for the first time with only half the money he had slaved for and his self-esteem at a new low. And yet, revitalized by the newness of it all, he was delighted by Los Angeles. Service loved cities almost as much as he loved nature. Cities were for him a giant panorama of people to be studied—people who always seemed to amaze, intrigue and inspire him.

He found a tiny room in an evangelical mission for one dollar a week and threw himself on the bed with a sigh of satisfaction. He lay there thinking about how far the nine dollars he had left would take him. To last a month, he calculated, he would have to eat on one dollar a week.

Los Angeles was a magical city for Robert. More than 40 years later he would return and renew his love for southern California. For now it was a heavenly haven, providing solace to a wounded spirit. Robert could always find charm in urban atmospheres, and in lazy abandon he surrendered to "the city of angels," roaming her streets and reading, writing, observing and escaping. Only rarely did he connect with the people around him.

Loneliness was rarely a problem. When he had lived with his grandparents and aunts in Kilwinning, learning to read had given him entry to an exciting world far from the pampered but stifling atmosphere of their home; when he moved back to Glasgow to a house overflowing with siblings, he escaped to the public library or found respite reading in the middle of the night.

The need to escape seemed to have infected the entire Service family. They moved frequently, and by the end of the 1890s four sons had sought worldly adventure, one in Australia, one in South Africa, one working on a boat between Ireland and Scotland, and Robert in North America.

Robert's new "family" in Los Angeles became the old men and derelicts at his mission house. Robert listened to the life story of each, and years later, while never naming them, he characterized them in *Ploughman of the Moon*: the socialist, the hypochondriac, the corn doctor, the quartz miner, the section foreman, the book agent. The mission was a school for Robert; the subject studied was humanity.

Every day he walked joyfully among the acacias, magnolias, palms and pepper trees. In the library, he found a corner where he could look out on magnolia trees and read poetry. San Francisco had made him want to write prose; here he wrote poetry. He sent pieces to the local newspaper and saw them in print, including "The Hobo's Lullaby."

But if this was heaven, it was a hungry one. Robert's eating regimen began at ten o'clock with coffee and three doughnuts for five cents—he imagined there were six doughnuts. In the afternoon he could have soup, salad, meat, two vegetables and a small portion of hotcakes and coffee for 10 cents at a cheap restaurant. In the evening he checked the markets for fruit fallen in the gutter. At seven he turned up at the Pacific Gospel Saloon, not for the saving grace but for the dry bread and coffee. Then he offered to wash the coffee cups, giving him access to more bread.

In this state of semi-starvation he explored the city and turned 24. There were moments of panic, and his birthday was one of them. His future looked grim.

Several writers have put Robert Service in the class of remittance men, but he doesn't fit the picture. He had no stipend from home, and writing later of that hungry winter he claimed that it never occurred to him to write to his parents for help.

Rather than leaning on his family, he appeared to be escaping from it. This became clear in the 1970s, when his younger brother Stanley, by then a retired Ottawa doctor, wrote a memoir "to set the story straight." It revealed the acute embarrassment that he and his siblings felt because of their alcoholic father. Nevertheless, the family had instilled in Robert an abundant measure of Scottish pride and stoic perseverance. Writing of that hungry January 1898, Robert said, "I would have died rather than confess my humiliating plight."[4]

Service's own writings never deal with the larger picture, even though his youthful plight was part of a widespread economic depression. North American settlement had reached the Pacific, and the manifest destiny mentality had come up against the fact that there was nowhere left to go. Commerce was stymied. Good jobs became scarce; Robert was not the only one going hungry. What was needed was a new frontier, and that winter thousands of people had sighted it and were packing for the Klondike gold fields.

As Robert's money ran out, he was temporarily saved by carrying an advertisement banner for a retirement sale, which earned him a dollar a day for three days. After that he found work as a fruit picker, which he loved. When that ended he placed an ad in the newspaper. His only reply took him farther south, to a job in San Diego tutoring three young women. The place of employment turned out to be a high-class brothel, and along with tutoring he had handyman and gardening duties. The job ended with the return of the regular handyman, "Big Pete." When Robert left, one of the girls gave him a parting gift—her guitar, which he had learned to play.

He left with $30, a pack and the guitar on his back, bound for Mexico. For 10 days he wandered south, eating hard biscuits and sleeping on the bare ground Sometimes friendly farmers offered food and shelter, and in return Robert played his guitar and sang.

Although he may have been escaping from his father, there is evidence of a bond between them. Years later he devoted an entire chapter of his autobiography to "Profiles of Papa," putting as good a face on the old man as possible. While in Mexico he bought a gaudy postcard to send home to Scotland, so his father could tell his friends that Robert was taking a holiday in Mexico. What his father thought about him still mattered.

Heading north, he enjoyed two square meals in San Diego. He replenished his supply of hard tack and tea and bought a set of steel strings for the guitar, which had become an extension of himself. Setting out north along the railway, he slept by day and walked by night, when it was too cold to sleep. As he tramped through the night, the full moon affected his imagination, "giving me a crazy feeling as if I were an unreal person walking in a world of dream. I have always been a minion of the moon. From the tropics to near the Pole I have worshipped it, deeming it the most beautiful sight in all creation. So in that tramp the white fire of fantasy glowed in me."[5]

Lacking adequate food, pushing his body to walk up to 30 miles a day and talking to no one but himself, he was alternately depressed and elated. At one point he gave up night travel because he feared missing his footing on the trestle bridges.

In dramatic prose in *Ploughman of the Moon*, Robert described a brush with death, one of many he would have in his lifetime. (His critics have accused him of exaggeration in his autobiographical writings, of "telling a good story." In some cases he juggled different times and characters to suit his narratives, but the stories of his trek along the California coast ring true with first-person intensity.) Beside the sea, under a gunpowder dark sky, he came upon a lonely beach. Suddenly the black shape of a whale appeared near shore, and he had a strange impulse to swim with the creature. Although he felt uneasy about the dark beach, he entered the water, but he had not taken three steps when he was caught in quicksand. Soon he was engulfed to the waist. With a quick twist and a desperate effort he got his legs free and, half floating, got back on solid land.

As he lay there the sun broke through a gap of cloud above the sea, turning the waves to molten gold, then fierce ruby.

As the sun centre passed the gap, the effect was terrific. Furious blades of light smote sea and cloud, transforming them into a raging furnace. The intensity of the conflagration was almost unbearable. Half blinded by that garnet glare, I danced naked on the beach and yelled with joy. Then the barbaric splendour passed, and the glow that followed was baleful. And I thought that only I had seen that pyrotechnic splendour; that last frenzy of the dying sun was for me alone.[6]

When the light faded he sat alone, drinking sweet hot tea and eating hardtack, and smoking his pipe. " ... I had that queer feeling of unreality that often came to me in those days. I was going forward in a dream in which I seemed to have lost all contact with the past."

The next night he met three hobos who warned him of a killer on the road. A drifter had been found dead, evidently robbed. The following evening, just as Robert had finished building a hut for himself from old railway ties by the side of the track, a man appeared in the doorway. Robert spoke, but got no reply. Then the man built a fire beside Robert's hut, stretched out and seemed instantly to be asleep. Too nervous in his hut to sleep, Service crawled out and slept instead in a grove of chestnut trees farther up the hill. In the morning, he watched from his hiding place as the man rose, walked to the hut and pushed it over with his foot. Robert wondered if the man had purposely wanted to crush him, and watched in shock as he vanished into the mist.

On another day, he stopped to ask a section boss for a job and felt the man's distaste as he turned him down. In *Ploughman*, Robert wrote that one refusal left him depressed for the whole day, overcome by self-doubt, fear, even a sense that he deserved his fate. Few writers have expressed more eloquently how it feels to be homeless and jobless.

Near Los Angeles he met Jimmy Service, a boy whose father came from Ayrshire—the county from which Robert's father hailed. The lad wanted to take Robert home to meet his own father; maybe he could give Robert a job? Shame at his appearance held Robert back. The theme of predestination, appropriate to his Calvinist upbringing in his grandparents' house, appears in Robert's accounts of such moments. While he saw the possibility of comfort and security, some unknown force controlled him, and he refused the lad's offer.

Early the next morning he entered Los Angeles "like a whipped dog." It was back to the Salvation Army mission, eating beans and bread and pondering his fate. He tried a pick-and-shovel and a dishwashing job. He marveled that he could fail even at dishwashing and resigned himself to life among "the great unfit" and his fatalist philosophy: what had to be would be, and there was nothing he could do about it.

On a bench in the public square, he found a discarded newspaper beside him. The headline read: A TON OF GOLD COMES OUT OF FROZEN NORTH. "Another gold rush like that of forty-nine. Maybe it will have its dramatic aspects. No doubt another Bret Harte will arise and sing of it in colorful verse."[7] But the man who would become the bard of the Yukon and make himself richer than all but the luckiest miners put down the paper with no notion of heading north. It was bad enough to be hungry and down-and-out in the sunshine of California, never mind the icy Klondike.

The man whose verse would one day give the Yukon its voice chose instead to head into the desert. One phrase in the Klondike article *did* excite Robert: that a poet would "arise and sing" of it in colorful verse. But he would arise and sing here where it was warm.

For the next few months, with his guitar on his back, he followed the open road through Arizona, Nevada and Colorado, feeling the magic of places he had read about in the adventure stories of his youth. In return for his supper at various desert houses, he sang cowboy songs like "Home on the Range," "Yellow Rose of Texas," "The Red River Valley"—even songs he had made up himself.

At the end of the day he would watch the orange light of sunset fade from the cacti and yuccas, then listen to the night wind in the ocotillo and the coyotes on the hills. The mountains stood in a dark line against the night sky, the stars seemed to sit just above them. In the morning he woke up to the sound of bees working the tiny flowers of the desert shrubs, the scamper of wood rats and the querulous four-note call of the Gambel's quail. Complete and utter solitude.

Mostly he was happy. There were times when he was wet and wretched. And there were hot, dry days of torment and exhaustion, made worse by hunger. But it was the loss of his guitar that turned him back to the city.

He was in the Tehachapi Mountains of the Mojave Desert, crossing a long trestle bridge, when he was nearly killed by an unexpected train.

The Mojave Desert where Robert wandered in 1898 on the edge of the Tehachapi Mountains, often sleeping on the ground in complete and utter solitude.

PHOTO: ENID MALLORY

To save himself he dropped his pack and guitar and crawled out on a tie jutting over the chasm. Deafened by the noise and shaken so hard he could barely hold on, he desperately dug his fingers into the tie until what seemed the longest train in the world had swept past.

In the stillness afterward he climbed down to where his pack and guitar had landed. The guitar was smashed. It had been his friend of the road, and its loss, he said later, took the heart out of him. Wearily he made his way back to Los Angeles.

Again he found himself sitting on a park bench with a paper that someone had left behind. He read a piece of news about British Columbia. That night he took a boat going north, and when money for transportation ran out, he walked, following the springtime north by milking cows and doing whatever he could to earn his food along the way. Three weeks later he was feeding the pigs on Corfield's farm at Cowichan.

The hordes of people leaving San Francisco, Seattle, Victoria and Vancouver for Skagway then had to climb over the White Pass or the Chilkoot. Men desperate to reach the gold fields, aiming to be on Lake Lindemann or Lake Bennett at the head of Yukon River navigation when the ice went out, made the trek in terrible winter conditions. They crawled over terrain turned to mud by countless feet before them and climbed slippery slopes where howling winds threatened to push them off into oblivion. On the Chilkoot they plodded upward, bent like beasts of burden under heavy packs. And they did it not just once but as many as 40 times to carry a year's supplies over the pass. Only then would the North West Mounted Police (NWMP) allow a would-be prospector to cross the border onto Canadian soil.

SS *City of Seattle* was one of the many ships carrying stampeders to the Klondike.
PHOTO: YUKON ARCHIVES, H.C. BARLEY FONDS, #5138

On the less steep White Pass, men set out with horses, goats and dogs, hoping these beasts would carry their burdens. The jumbled rocks left no level footing for the horses, and their packs, put on by men who did not know how to throw a diamond hitch, slipped off their backs. Their feet slipped. They fell over cliffs. They floundered in swamps. Panicked owners cursed and whipped them to their last ounce of strength until thousands of the poor beasts gave up. One witness reported seeing a horse deliberately walk off a cliff to escape its misery.

People with money to spare could hire packers and thus ease their climb. Those who needed to earn money immediately became packers. Most of them carried 100 pounds at a time. Among those packers was a man named Sam McGee, one of thousands who would never strike it rich, but whose name, through a quirk of fate, would become immortal.

From the two pencil-shaped lakes, Lindemann and Bennett, water flows 2,000 miles down the Yukon river system to St. Michael's on the Bering Sea. Some 300 miles along the way, the Yukon is joined from the east by a river called the Klondike. Into the Klondike, near this junction, runs what is now known as Bonanza Creek. This was the destination of the 30.000 men and women who waited for spring on the shores of lakes Lindemann and Bennett. In a tent city stretching nearly 60 miles along the shores of these two lakes, they built 7,000 boats in the spring of 1898 to carry them down the Yukon.

At the end of May, when ice broke up and the grand flotilla left Lake Bennett, Superintendent Sam Steele of the NWMP hurried to the rapids at Miles Canyon, where 10 men had drowned the day before. Steele put Corporal Dixon, a competent "white-water man," in charge and decreed that women and children walk the portage trail around the canyon and rapids; that no boat go through without a competent crew (pilots could be taken on for $25 a time) and sufficient freeboard. A man named Norm Macauley had built a tramway on the east side of the canyon and rapids, where goods were hauled by horses on flat cars along a track made of hewn poles. At the end of the tramway stood the town of Whitehorse, on the eastern bank of the river; with the arrival of the railway two years later, the town would be moved to the opposite bank.

chapter 3

The name Cowichan comes from the Coast Salish word *khowutzun,* which means "back warmed by the sun." The city of Duncan and the surrounding Cowichan Valley area have warmer year-round temperatures and more hours of sunshine than any other place in Canada. Today it also claims the largest number of artists per capita in the country. If a would-be poet had to feed pigs at the turn of the century, this was not a bad place to do it.

Two rivers, the Cowichan and the Koksilah, run down from the mountainous backbone of Vancouver Island into Cowichan Bay. On the alluvial land between the two streams George Corfield had established the biggest farm in the district and had diked the watery meadows to pasture his Holstein cows and plant fields of grain.

The sheltered saltwater bay to the east was protected by Saltspring Island, where Mount Maxwell, the highest point in the Gulf Islands, looked down on Corfield's farm. Gentle summer sea breezes moved in across the land. Fields rolled up from the bay—some green, some brown from the plough—toward Mount Tzouhalem to the north, the bulk of that mountain blue with shadow, the sky bluer still.

If Service had any home in North America, this was it. "Back to the farm for little Willie. There at least was work I could handle and I was duly appointed official cattleman." He took pleasure in driving the cows to and from the meadows among the sloughs by the bay, where they pastured. The Koksilah River would overflow its banks at high tide, so the cows would

Corfield's store was on the bank of the Koksilah River where it runs down to Cowichan Bay. Service spent four years of his life here, first as a cowhand, then as storekeeper.
PHOTO: COWICHAN VALLEY MUSEUM AND ARCHIVES

have to swim. "Driving them home they looked so sleek and clean. In the fields the men were getting in the hay, and its fragrance mingled with the milk-sweet scent of the cows. There, with the sun declining, it was one of those idyllic scenes of farm life that live in the memory."[1]

Work, of course, was unending; the cows had to be in for milking by six in the morning and the 20 cans of milk carried across the barnyard for the calves by seven. From that beginning the chores went on until the day was done—12 hours at least.

By December, Service was wondering if he could stick out the winter. And one day a moment of carelessness almost cost him his life. Lost in thought while leading the farm's bull to pasture, he was suddenly thrown violently into the air, landing to see the black beast above him, head poised to gore him. Winded and unable to move, he waited, terror stricken, until a great shout from a fellow worker who had jumped over the fence attracted the bull's attention. Service forced himself to crawl through the fence.

He was put to bed with cracked ribs, and as he lay there morosely pondering his future Bill, the ranch storekeeper, appeared and announced that he was quitting his job. Service was to get out of bed and go over the stock with him because Mr. Corfield was giving Robert the storekeeping job. Bill's announcement that day numbered among the great moments of happiness that Service had in his life.

For three years he served as storekeeper on the Corfield ranch. Looking back, he saw himself leaning against the store porch, his pipe in his mouth and his hands in his pocket. In fact he performed all the duties necessary for managing a country store and post office. He spent two hours a day on a wagon pulled by a pony, collecting milk cans for the creamery and delivering the mail to the station, then stopping again on the way back for the incoming mail. He also had the butchering to do to keep the crew of eight farm hands and the family of nine in meat. He learned to kill and dress a sheep in 12 minutes. A neighbor remembered him doing evening chores, washing the pails, separators, etc. To communicate with Native customers in the store, he learned Chinook, the traditional trading language of the Northwest coast.

George Corfield also hired Robert to tutor his sons. This work had to be fitted in around customers and took place when the boys were not in school. What his young charges could still remember more than 70 years later was the storytelling skill of their tutor. "He told some wild-and-wooly ones to us boys and anyone else who would listen," remembered Norman Corfield.[2]

Another Corfield brother, who was still running the store in 1939, reminisced to a reporter about the stories Service used to tell.

> He was a great one for making up stories. We used to follow him around, hoping he would tell us one—used to go over to the barn if he was working there and try to get him started. They were always adventure yarns, with the hero either getting in the way of an erupting volcano or else attacking a jungle beast single handed. We would sit around in the hay, breathless with excitement—our eyes popping. Just when the hero was in a spot from which there didn't seem any escape, Service would laugh, drop his pitchfork and streak out of the barn. We would come back to reality with a start, find that he had left us and the hero flat, and go running after him begging him to finish it. Once he left his hero hanging from a branch over a precipice.[3]

St. Peter's Anglican Church, where Service sang in the choir and performed in musical skits at Saturday-night community dances.
PHOTO: ENID MALLORY

Fred Corfield recalled a story in which Service claimed that, on a trek, he had made a fire on a stretcher and carried the flames to keep the wolves at bay. Fred was the eldest son, and the nearest in age to Robert—about 15 when Robert was 25. They often worked together and went to theatricals and dances in local schoolhouses and halls in Duncan.

Fred also introduced Robert to the ritual of a frigid morning dip in the nearby river. When the Boer War broke out in 1899, Fred enrolled in a volunteer reserve unit in Victoria. A morning swim was part of the training, and when he came home he persuaded Robert to join him in the Koksilah River. Robert quit when Fred found it necessary to break the ice before they could swim, but by then he had acquired the habit of bathing in cold water. While still a teenager, Robert had, presciently, written a poem that described the trauma of a morning dip in Scotland ("It Must be Done" was published in the *Glasgow Weekly Herald* at the time). Now, in his storekeeping days, in honor of his and Fred's early-morning escapades, he sent it to the *Duncan Enterprise,* which reprinted it in 1903.

He stands alone by the water's edge,
With pale and anguished brow,
And shudders as he murmurs low;
"It must be done and now."

He looks into those icy depths,
With wildly staring eye;
And from the panting breast there breaks,
A deep and bitter sigh.

Through all his tense and rigid frame
Great thrills of horror run;
And once again he murmurs hoarse;
"It must and shall be done."

His mind made up, A long, last look!
A plunge: And all is o'er.
He's taken—what was his intent—
His morning bath—no more.[4]

Looking back, Service saw his four years at Corfield's as time wasted; he was being indolent, too lazy or insecure to get on with establishing himself in life. His days were agreeable, even idyllic. He had a horse to ride, he was popular at theatricals and dances, where he performed with a borrowed banjo. He sang in the choir of St. Peter's. In 1901 he joined the South Cowichan Lawn Tennis Club—the earliest such club in Canada, established around 1887 on the Pimbury farm and later relocated to the Corfield farm. Life on the road had brought him enough hunger and loneliness that the comfort of his country store job and his inclusion in the life of the Corfield family and their community proved to be a powerful opiate. He would later conclude that this easy rural life had kept him from moving ahead.

The young Cowichan men found time in the summer to hunt for grouse and pheasant in the woods. Mallard, widgeon and teal gathered in the pools of the bay flats, the air clamorous with their cries on moonlit nights. There were trout in the rivers and abundant salmon in the bay. Robert had a dugout canoe that he took out on Cowichan Bay, even in stormy weather, confident that if it capsized he could get the water out and climb back in.

On winter evenings, with the coal-oil lamp lit and a fire blazing in the stove, Robert was content. He loved the time he had to dream, and the hours after work in his tiny attic room, where he could chew chocolate bars and read the novels he got out from the Duncan library.

He later wrote that he made no music and composed no verse during those years—which perhaps accounts for his sense that it had been time wasted—but this is scarcely true. Several of his poems appeared in Victoria's *Daily Colonist* after an editor on the paper named Charles Harrison Gibbons met him while on a fishing trip to Cowichan. The Yukon Archives preserves a newspaper clipping by Gibbons that vividly recalls a weekend when trout were "leaping to the lure of March Brown and Silver Doctor and the blue grouse drummed on his hollow log or chirred thicketward ..." Then as "velvety darkness" fell on the hills he sat in the old store and talked poetry with the young clerk.[5] When Robert showed him some lines entitled "The Christmas Card," which he had written about the Boer War then raging in South Africa, Gibbons begged to have the poem to print in his paper.

When gold and diamonds were discovered near Johannesburg, British troop numbers were noticeably increased. Dutch farmers—the Boers—who had been in South Africa 150 years before the British had a presence there, now clamoured for the removal of the troops. The British refused, and by October 1899 the Boers and British were at war.

In Robert's poem, the message on the Christmas card was "A merry Christmas to my dearest Dad," sent from a "kid in Canada" to a Sergeant Scott. It arrived the day after Scott fell in battle. The poem ends:

> *They stretched his mangled limbs in shape of rest;*
> *And ere they placed him in the common grave,*
> *They laid the little card upon his breast.*[6]

Robert Service had a brother in a prison camp in South Africa by this time. "Alick"—John Alexander—was a year younger than Robert and was the brother who had gone with him to live with aunts and grandparents at Kilwinning. There is no evidence that Robert knew when he wrote the poem what had happened to his brother. When the tale of Alick's incarceration emerged, it seemed like an episode from one of the adventure stories Robert had devoured as a boy.

Ladysmith, a British stronghold, had been besieged by the Boers, and they were threatening to advance on Durban. Captain Aylmer Haldane was sent on a reconnaissance mission on an armoured train. Among the troops on board were Alick Service and a young reporter for London's *Morning Post* named Winston Churchill. Alick and Winston were both 24 years old.

The train had gone 12 miles when the Boers attacked. The engineer tried to outrun them, but crashed into a mine trap set by the Boers. Three coaches at the front were derailed, but the engine in the middle and two trucks loaded with troops stayed upright. Haldane, keeping the Boers at bay, yelled at Churchill to help free the engine from the jammed forward coaches. In a hail of bullets, Churchill directed the men and the injured engineer until they finally freed the engine.

Wounded men were crammed into the tender and engine while the mobile troops who had been on the derailed wagons retreated on foot, moving parallel to the engine and keeping it between them and enemy fire. When they lagged behind, Churchill stopped the engine, got off and went back to rally the troops. Instead he found himself surrounded by Boer guns. As the engine sped on to safety, Captain Haldane, Winston Churchill and Alick Service were among those who found themselves taken prisoner, soon to be marched off to a camp in Pretoria.

The State Model School that served as the Boer prison camp was enclosed by a 10-foot-high corrugated-iron fence. Churchill, along with Haldane and a sergeant, made plans to escape by climbing onto the roof of a seven-foot-high outhouse. Churchill reached the latrine in darkness and lost no time in getting over the fence. The other two men were not so fast, and Churchill soon realized he was alone, without map or compass, without the food carried by the other men, and without the sergeant's ability to speak Afrikaans.

At first he hid by day and traveled by night, until he was so desperately tired and hungry that he knocked on a door. With incredible luck he had chosen the house of a colliery manager who was English. The man hid him in his mine, then packed him in a trainload of wool heading for Portuguese East Africa. Three days later Churchill crossed the border to freedom and became an instant British hero.

Stanley Service, in his memoir says, "The whole world knows of Churchill's sensational escape and the whole world is the better for it; but Alick remained a prisoner of war in Pretoria for two years and nobody knew anything about it but us. Yet to our family, Alick was more important than Winston Churchill."[7]

In fact, it was less than a year later that the troops held in Pretoria were freed. Churchill, after his escape, persuaded the British commander-in-chief, Sir Redvers Buller, to give him a commission, and he became a lieutenant in the South African Light Horse. By the summer of 1900 the British had captured Johannesburg and Pretoria. The two British officers who rode up to the prisoner-of-war camp where Alick and his comrades were held and ordered the sentries to put down their arms were Churchill and his cousin, the 9th Duke of Marlborough. Then, amid the cheers of the prisoners, Churchill tore down the flag of the South African Republic and ran up a Union flag. Alick Service marched out with the rest of the prisoners.

Robert would follow "The Christmas Card" with further patriotic poems catching the excitement generated by the Boer War. In 1899 he sent one of them to the *Glasgow Weekly Herald* in memory of a friend who died. Arthur Morrison was one of seven young men who had been Robert's literary friends in Glasgow. Service captures both the sharp beauty of youth and the cold finality of death in the poem's first verse.

> *But you my friend, who, even as I,*
> *Were ever in love with the blue of the sky,*
> *And song and summer's gold;*
> *Under the smoky sod you lie,*
> *While over the city the winds go by,*
> *Harsh, and bitter, and cold.*[8]

But a poem published by the *Daily Colonist* in June 1902 had a different theme; "Song of the Social Failure," another early Glasgow piece, is about Robert's view of himself. The second verse begins:

> *Ours was a banquet: remain but crumbs,*
> *Sad is the heart, the fire is low.*
> *Hark! With his stealthy tread he comes—*
> *Comes like a fiend to mock our woe.*
> *"Sit ye here, starveling!" hear his cry;*
> *"others the golden harvest glean;*
> *Yours are the poppies, reap! They die,"*
> *Such is the jeer of the might-have-been,*
> *The leering, sneering might-have-been; ...*[9]

If his days were adrift with idleness, they may not have been altogether wasted, because the country store was a perfect place to practice listening, an art he perfected in the Yukon as he collected and assimilated the stories of the "Trail of '98." His nights of reading were not wasted either; John Spears, a neighbor on land adjoining Corfield's, recounts that Robert knew the meaning of—and could spell every word in—the dictionary. John remembered Robert as a humble person but sensed in him an awareness of a destiny better than his role at Corfield's. He and Robert shared artistic efforts as John, an artist, tried to teach Robert to draw and Robert tried to teach John to write. Each of them came to the conclusion that "what one hasn't got in them, can't be got out."[10]

Sometime in 1902 Robert made a decision. As he tells the story, an elderly customer suggested he become a teacher. He had experience tutoring the Corfield boys; maybe he could do it. He quit reading novels and began serious study, saving every penny he could from his wage of $15 a month. But in late fall he complicated his situation by falling in love.

In Robert's own account of his early life, women are almost non-existent. While he devoted a whole chapter in *Ploughman of the Moon* to his father, his mother was hardly mentioned. Perhaps she bore all the blame for sending him away at age four to the grandparents and aunts. He got his first view of a naked woman—one of his aunts—when he was somewhere between four and eight years old. He recalled quickly deciding that if this was what a woman looked like, he would never marry one.

He also remembered that as a teenager he fell hopelessly in love with a girl but hadn't the nerve to ever speak to her. Later, as a young man, he understood that women could be dangerous. A school friend of his—one he thought had a golden future—got a girl pregnant and ended up in a row house with a job in the local mill. The lesson Robert took from this was that a woman could destroy a man's chance to attain freedom. And freedom was his most precious goal.

During his first stint at Corfield's, before traveling south, he had been attracted to a young Siwash girl who worked at the farm. She already had a Native boyfriend, however, who was in no mood to give her up. One day at noon as Robert lay dozing in the hay, a pitchfork hurled from above just missed his stomach and actually circled his thigh. After that he left the girl alone.

From his year of wandering to the south we have only his own words. If he studied the women of the Barbary Coast or at the San Diego brothel where he worked with more than passing interest, a reader would never know. By his own account he kept to himself, saving his meager earnings and keeping his dreams alive.

In his storekeeping years at Cowichan, he was in his mid-20s and feeling reasonably good about himself. Elizabeth Norcross, a neighbor, later recalled that "Service was my Uncle Norman Norcross's best man at his wedding in 1904." Her uncle's bride remembered that "he was a very modest man, quite moody by nature and loved being alone, quite shy, not very tall, very nice-looking, and most interesting company."[11]

With the Corfield boys Robert rode his borrowed bicycle or walked to the nearby town of Duncan to whatever hall or schoolhouse was holding a dance on Saturday night. Fred Corfield, when he was in his 90s, recalled some of the fun they had. "Service and I worked together on the dairy part of the farm—the churning of milk, with the old hand separator, and while doing that we'd whistle a tune and practice dance steps. We'd go to the agricultural ball, or the bachelors' ball, or some other ball, in starched shirts, bow ties, tail coats, head for Duncan, a four-mile walk, over the railway trestle bridge, and get back at 3 or 4 in the morning in time to change to go to work."[12] Then, one snowy December night at a Duncan dance, there was a new face in the crowd, and Robert fell in love.

chapter 4

Constance MacLean was the daughter of Vancouver's first mayor. In 1886 Malcolm MacLean, born on the island of Tiree in Scotland, had just moved from Winnipeg and had to be persuaded to run in the city's first civic election. The little stump-and-brush city of 400 souls and wooden buildings had two candidates: Richard Alexander, manager of the Hastings Sawmill, and MacLean, who was a realtor by trade. Those who considered Alexander an arrogant tyrant bent all the rules to get MacLean elected. Hotel managers helped people vote who weren't eligible, made up fictitious tenants and backdated receipts for residency. MacLean won by 17 votes.

MacLean expected his questionable electoral win to be challenged by his opponents, but the challenge never materialized because one month later Vancouver's Great Fire of June 13, 1886, burned the city flat. MacLean—who had lost all his own possessions—rose to the occasion. In a tent he pulled the council together and organized relief for the devastated citizens. He was a popular, well-loved and far-sighted mayor; one of the first pieces of legislation he dealt with set aside the land that became Stanley Park. A year later, when the first scheduled-service transcontinental train pulled into Vancouver, his city was ready to play its role as the western terminus of the Canadian Pacific Railway. When his term ended in 1887 he became police magistrate of the city.

When Malcolm MacLean died in 1895, Constance, her sister Isabel and their mother had to learn independence. By 1902, when she visited her cousin, Dr. Perry, in Duncan and appeared at the local dance, Connie (as she was known to her friends) was a mature, poised young woman.

Back in his attic room after the dance, Robert burned the midnight oil writing a poem entitled "The Coming of Miss McLean." The next day he mailed it to her care of Dr. Perry. Her last name was misspelled and he had been distracted enough by her presence that he had failed to hear her first name when he was introduced to her. A note at the top of the poem read: "The author regrets that, being ignorant of the Christian appellation of the lady, he was unable to work it into his verse."[1]

Constance wrote back telling him her name and saying that she would be at the annual hospital ball at Chemainus the following Friday. At first Robert's letters to her were teasing—he pretended some other poor bloke had written the poem and he was getting the credit.

Chemainus is 17 miles north of Duncan, so Robert would have taken the train to get there. Possibly Connie was on the same train. Her dance program from the ball, which survives, shows that she either danced or sat out most of the dances with Robert Service.

Connie went back to Vancouver and Robert tried to settle down again to study. Some time in the new year he quit his store job, intent on bettering himself, and moved into a friend's shack near St. Mary's cemetery on Somenos Road. Mrs. David Evans, a relative of Harry Evans, the old bachelor Robert had wintered with years earlier, supplied him with meals. Here, he aimed to study full time for two months in preparation for the entrance exams for university. After that he had been promised two months of road work, which would take him to exam time.

Alone in his shack, trying to keep his mind on algebra and Latin, he would be set dreaming by the smallest distraction. Years later he recalled that he felt like throwing the hated books out the window and writing sonnets to the moon. One night he found himself outside, pacing back and forth while the moon hung above the pines. A poem formed in his head, and he had a eureka moment of certainty that poetry, not algebra, was what his mind and soul craved. He put the poem down on paper and sent it to *Munsey's Magazine*, a New York-based publication with a circulation of 700,000. Two months later, "Apart and Yet Together" was printed, and, to Robert's amazement, he received a check for five dollars.

The Coming of Miss McLean

The snow lay deep in Duncans at the dying of the day;
A hundred happy hearths were gleaming bright;
The rancher chewed his supper in a cheerful sort of way,
And murmured: "There's a dance on for tonight."

There was hurry, there was flurry, mid the eager belles and beaux;
Refurbishing their charms to highest mark;
A-cleaning gloves with benzene, a-fixing Evening Clothes,
A-hitching up of horses in the dark.
And now the dance goes gaily, the music swells o'er all;
A radiance illumes each beaming swain;
Till suddenly a whisper goes round the giddy hall:
"Have you been introduced to Miss McLean."

They come the unsuspecting ones, they come with smiles so bland;
They dance, they talk things trivial and vain;
Then somehow in a manner it is hard to understand
They surrender to the Charms of Miss McLean.

They go away; they fain would stay, but others take their place;
And round their hearts in turn she winds a chain;
The dance is done, and one by one, they hurry home to trace
In dreams a face, the face of Miss McLean.

She came, she saw, she Conquered; now they would fain forget;
Alas! Their loss must be Vancouver's gain.
They'll hide their grief in ashes—ashes-a-la-cigarette,
For that dear departed darling Miss McLean.

Envoi
Yes, she'll go away from Duncan's on the train
And their hearts will ever beat a sad refrain;
For the one they can't forget, the One they'll e'er regret,
The dancing fair, entrancing Miss McLean.

A century later, we can only half imagine the importance of poetry as a public medium at the beginning of the 20th century, when there was no television or radio and the phonograph and cinema were in their infancy and had yet to reach a wide audience. For entertainment, people in the countryside had newspapers, magazines, the weekly sermon, family music-making and the social milieu of the corner store or the ladies' sewing circle. In genteel society there were at-home teas with calling cards; in less polite society there were saloons. Evening entertainments included amateur performances got up in private homes, churches, halls or schools. At these, people performed on stage, singing, playing the organ or the fiddle or the mouth organ; they step-danced while someone played the bones (pig's rib bones, held in the fingers and snapped together in rhythm); they performed skits—and they recited poetry. A new poem with mass appeal could move quickly across the country from one hall to another—and after 1887 the transcontinental train would speed its dissemination.

Once he had started the road work, Robert had to study at night by the light of a candle in his tent. And after a day of cutting brush, grading roads and mending culverts, it was a weary brain that was left for the books.

When the job ended he wrote the exams that would qualify him for McGill, although there is some confusion as to the career he had in mind. In his autobiography he speaks of becoming a teacher, though in a letter to Connie, and in other letters written later in his life, he says that he intended to study medicine. In 1903 the University of Victoria opened as an affiliate of McGill, so Victoria would seem the logical place for him to do his exams. But instead Robert headed for Vancouver, where Vancouver College was also an affiliate of McGill " … in so far as regards the work of the First Year in Arts."[2] (The University of British Columbia in Vancouver did not open until 1908.)

Robert arrived in Vancouver with $200 in his pocket, which would have to be stretched to cover six months of college. He went first to a boarding house costing $30 a month, but soon moved to a private house at 605 Cambie Street where he paid only $15 a month. In his small room he began cutting his food to the semi-starvation point, a pattern familiar from his California days. Looking back, Robert said that his whole future then had been based on innocent hope.

On arriving in Vancouver he received what he called a "terrible letter" from Connie. Before he left Duncan, Robert had heard that she was corresponding with two other men in Duncan; overcome with jealousy, he wrote her an accusing letter. Connie was so offended that she wanted to return his gifts and end their relationship. In his next letter to her, he repented bitterly and arranged to see her on a Thursday afternoon after an exam that was scheduled to end at four o'clock.

Algebra was Robert's last exam. He went to write it at nine o'clock on a "bleak Friday morning"—a morning made bleak by his Thursday-evening visit with Connie, when he had been "excommunicated." He stared at his exam paper, saw eight questions—all beyond him—and knew it was hopeless. He handed the paper back to the examiner and walked out.

A week later he went back to get his results: Arithmetic, 100 percent; Literature, 90 percent; Euclid and Latin, barely passed; Canadian History, 70 percent; Algebra, 0 percent; French, 1 percent. In French he had tried very hard, and he felt a surge of rage toward the pompous examiner who had given him a mark of 1. (Ten years later, Robert would learn his French in France from the best possible teacher, a woman he loved. He would become as fluent in French as in English.)

Robert's assessment of himself and his plight was harsh and blunt: he called himself a "failure and misfit." The Vancouver College headmaster who specialized in literature recognized his talent and encouraged him to enrol in an arts program. But he now had two supplementary exams to face as he started the six-month course that would cover the first year of McGill.

Four letters written to Connie in September and early October 1903 survive, and they show the turmoil he was suffering. In them he described her letters to him as teasing, even mocking. In a September 15 letter to Connie he spoke of a dressing-down she gave him and said he intended to follow the course she indicated. She had prescribed for him "The Gospel of Work," and he responded that he would do his best to get himself through university. He was not sure how he would do this financially; he might have to teach for a year or two. "It may take a long time, and in the end I fear I may lose you … "[3] Although he would not be seeing Connie, he felt he must be allowed to write sometimes until she saw fit to remove his "excommunication." Connie's letters to Robert have not survived, so we have only his own account of their relationship from which to guess at her feelings.

The other young men at the University were 10 years younger than Robert and impeccably dressed. In an effort to raise his morale, Robert spent his precious money on a blue serge suit and overcoat, a shirt, shoes and underclothing. By the time he bought textbooks he was down to $60.

His room was cold. The grey fall rains of Vancouver were eating away at his spirit. As usual he was starving, worried about money, and falling behind in his studies. Along with loneliness, he had to deal with bad news from home—his mother was seriously ill, and he might have to go home. Robert does not identify her illness, but in fact Emily Service recovered and lived joyfully for another 35 years.

A September 29 letter to Connie, written for her birthday the following day, reveals Robert at the low point of his life. "I cannot read at all, I scarcely eat anything and although I do not show it half the time I am desperate with misery." Then he describes a breakdown after re-reading her letter that evening. "A queer feeling came over me, an agony of loss ... I threw myself down on my bed and cried like a woman ... I have always boasted I did not know how to cry, but you have taught me."[4]

His autobiography also described this breakdown, although Connie, who does not appear in *Ploughman of the Moon,* was not mentioned as its cause. He spoke of a morning when he ate his bread and coffee and "rose heavily to go to class." The sun shone and a breeze blew in from the sea. He found himself walking wildly in the woods of Stanley Park. He walked for hours, then went to a good restaurant and had a real meal. "Nerve-racked and exhausted," he was unable to sleep that night.

His university career was over; he knew he could not make it. He "had tried to storm the citadel of decent society, and been thrown into the ditch."[5] He saw himself going back to Corfield's, still a lowly farm worker at the age of 30. "I tasted the dregs of defeat and felt cast into the outer darkness."

His next letter to Connie was full of despair. "I came home tired tonight, and I went to draw a pitcher of cool water from the well. The moon was brilliant, so I sat by the door and thought of you ... A long time I sat there alone in the moonlight just staring right into the moon's face. And then a reaction of intense sadness came over me and I sat for a long time with my face buried in my hands ... Oh Connie, Connie, we are fellow travelers, and this world's not all gladness and sunshine and I just want to travel by your side, always, always ... If I haven't won you now I never will. And sometimes, as tonight, I am despairful."[6]

His only antidote to depression was exercise, so he walked, usually at night, to a state of exhaustion and a sense of temporary euphoria. Then he would try to imagine jobs he might be able to do: a ragtime kid in a honky-tonk, a rose gardener, a "Parisian apache" (a gangster), a librarian, a rural delivery postman, a herring fisherman. Desperately he began to answer ads for work, but the mildest rebuff would discourage him for days.

Robert was at the end of his tether. Dressed in his new suit he had just applied for a clerking job and been turned down. He was standing in total dejection on a street corner in Vancouver when a hearty voice accosted him.

Here was a biscuit salesman Robert knew from his storekeeping days at Cowichan. When he heard that Service was job hunting, he asked what business he knew. Robert told him he had been trained as a bank clerk. The man asked what was the matter with the bank they were looking at. Robert stared up at the Bank of Commerce building that they were standing beside. He told the salesman he assumed he couldn't get a bank job again, since he had voluntarily left one. His friend told him things didn't work that way in Canada.

This is how the encounter is presented in *Ploughman of the Moon*, but another version comes from Charles Gibbons, the *Daily Colonist* editor from Victoria who published Service's early poems, and who by this time had moved to a Vancouver paper. Gibbons says it was he who helped Robert get a job at the bank. Service may have changed Gibbons into a biscuit salesman to preserve anonymity, in keeping with his aversion to using real names and dates in his autobiographical writings.

Through all his years of wandering, Robert had held on to his old bank manager's letter of recommendation, now tattered and dirty. Clutching that faint hope, but wearing his fine blue suit, he faced the bank's accountant and was sent upstairs to the inspector.

Knowing his 29 years was older than they would like, he passed himself off as 27. The inspector liked the Scottish recommendation, but said he would need three sponsors in Canada. Robert gave him three names, and was told to come back in a week.

When he returned he was told he'd be given a six-month trial at the bank's Victoria branch, at $50 a month. So amazed was Robert that he replied that since he was "Scotch" he didn't need $50 a month—$25 would be lots.

"No matter how Scotch you are you cannot live on twenty-five dollars a month. No, it's fifty of nothing."

"I'll accept fifty,"[7] Robert said meekly.

Service always said later that his success that day depended on three

The Bank of Commerce building at Government and Fort streets in Victoria, where Robert got his chance to turn his life around.
PHOTO: HERITAGE HOUSE COLLECTION

throws of the dice. If he had not kept his tattered recommendation; if he had not bought the new suit; if the "biscuit salesman" had not come along ... Suddenly he loved the whole world. His wounded spirit soared; he walked on air.

When he arrived at the Victoria branch of the Bank of Commerce, at the corner of Fort and Government streets, he had already spent his last half-dollar at a boarding house. Fortune smiled on him again as the accountant offered him the guardroom, a nice apartment above the bank. He rented a piano and taught himself to play it. He had friends at the bank as well as at the boarding house where he took his meals. Life was good again. There are no letters to Connie surviving from this period, so it is not known whether Robert's romance with her revived after his bank job had given him new financial and emotional stability, or even at what point she knew of the development.

One of his bank friends was Leonard F. Solly, who trained the new employee and taught him to type. Leonard had been born in Victoria but he would later move to Somenos, near Duncan, to become a chicken farmer. He and Service kept in touch in later years, reminiscing about Victoria and talking about the Cowichan country as well. A beautiful postcard that Robert sent to Solly from the Yukon, showing the winter stage between Whitehorse and Dawson, is preserved in the Cowichan Valley Archives.

For the present, all Robert's romantic notions and dreams of adventure were gone; his only determination now was to be a "nice fat little banker." He was grateful for another chance, anxious to please, and determined to do well.

In early summer 1904, when the trial period ended satisfactorily, the accountant announced that Robert was being transferred to Kamloops, some 200 miles from Victoria in the Interior. He left with regret, but his old sense of adventure was stirring too. His seven years of struggle, the wonderful highs and soul-black lows, had given him an education in what he called "low-life," and knowledge of the human spirit, with its aspirations and foibles and the resultant glories and tragedies. His travels had also taught him to love the land: Nevada, Mexico, the Arizona desert, the Colorado canyons, the American Pacific coast, the Oregon forest, the soft beauty of Vancouver Island. And the cities: San Diego, Los Angeles, San Francisco, Seattle, Vancouver and Victoria. Now, with new excitement—but a less reckless frame of mind—he was headed inland in Canada.

chapter 5

Kamloops lies northeast of Vancouver in the heart of cattle country, a 220-mile trip by train. Robert remembered with amusement his trans-Canada journey dressed as a would-be wrangler. Now he had a second chance to be a cowboy, so instead of renting another piano in Kamloops, he bought a pony. By four o'clock most afternoons, he and two co-workers were in their saddles, riding the ridges or exploring the gulches. The countryside reminded him of Mexico, desolate and dry. Sometimes they rode to dances at distant ranches.

By this time Robert had traded his creative muse for the safety and prestige of the bank. "My sense of poetry, so strong in my poverty and my desert wanderings, now seemed to have deserted me. My whole ambition was to get on in the bank … "

He had no illusions that he was good at banking; his mind didn't handle figures well—it wanted words and lyrics. But he gave the ledger his full attention and did well enough. Once a voracious reader, he reports that he never looked at a book during his time in Kamloops. He did buy a banjo, however, tuned it like a guitar and enjoyed his music immensely.

When employees got together at parties or around a campfire, there was always talk about the branches in the Yukon. The Bank of Commerce had set up a branch in Dawson in 1898, and Robert later wrote that stories about it were already the stuff of romance in the bank's history. There was talk of the special allowance men got to go there, but of the temptations too, and how many of the boys "went to the devil" there. But the best stories told were about the first "bank boys" who had gone into the Klondike in the spring of 1898 during the great stampede, famous in gold-rush history as the "Trail of '98."

In 1897 the minister of the interior had asked the Bank of Commerce to open a branch office in Dawson City, not only to act as a public banker but also to be the government's agent for assaying gold dust. The bank did not go to the Yukon unprepared. One of their men went to New York that winter to study assaying with U.S. Treasury officials. One worked with an industrial chemist in Boston, while another studied at the School of Practical Science in Toronto. Meanwhile, myriad details were worked out at head office: a supply of acids and fire bricks for the assaying operation, stationery and banking notes, ink powder, food for the staff, clothing suitable to sub-Arctic conditions, and a Peterborough canoe to get the advance contingent down the Yukon River.

The six men chosen to go in were carefully selected, and they were to travel in two groups. In the first, a manager, an officer and a messenger (who was also to be the group's cook) set out from Toronto on April 11, 1898, but the manager, H.T. Wills, was delayed at Vancouver, so on April 26, assistant manager Thomas McMullen left Victoria alone, bound for Skagway aboard the *City of Seattle*. With him were six tons of supplies to be freighted over the mountains to the head of navigation.

In Skagway McMullen arranged to have his supplies carted over the White Pass route. An avalanche had just occurred on the Chilkoot Trail, making it even less attractive than the already notorious White Pass. McMullen then climbed the White Pass himself, reaching Lake Bennett on May 1. Five days later Wills, now arrived from Vancouver with Thomas Comloquoy, messenger and cook, crested the White Pass and joined him on Lake Bennett. The mud and the misery of that slippery climb remained vivid in the telling years later, but it was the image of dead horses littering the trail that most horrified listeners. By the spring of 1898 the North West Mounted Police (NWMP) estimated that 3,000 horses had been killed by accident, abuse and overwork. There would be more.

The bank's second party left Toronto on April 30 and had to wait a week in Vancouver for passage on the *City of Seattle*. This party of two officers and one messenger had with them a supply of bank notes carefully sealed in a large box. It was never let out of their sight aboard ship. But tales of Soapy Smith and his outlaw gang in Skagway circulated on every Alaska-bound ship and were making the officers nervous. Soapy had been born Jefferson Randolph Smith in Georgia, and had practiced the con game from which he got his name (selling bars of soap on the promise that the wrapping might contain bills up to $100 in value—they never did)

Tons of supplies littered the beaches at Skagway and Dyea. The "bank boys" threw their kit bags nonchalantly on the ground, but never took their eyes off them, for in those bags, hidden from Soapy Smith's outlaws, was a small fortune in bank notes.
PHOTO: YUKON ARCHIVES, ANTON VOGEE FONDS, #114

across America, expanding his con schemes in Skagway and honing them to a fine art. He controlled the town through his large gang and infiltrated every public office (the deputy U.S. Marshal there was on his payroll). His small army of henchmen offered "help" to newcomers, and in various ways relieved them of their money.

Could the bank party get that obvious box, with its countersunk sealed screw heads covered with sealing wax, past Soapy Smith and safely over the trail to Canadian soil? Probably not, they decided. One night in the privacy of their cabin the three men broke up the box and threw it out of the porthole. The precious contents were divided and hidden in each officer's kit bag, with clothes stuffed around the packages of money.

At Skagway the kit bags were thrown "carelessly" on the shore with the other gear, but two officers remained within feet of them at all times. The third member of the party searched Skagway in vain for the North West Mounted Police escort that was supposed to meet the party in Skagway. A search in Dyea, a few miles to the west where the Chilkoot Trail began, was also unsuccessful.

When the Mounties finally arrived over the White Pass Trail, they suggested that the Chilkoot Trail might be better. So the second bank party set out from Dyea on the trail that led to the Scales, a large flat area near the head of the pass where prospectors' loads were weighed and packers raised their rates to a dollar a pound for the final steep ascent. This 35-degree climb would become the iconic image of the Klondike gold rush, engraved on the memory of the world: a black ant-like column of human beings bent double under their loads, etched against snow-white mountains, toiling forever upward.

The bank party, unlike the average stampeder, had the guidance and protection of the NWMP. After their first night in a tent on the summit they awoke covered in snow, which had drifted under the canvas. With a dog team to haul their baggage, they left the summit and floundered knee-high, sometimes waist-high through soft snow to Lake Lindemann, which they reached at 3:00 p.m. Other groups attempting to travel over the lake ice were breaking through it that day, so the bank party's dog-driver chose to wait until 4:00 a.m., when the night's cold had firmed the ice.

On a zigzag course, sounding the ice with a pole as they went, they made it to Lake Bennett and deposited $2 million in bank notes with Superintendent Sam Steele (he stowed them under his cot),[1] then joined the manager, officer and cook already at Bennett.

The bank party, on the advice of the NWMP, chose the 35,000-foot Chilkoot Pass route, which is immortalized in this image.
PHOTO: YUKON ARCHIVES, MCBRIDE MUSEUM COLLECTION 3626

The scene at Bennett, as reported in newspapers and by those who were there, was animated chaos: thousands of people living in tents, chopping trees, whip-sawing lumber and building boats, the whole place alive with anticipation and the tension of the danger ahead.

Against the advice of Superintendent Steele, but in keeping with their mandate to make all haste to Dawson City, the "bank boys" decided to start at once by pushing their 20-foot Peterborough canoe through the softer ice along shore, a gutsy move that put them about three days ahead of the grand flotilla of craft setting out from Bennett.

The manager, Wills ("a very heavy man who should never have attempted the trip"[2]), and the cook, Comloquoy, along with one of the accountants from the second party and Stewart, an outsider known to the manager, set out on the 600-mile journey down the lakes and rivers of the upper Yukon system, which would take them into the swift-flowing river itself and eventually to Dawson.

After a gruelling day and only 10 miles of progress, they pitched their tent. On subsequent days they would be too tired to pitch it and would simply fall into their blankets after a quick bite to eat. At a police post they obtained a sled, enabling them, when the ice was solid, to unload the canoe, put it on the sled, reload it, then push and pull the sled for hours over rotten ice, expecting every moment to fall through, before relaunching the canoe when open water appeared.

On the third day the manager developed a sore throat and swollen legs, which meant a day's layover. The day after that they were blocked by an ice jam until a heavy scow broke a channel through the ice and they followed it in their Peterborough canoe.

On Marsh Lake shallow water made it necessary to unload and portage the gear, then go back and push the canoe, wading in mud up to their knees while mosquitoes attacked without mercy. Mosquitoes also made sleep impossible that night, and the manager was now quite ill. On May 28, while trying to reach an island in Marsh Lake, they broke through rotten ice but escaped with only a partial wetting. Open water appeared and they paddled hard down the Fifty Mile River to Miles Canyon, where they prudently portaged their canoe around the rapids.

On Lake Laberge they were able to paddle on open water to a large island, then had to resume pushing through rotten ice. On the Yukon River they stopped to weigh the danger as the high rocks of Five Finger Rapids loomed ahead. "After two or three hours of argument, the manager and two members of another party, one of whom could not swim, were prevailed on to walk around the rapids."

This plan lightened the canoe by nearly 300 pounds. Some of the gear was also put in the other party's canoe, which the Peterborough could tow. In the middle of the run the smaller canoe ran aboard the Peterborough, almost knocking one man overboard. It was all over in seconds as they ended the course with the canoe facing backwards in the water. Two or three hours later, "the manager arrived at the foot [of the rapids], bitten to pieces by mosquitoes and exceedingly wroth."[3] He announced in no uncertain terms that there would be no more climbing around rapids for him.

Farther downstream, Rink Rapids appeared much easier, with a good channel on the right-hand shore. But a fallen tree thrashing up and down in the channel forced them out into the worst of the rapids, where smashing waves assailed them, one almost filling the canoe. They made it through

The sternwheeler *Whitehorse*, ca. 1901, in the 80-foot-wide Five Finger Rapids on the Yukon River.
PHOTO: HERITAGE HOUSE COLLECTION

with an inch or two of freeboard to spare—and with themselves, their flour supply and gear soaking wet.

Rain began to fall on June 3, and continued for three days and nights. On June 4, with a swift current and prodded by sheer misery, they made 100 miles in a 17-hour day.

At midnight on June 5 these cold, wet, battered men, who had begun as sedentary office workers and graduated as veterans of North America's most notorious trail, landed with great joy at the police barracks in Dawson City.[4] Food was scarce in Dawson after a hard winter, but the Mounties scraped up a snack for the bank boys, who were finally able to stretch out to sleep on the guardhouse floor, their heads resting peacefully on their precious kit bags full of money. In the morning a small building clad with galvanized iron, formerly used for storing fish for sled dogs, became the first quarters of the Bank of Commerce in the Yukon.

On June 5, as this first party reached Dawson, the second party left Lake Bennett, part of a flotilla of a thousand boats, scows, rafts and canoes, all bound for Dawson, that would soon be followed by 6,000 more vessels of all descriptions. The bank party had a big scow built to cart their six tons of freight, and had arranged for a small sternwheeler to tow it. On June 14 it arrived in Dawson, and the next day a canvas sign nailed to a board read:

THE CANADIAN BANK OF COMMERCE
CAPITAL PAID UP SIX MILLION DOLLARS

The Bank of Commerce in the Yukon was open for business.

Six years later, in 1904, it was well known among Bank of Commerce employees that anyone assigned to one of the Yukon branches did very well financially, with a special allowance of $50 a month for food, living quarters provided, even their laundry looked after—and a $200 allowance to buy woollies and a coonskin coat.

By Robert's own account, he professed complete surprise when the accountant announced, just a few months into Robert's stint at Kamloops, that he'd been chosen to go to the Whitehorse branch. But Fred Corfield, who kept in touch with him, says Robert asked for a transfer to escape an unhappy love affair. This would seem to be a reference to Connie MacLean, who would have been known to Fred. Since Robert could only communicate with Connie by mail in Kamloops, and would still have to do so in Whitehorse, it is unclear what purpose he thought would be served by his moving farther away than he already was. Whatever the reason, Robert sold his pony, gave away his banjo and said goodbye to friends—with regret, but also with a feeling that something remarkable was happening in his life.

Robert returned to Vancouver to travel north from there by sea, although he does not record in his autobiography whether he saw Connie there before he left. Her daughter says that Connie was also heading north; in 1905 she worked as a governess to the children of Gold Commissioner James Allen Fraser in Atlin, British Columbia, which is 113 miles southeast of Whitehorse. Without letters from this period it is impossible to know how their relationship stood; it may have been coincidence that Robert and Connie went north at about the same time, or one of them may have followed the other.

Robert said his goodbyes, collected his allowance, bought his coonskin coat, pocketed the remainder of his allowance and got on the boat for Skagway.

Part 2

The *Yukon* Years

"There are strange things done in the midnight sun
By the men who moil for gold …"

"The Cremation of Sam McGee"

chapter 6

As Service steamed north in November 1904, the savage splendor of mountains and blue glaciers began to work on the head and heart of the firmly industrious, committed bank clerk. He was thrilled, for a start, that this wonderful journey was costing him not a cent. In fact, he was being paid two dollars a day.

The idea of being paid to have a marvelous time literally went to his head. His banking experience told him that if he could save enough money in the North, he could one day live, frugally, on the interest. A capital sum of $5,000 could yield $20 a month, and he certainly had experience living on less.

Critics of Robert's career often regret that he gave us so little description of the places he traveled. Instead, he absorbed places; he generated a kind of electric excitement from landscape and used it to create his poems.

So at Skagway, in the rain, he set out for Whitehorse on the Whitehorse and Yukon Railway. In 1899 the British Yukon Mining, Trading and Transportation Company had begun construction on this railroad over the White Pass, and in 1900 the first train reached Whitehorse.

As Robert's train climbed toward the pass, the rain turned to snow and the windows iced up, but neither in his autobiography nor in his known letters is there any description of the trail outside, of the rocks piled like packing boxes, or of the trestle above the graveyard of bones known as Dead Horse Gulch, where men had tried to pack 1,200 pounds on the backs of horses and make their way over slippery, slanted rocks in blizzard

The grandeur of mountains and sea and shore, as seen in this photograph, held Robert spellbound as *Princess Beatrice* steamed north to Skagway.
PHOTO: ENID MALLORY

The White Pass and Yukon Railway began operating from Skagway to Whitehorse in 1900. Visitors today can still take a train over the White Pass Summit as far as Carcross and Bennett.
PHOTO: GORD MALLORY

conditions only six years before. If Service knew of the tragic events that had taken place here, he made no mention of them.

Robert's train chugged over the pass, hugged the eastern shore of Lake Bennett and entered the Yukon Territory at Caribou Crossing. He arrived at Whitehorse to find a collection of wooden buildings on the left bank of the Yukon River, just downstream from Miles Canyon and the White Horse Rapids. It had grown up as a place of rest and recuperation for people going "in" to the goldfields or "out" via Skagway. When Robert first saw it, it was appropriately dressed in snow. He alighted from the train to a platform full of men in coonskin coats; one of them introduced himself as his new manager, Leonard De Gex.

One of the best things Robert would recall about Whitehorse was the sense of finding a home. He, the teller and the bank manager and his wife shared living quarters. For the past seven years, the closest he had come to having a home was the little room above Corfield's store—he had put down some tentative roots there. For the past year, "home" had been a room above a bank, first in Victoria, then in Kamloops. Even in Scotland, "home" had often been something uncertain and provisional, as the grandparents and aunts who raised him tried to make up for the lack of mother and father. When he did go to live with his parents he no longer knew them, or his brothers and sisters (in his writings, he never seemed exactly sure even how many siblings he had). Now, in Whitehorse, he had a sense of kinship with his banking family. De Gex was an ex-sea captain—someone who had actually sailed the seven seas as Robert himself had longed to do. Robert described him as a "virtuoso in slang," who was full of humor and stories. His young wife was charming and had a motherly fondness for "her boys." The teller, Harold Tylor, seemed "brilliant" to Robert, filled with energy and good at any sport, a hunter and fisherman and extremely popular. Robert described their meals together as "sheer merriment."

One of his most vivid memories of Whitehorse was the fire that raged through the town in the spring of 1905. In a town of wood-framed buildings, log cabins and flimsy shacks, when stoves overheated in the sub-Arctic cold, fire was a fact of life. Although relatively new to town, Service was a member of the fire brigade, so this was not the first time he had been called from his bed in temperatures that could be −50 degrees F, to perform the ghastly work of coupling hoses, dealing with frozen lines, playing water on the flames and getting wet—until he and the other firefighters became figures encased in ice.

But the great fire of 1905 was in May, and it occurred only one day after the department received new firefighting equipment. It started at the White Pass Hotel on First Street, across from the White Pass Railway station. Smoke was pouring out of the building, but the pumphouse engineer could not be found. Furious men searched bars and the red-light district until they found the miscreant. Service and his comrades waited in panic, hoses in hand, until finally the pump was started. Water! And then it stopped. The engineer in charge had let the water tanks run dry.

As if to mock their plight, the flames shot up again. Now the stores around the hotel ignited. With buckets of water, men climbed to the roofs trying to save their buildings. Others salvaged store contents, dragging assets into the street. Flames jumped across the street to the railway station, then to the freight shed and storehouses. Robert helped a grocer friend and his daughter carry out stock, including cans of gasoline.

By 1904, when Service arrived in Whitehorse, sternwheelers still plied the river, but many were tied up and abandoned.
PHOTO: HERITAGE HOUSE COLLECTION

Suddenly De Gex yelled at him that the fire had spread to Second Avenue, and the Bank of Commerce was threatened. There were four barrels of water beside the bank, and the men feverishly doused boards that were smoking from the heat, while across the street a small building burned to the ground. The captain climbed up to the balcony while Mrs. De Gex worked alongside Robert and another man to pass buckets of water up to him. Together they saved the bank, but when it was over the town that had stood around it was a charred ruin.

That spring and summer was so hectic that all dreaming was put on the shelf. Carpenters poured over the White Pass, and a new Whitehorse sprang to life. Businesses reopened in tents, as they had begun in 1897, and soon there were new buildings, and even prosperity. When it was over, and the last boat of the season arrived from Dawson and the train had carried the departees out to Skagway, the calm in Whitehorse was euphoric.

Soon after his arrival in Whitehorse, Robert followed the example of his new mentor, Harold Tylor, who was saving up to marry a girl back in Ontario. He gave up drinking and began to save every penny he could. According to *Ploughman*, he had no notion of getting married at this time, but he had his own dream—freedom from work, which in turn would give him freedom to write. It was well known that young men sent north by the bank often succumbed to the dance halls and the saloons and went home flat broke. Robert was determined not to follow their example.

Service watched his first Yukon summer arrive with its wonderful long days and its tide of new and returning residents—summer prospectors and people who had gone "outside" for the winter, workers and adventure-seekers. The steady influx of people and their bustling activity made life at the bank hectic. Then summer was over and the Great Cold clamped down on the town. To his own surprise, the man who had always steered a southern course found he loved winter in the North. As 1905 ended, work at the bank slowed to a quarter of the summer volume, and that meant free time in which to fuel his imagination.

At Cowichan, dreaming had seemed futile, misguided. Here in Whitehorse, however, he had a sense that this hiatus was taking him where he yearned to go. "Creative dreaming," he called it.

I have never been popular ... I was polite and pleasant, but leaned back socially. I became notorious as a solitary walker, going off by myself as soon as work was done, into the Great White Silence. My lonely walks were my real life; the sheer joy of them thrilled me. I exulted in my love of nature, and rarely have I been happier.[1]

Actually, from other accounts, his life in Whitehorse seemed reasonably well balanced. Social occasions were available every night: skating on the rink, toboggan slides, handball, indoor baseball, whist (which he hated) and dances (which he loved). His social assets were his banjo and his ability to sing and recite poetry. Although he never felt popular, he tagged along with Tylor and others who were, and he usually enjoyed himself.

Since De Gex was a churchman, he marched his "family" off to the Whitehorse Episcopal church, where Service, a professed agnostic, listened at first to the redoubtable Isaac Stringer, a dedicated missionary who later, in 1910, reputedly ate his boots to avoid starving on the trail between Fort McPherson and Dawson. Stringer left Whitehorse in 1906—after being made Bishop of the Yukon—and spent the next 25 years in Dawson, then the territory's most populous town. The man who replaced him at Whitehorse was Reverend Hiram A. Cody, who shared with Service a love affair with words. Cody would become a prolific writer, first publishing a biography of Bishop William Bompas, Stringer's predecessor, then going on to write popular novels and poetry, his poems often showing the influence of Robert Service. Encouraged by Captain De Gex, Robert served as secretary and treasurer of the church vestry, and passed the collection plate. Years later he wrote, "though I may not believe in religion, I believe in churches … I respect the spirit of religion, that reverence for the finer things of life. Churches are a rallying point in the fight for a heaven on earth."[2]

Meanwhile, as a young deacon in the Whitehorse church, he wrote ribald verse about his role: "Me that's a pillar of the church an' takes the rake-off there, An says: 'God damn you, dig for the Lord,' if the boys don't ante fair."[3] They were lines that a publisher later refused to print, considering them sacrilegious. Robert, the student of human nature, was observing the parishioners at church much as he did the denizens of the gambling halls and using the same irreverent language to describe them.

In a letter to Harold Tylor when both men were in their 80s, he recalled the time he tried to talk Harold into gambling with the church money. Harold, whom he described as moral and exemplary, declined. But according to that letter, Robert had a session at the blackjack table with the church's money.

Only one letter survives from Robert to Constance MacLean in these Whitehorse years. It was written to her Hornby Street address in Vancouver in October 1906 and concerned a friend named Lionel Cowper, who had died in a terrible steamboat accident. Service said Cowper was the nephew of an earl, "six-foot two with a physique like Adonis," and worked as a deck-hand on the boat (contemporary reports in the *Weekly Star* say he was the purser of the steamer *Columbia*). The *Columbia* was pushing a scow-load of barrels containing gunpowder. When a duck came winging up the river, the cabin boy ran for his gun, but on the way back he tripped and the gun went off, the bullet striking one of the tin barrels and igniting the three tons of gunpowder they contained. Flame enveloped the steamer. Captain J.O. Williams managed to run the boat ashore. Two men died instantly, and three more soon after. Two remained badly injured, one of them Cowper.

The accident was at Eagle Rock, about 20 miles above Tantalus and 5 miles below the Little Salmon River. The captain and his remaining men constructed a raft and took the news to Tantalus, where they wired Whitehorse for help. The steamer *Dawson* set out at once on the 100-mile rescue trip, with Dr. Pare and a nurse onboard. Meanwhile, the steamer *Victorian*, coming upriver, took on the injured and the dead, transferring them to the faster *Dawson* when the two boats met.

In Service's biography he has forgotten the time sequence and says that Cowper died the next day, but the Whitehorse *Weekly Star* puts the accident on Tuesday, September 26, and Cowper's death on Thursday, October 10. Service saw him the day before his death.

Service had the address of Cowper's mother, and the hard task of writing to her. But he turned to Connie first with his pen, telling her the story and how it affected him. He said Cowper had not been allowed visitors, so he did not make an effort to see him. But the previous day Cowper had asked to see Robert and had begged him to smuggle in some water because he was crazy with thirst.

The *Weekly Star* said: "Death came as a relief after such suffering as is rarely ever allotted to a human being."[4] In his letter to Connie, Robert described how shaken he was by Cowper's death. He asked if she was all right now, indicating that there had been previous contact or letters (if they survive, they have not yet come to light).

In *Ploughman,* years later, he pondered Cowper's death and his own life:

An insignificant shrimp like myself permitted to survive while so many fine fellows were stamped out. More and more I believed in my guardian angel, and the experience of a lifetime has strengthened that belief. I know it is absurd and irrational, but I have steered through so many troubled waters to a serene haven that I cannot help fancying a guiding hand on the rudder.[5]

chapter 7

In Whitehorse, Robert Service seems to have been neither troubled nor serene. His solitary tramps in the woods above the town were the highlight of his days. He exulted in the weather, whether sunshine, rain or snow, warm or deadly cold. With his cocker spaniel—and sometimes joined by four or five other dogs—he explored the trails that led to Miles Canyon, the magnificent watery hell that every newcomer had to pass through on his way to the gold fields. Coming around a bend, he faced the gorge where the river narrowed and boiled, where a terrifying whirlpool lurked at its center and rock walls rose a hundred feet high. If a man got his craft through the canyon he had to face the jagged rocks of Squaw Rapids, followed by the White Horse Rapids, named for the flying foam that looked like running white horses when the sun lit it up. Out here, Robert was soaking in the drama and suspense of the landscape, while in town he was learning the language of the gold rush. He knew by now that "cheechako" was a Chinook word for a tenderfoot or newcomer, while a "sourdough" was someone who had seen the Yukon River freeze in the fall and the ice go out again in the spring—and got his nickname from the bread he made in the winter when yeast was hard to come by. Excited by what he heard and saw, Robert often walked late at night, feeling the powerful pull of the moon and an urgent need to express the rapture it engendered in him.

Robert was also part of the social life that revolved around Christ Church. In June 1906 he organized a theatrical show consisting of six

Once sternwheelers like the *Clifford Sifton* (seen here shooting Miles Canyon, in July 1900) cleared the whitewater just above Whitehorse, they could not return upriver, making Whitehorse the head of navigation on the Yukon River.

PHOTO: HERITAGE HOUSE COLLECTION

musical selections and a monologue, which he composed, followed by a one-act farce in which local Mounties donned female costumes. One of them, Captain T.V. Fleming, later recalled how he borrowed frilly drawers from the red-light district and how, in the bank building, "Robert W. Service made me up." For safety reasons the bank had to be brightly lit at all times, with no curtains drawn. Next day he and Service were amused to find a dreadful scandal going around town about a bank employee "behaving

most disgracefully with a loose woman."[1] Robert directed as well as acted in this production. Reverend Cody described the show as "splendid" and later explained how the monologue Service originally planned led to the writing of "The Shooting of Dan McGrew."

Pondering what to recite for the monologue, Service ran into Stroller White, editor of the *Daily Evening Star* (predecessor of the *Weekly Star,* and of today's *Whitehorse Star*), in which Stroller had published some of his verse. Service asked him what theme he should take for his monologue, and the editor told him to write something original. "Give us something about our own bit of earth. We sure would appreciate it. There's a rich paystreak waiting for some one to work. Why don't you go in and stake it?"[2]

Stroller White knew his Yukon. He had worked for the *Skagway News* in the days when Soapy Smith had the town in his clutches, then moved on to the *Bennett Sun* and the *Klondike Nugget* in Dawson City. In Whitehorse his instinct for the dramatic attracted him to something he saw in Robert Service.

With Stroller's challenge in his head, Robert walked the streets. It was a Saturday night, and as he passed the saloons he could hear that a bunch of the boys were whooping it up. He had the first line of his piece, and the rest soon followed. Characters appeared in his head as if waiting to come on stage—Dangerous Dan McGrew, the Ragtime Kid, the lady known as Lou.

His "family" was asleep when he came into the bank building, so he slipped downstairs to his teller's cage wanting feverishly to get the words down on paper.

In *Ploughman of the Moon*, Robert says he had forgotten that the ledger-keeper in the guardroom packed a gun. "Suddenly the man, awakened out of a tennis-championship dream, heard a noise near the safe. Burglars! ... Fortunately he was a poor shot or the Shooting of Dan McGrew might never have been written ... Anyhow with the sensation of a bullet whizzing past my head and a detonation ringing in my ears, the ballad was achieved."[3]

This story, as Robert admitted to Pierre Berton in an interview shortly before his death, is not true. Just like Dan McGrew, he had made it up. Whatever did happen in the bank in the dark of that night, the phrases and rhymes of Dan McGrew burst from his head with the force of gunfire. By the time he went to bed at 5:00 a.m., the ballad was in the bag. Generations of poetry readers all over the world were destined to carry around in their heads the lyrical opening lines of the poem about a bunch of boys whooping it up in the Malamute saloon and the kid on piano who was "hitting a jag-time tune."

But "The Shooting of Dan McGrew" contained too many cuss words for the church concert. Cody says that Robert instead recited "Minding a Baby." According to Robert's autobiography, he wrote "The Cremation of Sam McGee" a month later, then put his verses away in a drawer for more than a year. This seems unlikely if the recollections of Cody and Fleming are valid. It *is* known that he sent his verses to a publisher in the fall of 1906. If Robert's "year in a drawer" is accurate, this would mean he wrote them in 1905. Most likely Dan McGrew first came to life in the summer of 1906 and spent only months in the drawer.

"The Cremation of Sam McGee" had its creation story too. One night at a party, a mining man from Dawson, when he heard that Robert wrote poetry, said he'd tell him a good story—one that "Jack London never got." He then proceeded to spin a tale of a man out on the trail who cremated the body of his pal. The surprise ending of the story brought loud laughter from others who had listened, but not from Robert. Overcome by the gift of a perfect story and perhaps a growing sense of his own destiny, he felt he had to get out of the house. "It was one of those nights of brilliant moonlight that almost goad me to madness. I took the woodland trail, my mind seething with excitement and a strange ecstasy."[4] He walked for six

The *Olive May* is believed to be the boat on which a cremation took place—the inspiration for Robert Service's famous poem.

PHOTO: HERITAGE HOUSE COLLECTION

hours in bright moonlight with words and images racing through his head. Finally he went home and slept, and the next day lines of verse continued to take shape as he put words to paper.

The Sam McGee poem is based on an actual event, but the real cremation story has to be unraveled out of confused reports concerning Lake Laberge and two different boats, *Olive May* and *Alice May*. The story begins in 1899, when the Bennett Lake and Klondike Company's *Olive May* ran through Bennett and Nares lakes to Tagish and down Taku Arm to the Taku townsite. That year *Olive May* struck a rock near Tagish and partially sunk.

That winter, a doctor, Leonard Sugden, got a report from the Mounted Police of a miner suffering from scurvy on Tagish Lake. "Doc" Sugden mushed there, but found the man dead. Burial was impossible, as the ground was frozen as stiff as the corpse. Sugden transported the body by sled to the telegraph station at Tagish and cabled the man's family, asking if he could cremate the body. The miner's name has been lost, but Sugden's grandson believed he really was from Tennessee, as Robert's fictional Sam McGee would be.

Dr. Leonard Sugden was the man
who cremated the famous miner
from Tennessee.
PHOTO COURTESY OF DOROTHY SUGDEN

The answer came back in favor of cremation. Sugden transported the
body to the *Olive May*, lit the firebox below her boiler (which was still above
the waterline), stuffed in the miner's body, and the rest is poetic history.

Leonard Sugden was born in Scotland and studied medicine at Christ
Church, Oxford. When his parents moved to Winnipeg he followed them,
and found that their next-door neighbor was Sam Steele, superintendent in
the NWMP. Possibly influenced by Steele, Leonard launched himself on a life
of adventure, first as surgeon on a sperm-whaling bark. In 1897 he joined the
stampede over the Chilkoot Pass and was one of hundreds frozen in before they
could reach the goldfields. He built a cabin where he had stopped, near the foot
of Marsh Lake and about 18 miles north of the NWMP Tagish Post.[5]

Some written accounts of Sugden's deed put *Olive May* on Lake
Laberge and the miner near Tagish Post. But Tagish Post was on Tagish
Lake, some 60 miles south of Lake Laberge. The confusion arises because
Service set the action on Lake Laberge (which he changed to "Labarge" for
the sake of euphony) and called the boat *Alice May*. As fate would have it,
a boat named Alice May actually came to grief on Lake Laberge years after
the poem was written. Its hull can still be seen today at the south end of
Richthofen Island.

This boat was originally launched as *May West* at St. Michael, Alaska, in 1896. It was sold to the Royal Northwest Mounted Police and renamed *Vidette,* and then sold again and named *Alice May.* She struck a sandbar and sank a decade after Service's "The Cremation of Sam McGee" was published, so her name most certainly was taken from Robert's poem, a case of life imitating art with almost disconcerting exactness.

It was *Olive May,* grounded on Tagish Lake in 1899, close to the cabin in which the unknown miner died of scurvy, that was the model for Robert's famous *Alice May* and Sam McGee's crematorium.

The original version of Robert's poem, which can be seen in the Yukon Archives, does not mention Lake Laberge. The action takes place "on the periphery of Lake McKiflery" (a wholly fictitious name). As Service reworked his poem, a moment of inspiration—and the need for a rhyme—gave him "the marge of Lake Lebarge."

In this first version, the man cremated was named Sam McKlot. That didn't satisfy Service either. Next day, with his mind not entirely on his bank work, he read the ledger, looking for a name that would trip liltingly off the tongue and rhyme with Tennessee. There it was: Sam McGee! Perfect! With innocent disregard for the bank client, and certainly no thought that the poem would be read around the world, he helped himself to the name.

In his autobiography, Service—careful not to reveal the identity of Sugden, a well-known resident of the Yukon—said the story came from a portly, pompous miner from Dawson. Sugden, on the other hand, was a fit, athletic doctor who by this time had lived a life of remarkable adventure, served as a surgeon in the Boer War and on both sides in the Sino–Japanese War. In Whitehorse he made over four hundred trips through the White Horse Rapids as a river pilot; he was now married and mining on Kluane Lake. While Service had lifted Sam's name from his bank ledger without qualms in 1905, he had become paranoid about names in 1940, as he began to write his autobiography. By that time he had not only experienced the embarrassment caused by the real Sam McGee objecting to the use of his name, but had been sued by a British baron for using a name similar to the baron's in one of his novels (though the latter resemblance was, it seems, accidental).

If Service wrote his two most famous poems in the summer of 1906, the sequence and development of his other Whitehorse poems remains a mystery. He describes one day in early spring, standing above Miles Canyon and looking

Tagish Lake broods under a dark sky.
PHOTO: GORD MALLORY

down on White Horse Rapids, drunk with the beauty of it. As he gazed on "naked grandeur" the poem that would become "The Call of the Wild" came to him, as if dictated by the wild scenery itself (Jack London's novel of the same title had been published just three years before). In the two months that followed he tramped the trails and wrote every day, he claimed. "The Spell of the Yukon" and "The Law of the Yukon" came to him in the great outdoors and were then put on paper in his room and stuffed in a drawer.

Service described this time in Whitehorse as a phase of almost manic happiness. He wrote that sometimes he thought he would burst with sheer delight. He mentioned early spring as the time of writing "The Call of the Wild"; there's a rampant form of spring fever that affects all Yukoners and makes them pack amazing levels of activity into the lengthening brightness around the summer solstice. Service spoke of the intense gusto of living. He was 31 years old, well fed by Mrs. De Gex, physically fit from his daily tramps, part of a family, coping well with the shyness and inferiority complex that sometimes made him socially awkward, secure in his job, and with enough free time to feed his soul.

Service chose to cloud the details of his Yukon years or had simply

Lake Laberge was made famous by Service's poem about Sam McGee.
PHOTO: GORD MALLORY

forgotten them by the time he wrote his autobiography. Exactly when he did his most creative work remains vague.

Vagueness also surrounds his relationship with Constance MacLean at this time. In 1905, when Robert and the rest of Whitehorse were still rueing the misdeeds of their fire brigade, their town reduced to ashes, Connie MacLean was living in Atlin, B.C., not far south of the B.C.–Yukon border, working as a governess. Atlin was accessible from Whitehorse in 1905 by taking the train to Carcross and then the steamer across Tagish Lake to Taku, where the Short Line Railway connected to Atlin Lake. It would have been easy for them to visit each other, but there is no record of either Service or Connie making the trip.

Two documents, however, do confirm that the two had stayed in touch: a letter Service wrote to her in October 1906 and a copy of Service's first poetry collection. Connie's family still has that copy of Service's collection, which is marked in Connie's handwriting as the "First copy issued of Songs of a Sourdough." She has also made annotations throughout that indicate she knew some details about the poems. The fly-leaf has his message to her:

This courthouse in Atlin, B.C., on the edge of the Yukon, housed the gold commissioner, James Allen Fraser. and his family in 1905. That year, Connie MacLean was governess to the family.

PHOTO: ENID MALLORY

To Connie
with Love & Gratitude
from the Author
(In absence of a formal Dedication)
WhiteHorse Y.T.
25th June 1907.

One day, about the same time Service wrote the 1906 letter to Connie, he reviewed his sheaf of verses. There is proof that he had reworked some if not all of them, and at this point they seemed not bad. Hesitantly he asked Mrs. De Gex to read them.

She agreed and suggested that he make a book out of the best of them and give it to friends for Christmas. She advised him to leave out the McGrew poem, the McGee one and the two called "Harpy" and "My Madonna."

When Robert heard from Mr. De Gex that he was to get a $100 Christmas bonus, he decided to squander it by getting his book published. Harold Tylor suggested the Methodist Book Room in Toronto as a suitable publisher. Robert's parents had immigrated to Canada in April 1906 and were living in Toronto. Robert sent off his manuscript to his father, asking him to deliver it to a firm that would publish work at the author's expense.

At the last moment, and against the advice of Mrs. De Gex, he included "McGrew," "McGee," "The Harpy" and "My Madonna." His order was for 100 copies or as many as his check would cover, and he prepared to make a fool of himself giving them away.

His father was delighted to help. Although Robert Sr. no longer worked in the conventional sense, he "considered the launching of his family his chief occupation." Stanley, Robert's brother, describes him going off to the publisher all dressed up "in his grey topper and fancy vest with his heavy gold watch chain, his cut-away tail-coat and loud checkered trousers ... and walking stick—a picture to behold."[6]

In January 1907 in the office of Reverend William Briggs, the Toronto Methodist publisher, was literary editor Edward Caswell and a young salesman named Russell Bond, who was about to make his annual trip west. Caswell thrust at Bond some proof sheets of the book of poetry they were producing for some fellow in the Yukon—at his expense, of course, since Canadian poetry did not often make money for a publisher. "Try to sell some for him, if you can," he told him. Bond shoved the proof sheets in his pocket as he made for the train station.

As the Canadian Pacific transcontinental sped through the early darkness of that winter night, Bond sat in the dining car and pulled out the page proofs. "It was the 'Cremation of Sam McGee,' and I became so enthralled I forgot my meal and burst out laughing as it finished with the lines about the man from Tennessee who finally got warm."

A commercial traveler sitting across from him wanted to know what was funny. Bond replied, "It's unusual and it's Canadian, and it might even sell."

That commercial traveler was the first person to hear "The Cremation of Sam McGee" read aloud. He laughed until he choked and had to leave the car. Later Bond passed through the smoking car and heard the man telling his friends about it. When Bond came back later for a smoke he was urged to read "that McGee poem" to the crowd. People passing through the car stopped and those who came late insisted he read it again.

By the time Bond reached his first stop at Fort William, at the top of Lake Superior, he knew "The Cremation of Sam McGee" by heart. Here he would not have a captive audience on a moving train, but a busy bookstore owner uninterested in a book salesman bearing poetry.

He was lucky. The owner had already heard of the poetry reading on the train, and he ordered five copies. At Portage la Prairie, the bookseller irritated Bond by saying, "If Billy Bill had that book, he'd really sell it." Bill was acknowledged as the best book salesman in Canada, while Bond was just 23 years old and new at the game. He made up his mind right there that he would push this book to the limit and sell it as well as Billy Bill ever could.

In Lethbridge, the bookseller–druggist listened to both "Dan McGrew" and "Sam McGee" and asked if he could read them to the men at the club for lunch. He came back with orders for 36.

In Calgary Bond was thrilled when Jim Linton of Linton Brothers bookstore ordered 25 copies. Linton had his own definition of a sourdough: a man who had seen the Yukon River both freeze up and thaw, and who "had shot a bear and slept with a squaw."

Early in March, in Revelstoke, the first sample copy of *Songs of a Sourdough,* with its dedication to someone whose initials were C.M., reached Bond hot off the press. "How I swore! It was a poor-looking, thin book, bound in green cloth, marked Author's Edition." And it was listed at 75 cents while Bond had been selling it for a dollar. Bond got a message off to Briggs, telling him to check the orders he had sent in at one dollar and note that the first edition was just about sold out. He suggested that the firm offer a contract and pay the author royalties. Briggs agreed, and kept the price at one dollar.

Service was at work in the bank that day in early spring 1907 when a letter arrived from Briggs. He hadn't time to read the long letter, but he could see that his check had been returned. So the Methodist publisher was refusing to print his stuff, he thought, thereby saving him from making a fool of himself. Relief was mixed with chagrin.

When work was done he read, then re-read, the letter with a growing sense of stupefaction. The letter told of Bond selling 1,700 copies from the galley proofs. The company wanted to publish at their expense and pay him royalties.

Robert writes in *Ploughman* that he telegraphed acceptance of the offer so quickly that they couldn't change their minds. But Bond told *Globe Magazine* in 1958: "I never will forget his surprised and pleased reply. He suggested that there might be some mistake, and asked how long the royalties might continue. I have no doubt he is still wondering, for certainly no Canadian poet, or possibly any poet, has received as much as Mr. Service has received—and continues to receive, for the sale goes on."[7]

It was typical of Robert's solitude—or maybe his disbelief—that he hugged the glad news to himself. He told only Mrs. De Gex until the two dozen copies he had ordered arrived on the first train up from Skagway.

It wasn't until people from outside began to arrive that Whitehorse residents realized they had a celebrity in their bank. When they did, the ladies of the sewing circle—using the deacon, Hiram Cody, as a mouthpiece—objected to the "bad women" in the book and the lack of good ones. Robert Service was someone who passed the collection plate in their church, a bank clerk and, after Harold Tylor's transfer to Dawson, a teller. He was expected to move in the right social circles. In *Ploughman of the Moon* he says: "I wrote of human nature, of the life of a mining camp, of the rough miners and the dance-hall girls. Vice seemed to me a more vital subject for poetry than virtue, more colourful, more dramatic, so I specialized in the Red Light atmosphere."[8] In a letter to Harold Tylor written in 1952, he recalled how respectable Harold was, and how shocked the church ladies had been with himself.

Cody invited Service to the rectory and they had a long talk. Service said that he had nothing against virtue, but readers tended to find it rather a bore—an answer that would have done nothing to redeem him in church circles. Yet the two came to an understanding that let them remain friends; they got together often to talk about writing and trade reading materials. Cody shared with Service his notes of missionary travel among the Native people, and in his poetry adopted the style, if not colorful language, of Service. Meanwhile the bank's local customers had to watch tourists line up to push their books through the wicket and get them signed by Robert Service. The town's moral vigilantes backed off and accepted Service's book and his success. He did, however, resign from his vestry job.

The first poem in *Songs of a Sourdough* is "The Law of the Yukon." In it the poet serves notice that he won't be writing conventionally "pretty" poetry about this iron-fisted land; he will tell it as hard and cold and unforgiving as it comes.

> *This is the law of the Yukon, and ever she makes it plain:*
> *"Send not your foolish and feeble; send me your strong and your sane ...*
> *Them will I gild with my treasure, them will I glut with my meat;*
> *But the others—the misfits, the failures—I trample under my feet..."*

In "The Call of the Wild" there are black canyons and roaring rapids and wind in the night. The poem ends with a beckoning to others like himself:

> *Let us probe the silent places, let us seek what luck betide us;*
> *Let us journey to a lonely land I know.*
> *There's a whisper on the night-wind, there's a star agleam to guide us,*
> *And the wild is calling, calling ... let us go.*

Service often stressed the smallness of man against the vast north land. In "The Heart of the Sourdough" he deals with the inevitability of death and defeat.

With the raw-ribbed Wild that abhors all life, the Wild that would crush and rend;
I have clinched and closed with the naked North, I have learned to defy and defend;
Shoulder to shoulder we've fought it out—Yet the Wild must win in the end.

No one has ever described this frozen land as well as Service in "The Spell of the Yukon" (it became the title for the U.S. edition of the collection). The entire poem has a ringing sharpness, with phrases that live in the memory: "the bighorn asleep on the hill ... the brightness that blinds you, the white land locked tight as a drum ... the silence that bludgeons you dumb ... valleys unpeopled and still."

The poem ends with a summation of how the Yukon speaks to his soul:

It's the beauty that thrills me with wonder,
It's the stillness that fills me with peace.

But the poems that tell a story are something else; these people-poems grab the reader and rivet the listener. In "The Harpy," a blunt portrait of an aging prostitute and the "wolf-pack" that preys upon her, Service shows such a depth of understanding for the "tarnished" women of the mining camp that even the sternest of the righteous women of Whitehorse society, even Bishop Stringer and the Pringle brothers, both Presbyterian ministers, must have felt a twinge of empathy.

There was a woman, and she was wise; woefully wise was she;
She was old, so old, yet her years all told were but a score and three;
And she knew by heart, from finish to start, the Book of Iniquity.[9]

He makes his point again in "Madonna," a poem about a woman of the street chosen by a painter to pose for his portrait of the Madonna, which was to hang in the church of Saint Hilaire.

But it was two of his people-poems in particular that stuck like glue to the public imagination: "The Cremation of Sam McGee" and "The Shooting of Dan McGrew." Their rhymes danced in the air when read. They got a grand reception in every dining room, drawing room, schoolhouse and saloon where they were recited. Fans across the entire English-speaking world would come to know these poems.

Fisher Unwin of London published a British edition and the New York publisher, Barse and Hopkins, as well as E. Stern and Co. of Philadelphia, rushed the poems into print. All of this happened in 1907. Each year thereafter edition after edition would be published or reprinted as the demand for Service's poems spread. *Songs of a Sourdough* had become a phenomenon in the publishing world.

On the first day of the stampede in 1898, 150 boats were lost and 10 men drowned in Miles Canyon and the White Horse Rapids. By 1899, the real Sam McGee was helping operate the tramway that carted goods and canoes and boats around the treacherous canyon and rapids.
PHOTO: YUKON ARCHIVES, T.R. LANE COLLECTION 1391

Sam McGee married Ruth Warnes in Peterborough, June 5, 1901, then headed back to the Yukon with his new wife. Sam was 33; Ruth was 18.

PHOTO: COURTESY OF BEVERLY GRAMMS

One hard-working man in Whitehorse was acutely aware of the commotion Robert's poems were causing. His name was Sam McGee. He could no longer meet a friend on the street or have a drink with his road-building crew without someone asking, "How's the furnace, Sam?" or "Hot enough yet?" or "Please close that door!" Robert Service's poem was everywhere you turned. One day the irritation got the best of him, and he marched into the Bank of Commerce and drew out his money. That would show that lousy little bank clerk!

Sam was born in 1868 on a bush farm between Bobcaygeon and Fenelon Falls in the Kawartha Lakes district of Ontario. He left home at 15—perhaps because of a dispute with his older brothers after the death of their father in May 1884. Fifteen years later he was on the west coast, probably San Francisco, when hordes of people were leaving for the Klondike, and he joined them.

Sam arrived in the North in the fall of 1898 and became a packer. By the time he reached Skagway, the mob of humanity, horses, dogs, goats, sheep, oxen and even cows had thinned, and a more orderly and generally more competent crowd of men worked to cart freight over the passes. A tramway had been built on the steepest portion of the Chilkoot Pass, which let those with money convey heavier goods 14 miles to the summit. The White Pass had no tramway, and the railway had not yet been built, so goods still had to be carted by the muscle power of man or beast. In places where the trail had been blocked by a pileup of injured horses and spilled goods mired in bogs, men had cut trees and made crude bridges and corduroy roads. In a letter written in 1938, Sam says: "I went to the Yukon in the fall of 1898, and that winter freighted the steamer 'Glenar' [i.e., *Gleaner*] from the White Pass to the head of Lake Bennett."

By the fall of 1898, enterprising men were building larger boats for the Yukon route. The John Irving Navigation Company brought in the makings for *Gleaner* and two other sternwheelers that year to construct at the headwaters of the Yukon River. All the parts to build them—wood, engines, boilers—had to be freighted from the sea over the Coast Mountains using either the Chilkoot or the White Pass route. Material for *Gleaner* and *Reaper* were carted to Lake Bennett for construction, while *Scotia* was built on Atlin Lake. *Gleaner* was launched on May 2, 1899, and made its first trip to Taku on May 6.

In the 1938 letter Sam says: "When we got through with that job we took horses to operate the tram road around Miles Canyon and White Horse Rapids on the Yukon river the summer of 1899."

Sam loved the Yukon from the start. All the news from Dawson suggested it was too late to strike it rich there, but what he saw around Whitehorse looked hopeful. "In July 1899," he says, "I staked copper property some miles from White Horse Rapids."[10] Like thousands of others in Dawson and Whitehorse, he was expecting the big break, but in the meantime he had lots of jobs, and he was happy working outside whatever the weather. Unlike the character who would become famous in Service's poem, he didn't mind the cold.

Sam built himself a log cabin that can still be seen today beside the Whitehorse Museum on First Avenue. After freighting the White Pass route and carting people, goods and canoes around Miles Canyon and the White Horse Rapids, he was occupied with building roads to the new mining properties or freighting goods to them. In the winter of 1901 he was freighting across the ice of Lake Laberge.

That spring he made his first trip back east to Ontario since he had left as a teenager. His mother, Ellen, had died in April 1900, and by 1901 Sam had decided to go east, sell the farm and come back to the Yukon where he belonged. While he was home he met 18-year-old Ruth Warnes, who had cared for his mother when she was ill. Sam and Ruth fell in love and were married in Peterborough in June. By August Sam had sold his land, and he and Ruth set out for Sam's Yukon.

Back in Whitehorse, while Sam pursued his work, Ruth gave birth to a son, Walter, followed a year later by a baby girl, Ethel; these were the first of four McGee children born in Whitehorse. Much of the time Ruth was on her own, dependent on neighbors for help. In 1903 Sam was involved in the gold rush centered on Canyon Creek (also known as the Aishihik River), west of Whitehorse on the wagon road leading to Silver City near Kluane Lake. He and a partner named Skelly built a bridge across Canyon Creek and in 1904 were running a roadhouse there.

By 1905 the action had shifted to Carcross (formerly Caribou Crossing) and Montana Mountain, south of Whitehorse on the shores of Tagish Lake's Windy Arm. Here, a new boom town was springing up, known as Conrad City; silver was the main attraction. As excitement mounted and men invested their savings here, Sam McGee built roads up Montana mountain, operated a sawmill on Tagish Lake and towed his lumber to the busy Conrad City townsite. In August 1905 he was foreman of a 20-man crew building an 11-mile road from Carcross to Conrad City. In September he started 16 men on a seven-mile pack trail from Carcross to the Big Thing Mine on the mountain. There were other mines—such as Mountain Hero, Venus, Thistle-Aurora, Montana, Caribou and Vega—and they all needed roads or pack trails to cart in their equipment.

In the winter of 1906 Sam and Frank Johnson leased an old sawmill at Tagish and worked steadily to get it into operation. By spring they had lumber ready for the busiest summer ever seen on the headwaters of the Yukon. On June 29 the *Weekly Star*'s "Conrad City News" section reported: "McGee and Johnson brought in a big raft of timber the other day containing 60,000 feet and another raft is expected this week. Mr. McGee informed the writer that the sale of lumber is advancing very rapidly."[11]

At a banquet in Whitehorse, Colonel Conrad, chief promoter of the silver stampede, suggested there would be 30,000 people in Conrad City within two years. It was not to be. Joseph Burr Tyrrell, Canada's top geologist of the day, was brought to Montana Mountain by William Mackenzie (co-owner of the Great Northern Railway) to assess his company's 84 claims. Tyrrell burst the Montana Mountain bubble when he found that the gold and silver petered out as the tunnels got deeper. By the end of 1906, the dreams of a whole army of investors and workmen, including Sam McGee, were shattered.

It is unlikely that Ruth saw much of her husband in these busy years; in the summer of 1906 she made a trip "outside" and came back convinced that she wanted to live somewhere warmer than the Yukon. To compensate, Sam built her a new house in Whitehorse on the corner of Fifth Avenue and Wood (this house survives today as a bed-and-breakfast).

The year 1907 was not a good one for Sam. Conrad City had been his Dawson, and now it was over, so he was not in a good mood to be "cremated" by an upstart poet as well. He first heard the poem when Service himself recited it at a banquet given for August Heinz, a copper magnate from Butte, Montana. After that he had no peace.

One of the stories that circulates to this day, especially popular in Whitehorse, concerns a trip through Miles Canyon. It may be true, or Sam may have invented it to get even with Service for using his name. In some versions the action takes place in a canoe, in others on a boat. One newspaper that quotes Sam himself puts the action on a raft.

"I got even with Bob [Service] once. He wanted to shoot the White Horse rapids on a log raft, so I took him along. He got a bigger thrill than he expected, and in the middle of the stream he yelled out to take it easy. I told Bob he had cremated me once, and now I was going to plant him in a watery grave.

"We came through all right, of course, but Bob said he would never abuse old Sam McGee again."[12]

chapter 8

In Whitehorse each year, the coming of winter brought Robert the stillness that filled him with peace, the white silence in which he could be creative again. But in the winter of 1907–8 he found himself cast out in the name of kindness. Bank regulations decreed that after three years at a Yukon posting, employees had a compulsory leave of three months outside, on full pay.

Service's holiday in early 1908, which he took in Vancouver, comes down to us in two versions—both of them his own. In one he is miserable and desperate to get back to the Yukon. In the other he is rapturously happy with Connie and devastated when he is forced to return to the Yukon.

In *Ploughman* Service wrote:

The climate here was indeed detestable, and I hated my enforced holiday. Then there was the chance I might not be sent back to the North. That would be a catastrophe. I realized how much I loved the Yukon, and how something in my nature linked me to it. I would be heart-broken if I could not return. Besides, I wanted to write more about it, to interpret it.[1]

He went on to describe three months in the Vancouver rain, living in a boarding house that had 20 tenants and only one bath—he was not about to let this vacation eat into his savings by spending money on personal comfort. He wrote of walking alone in the Stanley Park drizzle, feeling lonely and inferior, of beginning to fear that the Bank of Commerce would not send him back, but reassign him elsewhere.

The day came; he faced the same inspector who had hired him five years before. The man said nothing about his book, but, with a twinkle in his eye, said he had decided to send him to Dawson as teller. Service wrote: "As I went north again my mood was of serene happiness and of faith in the future."[2]

In contrast to Robert's later writings, three of the letters he wrote to Connie MacLean, which Beatrice Corbett and her sister, Constance, first found in 1960, tell a very different story. Two were written on board ship between Vancouver and Skagway at the end of the holiday, and the third was written after he arrived in Whitehorse, where he seemed to be standing in for the manager for a week before going on to Dawson.

There is nothing serene about these letters. "What a fool I was ever to agree to go back to the North," he wrote in the first letter (March 25) from the ship. "I feel like throwing myself over the side and trying to swim back to you. Oh I'm just crazy, crazy my dearest, dearest dear. I suppose I will get back my sanity in a little, but this is the most awful yet."

Service wrote that he had left Connie to go home and pack, expecting to be able to see her again before the boat sailed. But when he arrived at the dock he was told the ship would go immediately, so he rushed to the freight shed to phone her. When the boat finally sailed (after a long delay to load horses) he realized there would have been time for him to get to her Broughton Street home after all, and that made him feel even worse. In his second letter, on March 27, he wrote: "I cannot describe the feelings of despair with which I watched the lights of Vancouver disappear. I certainly left my heart there."

According to Robert's first letter, Connie had consented to marry him, and his comments throw an interesting light on the mores of the time. "If it weren't for the Bank regulation against marrying under thirteen hundred [dollars] I would marry you now and we would take a chance. But we must wait. But what a joy it is to know you would take me anyway for richer or poorer, for better or worse."[3] At the beginning of the 20th century, this was the norm for "respectable" couples of the aspiring middle classes. Laura Thompson, who came from Toronto to Dawson as a kindergarten teacher, waited four years to marry Frank Berton, until he got a job as mining recorder. The idea that an employer such as the Bank of Commerce could dictate when its employees married may seem far-fetched today, but in fact it was not uncommon a century ago. The North West Mounted Police had a similar rule: no married constables in the Territory. To get married, a man had to "purchase" out of the force.

In the second letter Service was still onboard ship and still "suffocated with wretchedness." In the third, written from Whitehorse on April 3, he seemed to have regained some composure. It ended with memories of their wonderful time together and how he loved her more than words could say.

Which version are we to believe—*Ploughman* or the letters? Possibly both. Service wrote his autobiography 35 years after these events, but it seems unlikely he could forget feelings so intense. In all his writings he did his best to protect the privacy of friends—and, to a large extent, himself—drawing a veil over events if necessary, changing names and locations, and omitting dates almost entirely. Where Connie MacLean was concerned, he decided to wipe the slate clean—for the purposes of posterity, she did not exist, so she does not appear in *Ploughman of the Moon*. Without any other particular reason to want to be in Vancouver, therefore, he must have been delighted to go back to the Yukon—hence the version presented in *Ploughman*.

Perhaps he had time to be both miserable and ecstatic. Just when the romance with Connie resumed, we do not know. In his 1906 letter about his friend's tragic boat accident, he addressed her, it seems, only as a friend: "Yours ever, Bob." But the tone of his 1908 letters implies that the romance flourished again during his time in Vancouver.

There seems no doubt that he was badly distraught as the boat left Vancouver, but he had made the decision to go north again. He loved Connie, but whatever his reason for going north had been in 1904, he went back now because he had also fallen in love with the Yukon.

Previous biographers dealing with this phase of his life took Robert's words in *Ploughman* at face value without seeing the letters he wrote to Connie. In addition, there are the warnings expressed in brother Stanley's memoir that Robert told the world only what he wanted it to know, and sometimes embellished or rearranged the facts.

At any rate, it seems the rekindled romance soon died down again. After the April message, either the letters stopped or Connie did not keep the later ones. When and in what circumstances the romance finally ended remains a mystery. Beatrice Corbett says that while her mother was a very social, outgoing person, she never talked about Robert Service. For his part, in all his public writings, Service never mentions Connie by name or by implication, and his granddaughter confirms that in their family he never spoke about Miss MacLean. Three biographies were written about Service before *Songs of a Sourdough's* dedicatee "C.M." was identified.[4] That came about in a CBC radio interview in October 1995 when James Mackay, author of *Vagabond of Verse* (1995), wondered on air who "C.M." could be. Connie's granddaughter, who happened to be listening, phoned in to tell program host Tom Allen what only her family had known until then.

In trying to understand what happened between Connie and Robert, Beatrice points to a particular poem in *Songs of a Sourdough*. "Our copy always fell open at this page. Mother was a very positive person. Her father died when she was young and the family members had to make their own way. She believed you could do whatever you put your mind to. Robert, on the other hand, had a strong streak of Calvinism, which he expresses in this poem, 'Quatrains':"[5]

> *One said: Thy life is thine to make or mar,*
> *To flicker feebly, or to soar, a star;*
> *It lies with thee—the choice is thine, is thine*
> *To hit the ties or drive thy auto-car.*
>
> *I answered Her: The choice is mine—ah no!*
> *We all were made or marred long, long ago.*
> *The parts are written: hear the super wail:*
> *"Who is stage-managing this cosmic show?"*
>
> *Blind fools of fate, and slaves of circumstance,*
> *Life is a fiddler, and we all must dance.*[6]

The *Weekly Star* reported Robert's arrival back in Whitehorse on Saturday, March 28, 1908: "R.W. Service, author, banker and all around good fellow, arrived Saturday evening and will be here two weeks before going on to Dawson where he will accept a position in the Canadian Bank of Commerce. Mr. Service has been outside three months looking after his publishing interests."[7]

There were other visitors passing through Whitehorse. Bishop and Lady Stringer and their three children had arrived on the stage on Sunday en route to London on church business. If Service attended Christ Church that evening he would have heard an address by the bishop. His friend Cody was moving on too, and a new minister, Reverend Sinclair, was announced.

His goodbye visit to Whitehorse lasted until April 9, when he boarded the stage for Dawson. "It was a brave little burg, birthplace of my prosperity. I had been brilliantly happy there. Everyday had been enjoyable ... I cherish the three years I spent there as one of my fondest memories."[8]

The distance from Whitehorse to Dawson is 325 miles (522 kilometres) by today's Klondike Highway; even now, it's a journey that people take at some risk in winter. When the temperature is as low as −40 degrees F, a flat tire can find you struggling to remove a frozen wheel, knowing that you must either succeed or freeze to death. But in 1908 the trip was made in an open sleigh, and it took five days. In early April, when Service boarded the stage, he recalls that the temperature was still −30 degrees F.

The Overland Trail was built by the White Pass & Yukon Route Co. to carry winter mail to Dawson. It was used until the highway was built in 1955.
PHOTO: COWICHAN VALLEY MUSEUM AND ARCHIVES

Parts of the Overland Trail are still visible near abandoned roadhouses like this one at Minto. Here the route follows the Yukon River.

PHOTO: GORD MALLORY

Day after day, with horse bells jingling and passengers wrapped in coonskin coats, they raced over the frozen beauty of a land so still you could almost hear the silence. Sometimes their path was along a trail that paralleled the Yukon River, but it was rarely on the river ice itself, because it was too uneven for travel.

Service wrote that they stopped at roadhouses twice a day. Laura Berton, traveling on the stage about this time, says they stopped every 22 miles—four times a day—to change horses and eat a heavy meal. She describes a giant heater and a long table loaded with roast moose, caribou, mountain sheep, blueberry pie and baked beans.

As they sped along, Service was both stunned and exhilarated by the cold and loneliness of a vast, unconquerable land. The Yukon's immensity seeped into his bones; his delight in the frozen landscape never left him during the five-day trip. He was heading north with a purpose, being given the chance of a lifetime to write the story of the Yukon from the inside, in the town that had been the center of the gold rush—maybe, after all, to be the Bret Harte of the Northland.

chapter 9

On arrival in Dawson the solitude ended with a jolt, and 35 years later Service had no trouble describing it in detail in *Ploughman of the Moon*. A lad who looked like Abe Lincoln (he was Abe Murphy, gold buyer at the bank) met the stage to take Robert to the bank mess—and also to warn him. He said that Service's reputation for bawdiness—derived from his poems—had preceded him, but the bank boys were on the pious side. As they walked along the frozen Yukon, a few dim lights in the cabins, the snow squeaking underfoot, Robert thanked him for the warning.

But there was no piety to be found in the bank mess that night. Instead, a blaze of light and a burst of cheer greeted them. A pianist and a dozen young men hailed Service as the "Bard of Bawdyville." They followed this up with ribald songs about Service and plied him with whisky. Exhausted, he sank into a big chair and drank the fiery stuff. Dinner followed: soup, roast beef, apple dumpling—and ribald conversation. By dessert time the Mounted Police, whose barracks were next door, began dropping in to join the fray.

Then an older man known as Sandy (Alex Ross, the bank's messenger and one of the original "bank boys" of 1898) arrived with the staff's mail, which had traveled with Service on the stage. It included a letter for the new clerk from his Toronto publisher. A check fluttered out of the envelope. Service, after three years as a teetotaller, was now seeing double from his sudden exposure to alcohol. "Looks like 10 dollars," he later recalled saying, but the man beside him, also drunk, said, "Looks like a hundred to me." Sandy, the only one sober, took the check in hand and announced, "My gosh, mon, yon cheque's for a thoosand dollars."[1]

The men called for more hooch to celebrate the event, and Service bought three bottles for the crowd. Finally the accountant realized that their new teller was worn out and showed him to his room, saying he wanted to rescue him from the boys who were whooping it up.

Gratefully, Service sank into a deep sleep, only to be awakened by four of the revellers announcing that two ladies wanted to meet the poet. They

Dawson City was home to some 30 to 40 thousand people at the turn of the century. When Service arrived in 1908, the population had shrunk to 4,000.

PHOTO: NAC C-6648

Dawson as seen from the Dome; the Klondike River comes in from the left to join the Yukon.
PHOTO: ENID MALLORY

seized him and, shrieking with laughter, carried him down in his pyjamas to dump him beside two dance-hall girls. Horrified, he grabbed a blanket from the couch and wrapped himself in it, then had to sit at the piano and sing some of his own songs. Some time later, thoroughly initiated into Dawson's social life, he managed to sneak back to bed.

From the moment of his arrival, Service loved Dawson. From a city of 30–40,000 souls in 1898–99, it had shrunk to 4,000—but that still made it five times bigger than Whitehorse. For someone of his sensitivity, Dawson City's dramatic past was still visible. That summer, as he wandered streets still alight at midnight, with birds still singing and flowers shining in the twilight, he could feel ghosts of the gold rush all around him.

Some of those ghosts were the original "bank boys" who had opened for business on June 15, 1898. In their galvanized iron shed, the four officers and two messengers had a counter to work from and a space about 5 by 20 feet for the public, who pressed in from the crowd outside. The first day established a pattern that would repeat itself each day thereafter, "... so great was the rush of business that the mess [a tent pitched against the shed] was abandoned, meals were obtained at a restaurant and the messenger and cook pressed into service as handy clerical assistants—to write supplementaries, label gold sacks, and perform other similar duties ... "[2] A day began at 7:00 a.m. when Tommy or Sandy would carry water from the river and the officers would come down from the loft with their basins to wash up in full view of the customers already lined up outside. Breakfast was gobbled down and business began. At 7:00 or 8:00 p.m. the cash was locked in a tin biscuit box, and the gold dust in tin-lined wooden chests. Until the assay plant was working, a customer's gold dust was weighed, and the weight credited to the customer; a pointed stick was dipped in ink to mark his sack of dust with his account number.

Manager H.T. Wills may have lacked the ideal physique for the Trail of '98, but once in Dawson he showed his true colors as a genial, flexible general, creating order in the midst of chaos, roughing it with his tiny advance army, sharing this great adventure with his boys and his customers and working from dawn to dusk.

Tappan Adney, who was in Dawson when the bank arrived, described the action.

> The agent, Mr. Wills, assisted by one or two clerks, received gold-dust, which he weighed in a pair of immense scales, issuing paper money or drafts in return. The "vaults" were two wooden tin-lined boxes, four feet long, three feet wide, and three feet deep, with a lid. Upon one occasion I saw these half-full of gold sacks, also five boxes of gold packed for shipment, each holding from 500 to 800 pounds of gold dust—close to a million dollars in all. On the table in front of the agent was a stack of notes a foot high, though the door was wide open, and there was not a weapon or a guard in sight.[3]

The *Klondike Nugget*, a Dawson newspaper published from 1898 to 1900, also had a description of the bank: "An unpainted counter with a giant pair of Gold Scales in place of the usual grating, a table and some chairs inside, the smiling countenance of Manager Wills with assistants ...."[4]

Sleep at night—in the heat of the galvanized building and with the

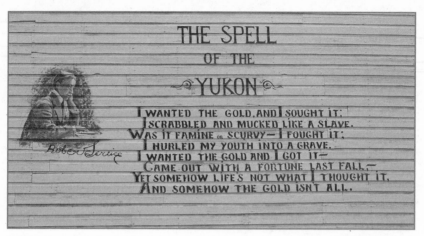

THE SPELL
OF THE
YUKON

I WANTED THE GOLD, AND I SOUGHT IT;
I SCRABBLED AND MUCKED LIKE A SLAVE.
WAS IT FAMINE or SCURVY— I FOUGHT IT;
I HURLED MY YOUTH INTO A GRAVE.
I WANTED THE GOLD AND I GOT IT—
CAME OUT WITH A FORTUNE LAST FALL,—
YET SOMEHOW LIFE'S NOT WHAT I THOUGHT IT,
AND SOMEHOW THE GOLD ISN'T ALL.

This first verse of "The Spell of the Yukon" is painted on a building wall in Dawson City.
PHOTO: ENID MALLORY

constant noise of dance-hall revelry—was sometimes impossible. This could work in the bank's favor; some of the bank's best contacts were made late at night when an officer who couldn't sleep joined the rowdies at the dance hall.

Manager Wills faced some tough moments. As quickly as possible the assay furnace was built; the acids, fluxes and Troemner balances were ready, and the furnace was fired in an attempt to melt 50 ounces (1,400 grams). Forty-eight hours later, unable to sustain the level of heat required, the dejected bankers stared at a conglomerate mass that could not be assayed. At that point, it had to be hidden from customers clamoring to have their gold valued so they could head "outside." Manager and staff pored over the furnace plans, unable to determine what had gone wrong. They kept a hot fire going to fool the public, and when a customer became too difficult, he would be invited out for a drink. Again the bar was good to the bank, for on one of these drinking forays an officer met an Austrian graduate of the School of Mines in Vienna and invited him back to the bank to see if he could help.

His name was Jorish. Unable to speak much English, Jorish had a look at the furnace and grinned. With a cold chisel and a mallet he knocked out a few bricks to enlarge the draft, and the bank's first successful melt was soon poured. Jorish worked several weeks as melting assistant at $15 a day before he left for the mines. One month after opening, the bank ledgers showed that $2.5 million in gold dust had passed through the bank.[5]

On June 23, 1898, at 4:00 a.m. the first consignment of gold—worth $758,520—went down the Yukon River aboard the North American Transportation and Trading Company's steamer *P.B. Weare*. Sandy Ross went with it, guarding it as far as St. Michael on the coast. There he met the bank's third incoming party. The senior officer of this party then turned back to guard the gold on its trip south while Ross and the junior officer brought the new supplies, including much-needed safes, up the Yukon to Dawson. There would be no further communication with the outside world until the long winter of 1898–99 gave way to spring.[6]

A log building was built in the late summer of 1898 to get them out of the galvanized shed. Logs were sawn on three sides but the bark was left on the outside. The roof had two layers of board overlaid with an inch of moss and three inches of mud, helping to keep the building cool in summer and warm in winter. It was two storeys high, with living quarters upstairs for the staff. The downstairs was divided, with a counter and public area in the front and the assay operation at the back. Window panes had to wait until one of the season's last scows brought glass in November. With lamps and a large wood-burning stove, they were ready for the cold and dark of winter.

This large bank, built in 1900, replaced the log building that then became living quarters for the bank staff.
PHOTO: GORD MALLORY

The bank was situated in good company, with the gold commissioner's office on one side and the Mounted Police on the other. From the beginning, the NWMP ruled Dawson with a firm hand. The city's woodpile was notoriously effective at dissuading any would-be criminal. Anyone convicted of theft or other villainy could be seen in the cold mist of winter, "sawing, chopping and hauling wood for Her Majesty, under an escort of Mounted Police in short buffalo coats and with loaded carbines ... "[7]

The rival Bank of British North America was not so lucky in its location. It actually arrived in Dawson a week ahead of the Bank of Commerce, setting up business in a tent, but their "office" was almost immediately wrecked by a flood. Then they built their office downtown, and lost it in the fire of April 1899.

The large Bank of Commerce building on Front Street, where Service now worked, had opened for business on January 10, 1901. The log building that had served for two years then became the bank mess, and was home to Robert Service in 1908–9. In their new premises the bank could operate with the order and dignity of banks in the south. The mad excitement of those first days was gone, but the stories told by men like Sandy Ross were part of the lore and legend that Service needed to hear.

By joining the Arctic Brotherhood Society, he found another way to meet the prospectors who had crossed the Trail of '98, and who delighted in telling their tales to a keen listener. The society had its origin in 1899 when the SS *City of Seattle* was heading up the Lynn Canal. The captain decided to organize his passengers into a group to entertain themselves. They had so much fun that they got together again in Skagway in March, and the Arctic Brotherhood became firmly established. Its insignia was a prospector's pan filled with gold nuggets, its motto "Fidelity and Friendship," and its watchword "Mush On."

The men of the brotherhood taught Robert about placer mining, how you dug down through the permafrost, thawing the ground with fires at night and digging by day until you hit "pay dirt" (the level at which ore was to be found), then "drifting" out on either side, uncovering the seam as you went. Working like badgers in your tunnels, you heaved the buckets of pay-dirt up to the top—first by hand, then when you got too deep, by means of a windlass. By spring a big pile of dirt known as a dump awaited the thaw and the running of water in the creeks. When the sluice was built you would shovel the dirt into it and run water through. "Riffles" were

The staff of the Bank of Commerce in Dawson; Robert Service is in the back, standing in front of the window, June 22, 1908.

PHOTO: HERITAGE HOUSE COLLECTION

slats positioned across the sluice bottom to catch the heavier gold, while the soil and gravel washed out. This was "clean-up"—the big moment of celebration or bitter disappointment after an entire year of work. From the old-timers Service learned how it felt to work in the cold mud of early fall, and in the depths of winter at −50 degrees F, thawing the frozen ground inch by inch. By 1908 giant dredges, first introduced by Joe Boyle's Klondike Mining Company, were operating on the creeks. But it was placer mining that made Klondike gold accessible to the average man, working alone and without elaborate machinery. Service was plying his own brand of placer mining, sifting and searching in the sluice for nuggets of pure gold to put in his ballads.

The transformation of human history into creative expression was now his real life's work. His job at the bank still earned him a living, but he never considered himself good at it: "not a success and far from happy" was how he described himself as a banker; he saw himself as overcautious, slow and nervous about balancing his cash at the end of each day, and never affable, relaxed or outgoing in the work environment.[8]

Probably his self-assessment was too harsh. There is no indication that the Bank of Commerce questioned his performance; in fact, they intended to promote him to relieving manager at Whitehorse. But his heart was never in banking, especially after he gained success as a poet, and his mind was often off in the hills. His aim in the bank was simply to accumulate $5,000, and then be free of it. But as royalties began to flow in, he raised his goal to $10,000 and fixed his sights on a less frugal plan for the rest of his life.

He knew he needed to write more poems, but he had his work in the bank by day and the rowdies in the bank mess by night. His solution was to sleep from 9 to 12 in the evening, make a pot of black tea and write from midnight until three; then, often too excited to sleep the rest of the night, he went in to work "hung-over," drunk on his own poems.

His second collection of verse, *Ballads of a Cheechako*, was published in 1909, but only after a spat with the publisher, W. Briggs, whose Methodist background made them question Robert's coarse language and what they considered his immoral viewpoint. When Service threatened to depart to another publisher, they reached a compromise: they would remove one poem dealing with the Tenderloin (a local term for the red-light district) but increase the royalty rate by 5 percent in compensation. For a diffident poet, it was a new experience to fight for both freedom of expression and more money, and—since he won—he discovered that he enjoyed the fray.

Service had worked with such "grim determination" on *Ballads of a Cheechako* that he wrote nothing for the two years following its completion. The public rushed to read his new book, and a royalty check for $3,000 made him happy. The critics did not quite know what to make of this poetic phenomenon coming out the Frozen North. They decided he must be something other than a poet—a versifier, a rhymer. Service didn't care what they called him as he watched the royalties roll in from Canada, the United States and Great Britain.

By his own account he dreamed and loafed as much as the bank would let him. Work was over by four o'clock, and he would head out for a snowy tramp along the Klondike River or a climb by moonlight to the Midnight Dome behind the town. Social life in Dawson was non-stop, and even Service was swept along to meet charming girls at the skating rink, climb the Dome in snowshoe parties bearing torches, or join sleigh rides, "singing to the jingle of bells as we returned to the mess for supper."[9]

Bobsledding from the hill behind the town down to the river was a favorite sport that one night put one of Service's nine lives on the line. Their steersman was a Mountie corporal with a daredevil reputation. Eight of them were packed onto a sled streaking toward Main Street and the river when a team of horses appeared out of the darkness, pulling a heavy load of goods bound for the creeks outside town.

Service heard the frightened whinny of the horses and the shouting driver; he shut his eyes, expecting to be killed. Suddenly they were on the river, the team disappearing behind them like a phantom in the night. The Mountie grinned and explained that he couldn't make it past the front of the team so he had to take them under the bellies. Was anyone kicked? No one was!

There were two dances a week, as well as balls for special occasions. Service remembered it as a glorious time: he was making money, his workload was light, and he was healthy, fit and happy.

Laura Berton's book *I Married the Klondike*, written with the help of her son Pierre, provides an intriguing glimpse of Robert Service. Already knowing his poetry, when she heard of his arrival in town she and another teacher hurried to the bank to see this "rip-roaring roisterer ... instead we found a shy and nondescript man in his mid-thirties, with a fresh complexion, clear blue eyes and a boyish figure that made him look much younger. He had a soft, well-modulated voice and spoke with a slight drawl."

Laura got to know him through the mostly unmarried young crowd made up of teachers, bank employees, nurses, stenographers, civil servants and "Guggies" (men who worked for the Yukon Gold Company owner, Solomon Guggenheim). Laura described Service as a good mixer among men, especially sourdoughs, but not a party man. When someone asked him to attend a social function, he would say, "Ask me sometime when you're by yourselves."[10]

Laura Berton tells the story of Governor General Earl Grey's August 1909 reception at Government House (Dawson was then the territorial capital). People had got out of the habit of inviting Service to social functions because he rarely came, so Earl Grey caused a turmoil by asking where Robert Service lived (he lived next door) and why he hadn't been invited.

Martha Black, who would become chatelaine of Government House a few years later, also tells this story. In 1898 she had climbed over the Chilkoot Pass with her brother after her husband deserted the party, delivered her baby in a Klondike cabin that winter, managed sawmills, then married the former prospector and Conservative politician George Black, who in 1912 would be named commissioner of the territory. As the commissioner's wife she would preside over the Yukon like a queen (Service once described her as a "marchioness"). In her autobiography, *My Seventy Years*, Martha says that after that dinner, the Governor General invited Service to have breakfast with him and Lady Grey. Service made a great impression on the vice-regal party that morning, especially when he presented Earl Grey's daughter, Lady Sybil, and her friend the Honourable Miss Middleton with signed copies of *Songs of a Sourdough*. "This royal recognition of Robert Service, the bank clerk 'who wrote verses,' had Dawson all agog. Till then Yukoners had not paid much attention to the shy young Scotsman who weighed gold dust and kept the ledgers of the Canadian Bank of Commerce."[11]

One social activity that did appeal to Robert was dancing. In his preface to Laura Berton's memoir, Service recalled escorting her to a Dawson dance. She remembered a dance at the A.B. Hall at which he danced with her and absent-mindedly forgot to remove his arm from her waist when the dance ended. They wandered intimately around the dance floor causing whispers and grins until he noticed his faux pax.

Laura remembered him "strolling curiously about in the spring sunshine, peering at the boarded-up gaming-houses," or "on the A.C. Trail [named for the American Commercial Company], swinging along athletically, looking a bit vacant-eyed. He was always cordial and pleasant but he had no close friends, as far as I know, and nobody knew him well."[12] Those long, solitary walks in the natural world were where his real life lay. Nature fed his mind and soul.

His love affair with nature was just that. It did not result in nature writing, systematic study or even description of nature's creatures. There is no mention of the high-pitched call of thousands of sandhill cranes winging north, or of a lynx hunting on padded feet along a creek bed. To know what Service actually saw on his walks we would have to go to Martha and George Black, who recorded the abundant willow ptarmigans and rock ptarmigans, the spruce and blue grouse and prairie chickens, the bald eagles and golden eagles, and the many species of owls. In summer there would be swallows and ducks and geese, mergansers and cranes and swans, and songbirds such as thrush, bluebirds, robins, warblers and juncos. And in winter and spring the chickadees and snow buntings, Arctic three-toed woodpeckers and hairy woodpeckers, ravens and Canada jays must have kept Service company as he tramped through the forest on his snowshoes. If he worried about meeting wolves or bears hungry after a winter's sleep, he makes no mention of it.

If he studied anything systematically, it was people. He was always on the outside looking in, trying to figure out what made people tick and then applying the knowledge to his writing and even to his own living. Social relationships did not come to him with any ease; he seemed to be painstakingly learning how to live with his fellow humans.

It may have been the foursome at the Whitehorse bank that first showed him how a "normal" family might live—Harold Tylor like a brother to him (one who knew the rules and had all the social skills), Mr. and Mrs. De Gex, convivial and full of fun, and, with no children of their own, treating these boys like sons, and all of them having a happy time.

But it was the people on the edge he studied most. The lives of such men and women seemed to be written in an exaggerated script that was easier to read, and in some ways he felt closer to them, since he considered himself a misfit too. The titles of his many books express his off-center position, referring to himself as a *rolling stone*, a *bohemian*, a *roughneck*, a *lowbrow*, a *rebel* and, finally, an *old codger*. Even such titles as *Songs of a Sourdough, Ballads of a Cheechako, The Pretender, Ploughman of the Moon, Harper of Heaven* and *Rhymes For My Rags* reflect his askew position.

In Whitehorse, and now in Dawson City, he had a wealth of colorful humanity to study. The gold rush was over, but its stories hung in the cold mist that hugged the valleys and the ghost city—the original townsite—on the flats. The die-hard prospectors were still in their cabins on the creeks, still grubbing for gold. Men dealt with loneliness and despair by crowding into the saloons on Saturday night, telling their stories to anyone who would listen, and Service was a great listener.

When he arrived in Dawson there was still a dance hall where girls performed, sipping champagne with any delirious, drunken man who had struck it rich and stealing his poke. The prostitutes who lived in Lousetown catered to a dwindling clientele. Many years later, Service wrote to Harold Tylor (who had been moved to Dawson ahead of Service and transferred out by the time Service arrived) recalling some of the girls by name, mentioning Violet deVere, Jew Jessie and Minnie Dale.

There may have been some fantasy in the letter's ramblings—written

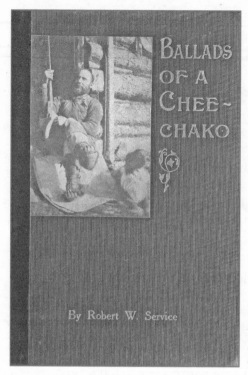

The man depicted on the 20th edition of *Ballads of a Cheechako* is Solomon Albert, who lost part of his feet to frostbite and walked on the feet of a grizzly bear.

by a man who by then was 78 and usually described himself as a prig. But there is no doubt from his writings of his empathy for these women. In another letter to Harold he spoke of the kindness and generosity of some of them. These women were shunned or derided by the circle in which Service and his co-workers moved, yet he saw each one as an individual human being, with a story in her past and significant emotions in the present.

Among the men he studied, there was villainy but very little actual crime—thanks to the presence of the NWMP and its dreaded woodpile. What Robert found was humor, courage, pathos and tragedy, the epic struggle with the elements, the obsession with gold, fear of the grizzly or the loup-garou (werewolf), loneliness that could make a man crazy, and the grim reality of scurvy and starvation. When the 20th edition of *Ballads of a Cheechako* was published with a picture on its cover of a man with the feet of a grizzly bear, this was no art of the imagination but an actual photograph. The man's toes had been amputated after they became frostbitten, and the resourceful sourdough made boots from the feet of a grizzly bear so he could walk again.[13] What Service wrote about was reality: *Ballads of a Cheechako* had behind it four years of study and discovery on the creeks and in the streets and saloons of Whitehorse and Dawson City.

Laura Berton tells a story that illustrates how seriously Service took his study of humankind. A man was to be hanged for murder at dawn one day in late September. The gibbet was erected on the banks of the Yukon behind the police barracks, and Service got permission to be one of the witnesses at the foot of the gallows.

"Service remained at the scene until the black flag fluttered up the mast, and then, pale and visibly unnerved, he moved with uncertain steps back to the bank mess-house, where he spoke not a word but poured himself a tumbler of straight Scotch and gulped it down."[14] She knew how unusual this was because, according to her, Service never drank while in Dawson. Studying human nature, in all its shade as well as its sunlight, had its price. But this experience would find poetic expression more than 30 years later.

chapter 10

While Dawsonites saw him as an often vacant-eyed wanderer, Service was preoccupied by a new inspiration. It had occurred to him that somebody must write a gold-rush novel, an epic story of that amazing stampede, with all its excitement and tragedy, set against the great canvas of the Yukon. Why not himself?

When he fished for graylings in the Klondike, not far from the site of George Carmack's gold strike that had set off the rush of '98, scenes of the novel danced in his head even as he pulled out trout. He turned over in his mind the tales told by sourdoughs; he could portray their hardships and rejoice in their triumphs, vicariously becoming one of them. More confident than he had ever been in his life, he was sure he could do this. He retreated from his fishing hole elated, eager to begin.

But when he tried to write in the pandemonium of the bank mess hall after a day of work, he couldn't do it. A novel was a far more complicated process than writing one poem at a time. He needed isolation, and there was none to be had.

Robert on the porch of his Dawson cabin.
PHOTO: YUKON ARCHIVES, GILLIS FAMILY FONDS 4531

One autumn day in 1909 Service's manager called him to the office to tell him he had been appointed relieving manager at Whitehorse, standing in for the regular manager there. Service was shocked for three reasons: first, that the bank would trust him with a manager's job; second, that the responsibility would be "perfect hell"; and third, that he couldn't bear to leave Dawson. Not now. Not with a gold-rush novel in his head.

He was even more shocked to hear his own voice announcing that he was resigning.

The manager stared at him, then asked how much money he was making. Robert replied that he was making $5,000 a year from his books and $1,000 from the bank. The manager gasped, then told him he was doing the right thing and congratulated him on taking a chance.

Service returned to his cage stunned. Once before, in Glasgow, he had quit the security of a bank, and his manager then had envied him for taking

a chance—yet for seven years he had almost starved. Was he making the same mistake twice? He opened his bank book, saw the five-figure number there and knew that this time it was different. His last day at the bank was November 15, 1909.

On Eighth Avenue, he found himself a home, a cabin on the hillside above Dawson. It had an inspiring view, all the isolation he craved and a pair of moose antlers above the door that seemed a symbol of success, his own Winged Victory.

It was a tiny place with a big Klondike heater, a contraption that had a drum fitted into the stovepipe to conserve heat and dry clothes. There were two rooms, adequate space in which to live and write. With winter coming on, he splurged on flannelette sheets for his double bed. For company he adopted Mike, an enormous Siberian bear hound, and a stray kitten he'd found on the trail. Meals became a variety of meats: caribou, moose, bear and mountain sheep, served in the Dawson restaurants. Breakfast, often eaten at 2:00 p.m. when the lunch crowd had thinned, was ham and eggs in a Norwegian bakery, his favorite place to meet up with friends.

Bert Parker, who went over the Trail of '98 when he was 18, was a Dawson friend of Robert Service.
PHOTO: COURTESY OF LIZ ROWLEY

R.J. Latshaw, a young surveyor who knew Service at this time, "liked him very much as a person." In a letter to his brother he described him as "an excellent elocutionist," and had warm praise for his poems. "I have never before come across verses that paint such vivid word pictures." He quotes for his brother the first lines of Dan McGrew and says, "... every line adds to the picture like a stroke from an artist's brush."

Latshaw asked Service about loneliness when he visited the cabin. Service answered that he was poor company if he was writing, and at other times he could go to see friends or invite them to his cabin.[1]

Among these friends was Bert Parker, who had left a farm in Guelph, Ontario, in 1898 and come to the Yukon at the age of 18. Fifty years later, Bert wrote a memoir entitled *Kid in the Klondike*. Bert loved to talk, and Service soaked up his stories—yarns about the trail and river trips, the odd jobs by which he survived, his six months in the Dawson hospital with typhoid fever, the characters he knew and the girls who sang at the Monte Carlo Theatre when gold fever was it its peak.

From the prospectors who came to town Robert got to know the lay of the land. He spent time out on the creeks, taking part in clean-up, and would get the old-timers talking about their adventures. He stayed in roadhouses and in prospector's cabins in the hills. He haunted the city's Carnegie library and read everything he could find on the Yukon, including government reports (so-called blue books) and *Dawson News* files stored in the basement.

Service became the proverbial writer sharpening his pencil, unable to get started. But he was doing the next best thing, immersing himself in his subject until he felt he had been there 11 years ago, had climbed the Chilkoot Pass himself, had run the Yukon rapids and dealt with both heady excitement and terrible despair. Finally, a letter from the New York publisher Dodd Mead, agreeing to a 15 percent royalty (well over the usual rate), got him started. For five months he figuratively lived, ate and slept on "The Trail of '98."

Service declared himself a slave to the task until it was completed, fully committing himself to a craft he had studied from an early age. By age 16 he had rejected the "nectar of mythology and nature worship in poetry." He was attracted to coarser themes, to hardship and vice, "to eating and drinking and lusts and common people."[2] Now, working in prose instead of poetry, influenced by Harte, Stevenson, Kipling and Morley Roberts, he brought his own voice to the written records of the stampede.

The hero of his novel, Athol Meldrum, was by the author's own admission a self-portrait, a character not tough enough to succeed in the harsh reality of a gold rush.[3] Service always claimed that he was meant to be a failure, but that chance saved him. His Athol would have no such luck.

Berna, his heroine, was not modeled on anyone he knew, although if we look for inspiration in Dawson, there was someone who figured in

Robert inside his cabin, writing.
PHOTO: YUKON ARCHIVES, GILLIS FAMILY FONDS, 4534

his life at this time. Laura Berton remembered, in her memoir, a pretty stenographer who worked in the government building. From his cabin on the hill, Service could see when she finished work, and he hiked or rode his bicycle down to meet her. In the Dawson Archives, a photo of the government administration staff identifies her. One of the two women in the picture is described as "Jean Clark, engaged to Robert Service."

But like Berna's with Athol, his romance did not go well. Laura Berton heard that Jean's family did not approve of the poet who wrote bawdy verse, and the gossip was that they believed he drank. (Later, after Robert had left the Yukon, Jean became a roommate of Helen Scott, Bert Parker's future wife.)

How much Jean contributed to Service's Berna in 1909–10 is only speculation. Likewise, some of the melodrama of the Athol–Berna romance could reflect his sporadic relationship with Connie MacLean. At any rate, the book has no dedication, and Service says in his biography that Berna was the name of a brand of condensed milk.

Despite the wild reputation of its early days, society in Dawson by 1909 was as "proper" and restrictive as you could find anywhere in Canada. Laura Berton described it as almost a caste system, with the commissioner

"Federal and Territorial Staff" on the steps of the Administration Building in Dawson. The first woman from the left in the second row is identified as Jean Clark, "fiancée of Robert Service."

PHOTO: DAWSON CITY ARCHIVES

and his wife at the top, followed by the judges, top police officers and civil servants, company heads, bishops and pastors, bankers and bank clerks, lawyers and nurses, and, finally, teachers like Berton herself, just hanging on "to the charmed group by our finger-nails." The next level was made up of merchants, laborers and policemen, while the lowest level comprised dance-hall girls, prostitutes, anyone of mixed race (irrespective of their occupation) and Natives. In such a society there was a lot of room for gossip about people such as Robert Service, who did not fit neatly into these social categories—an eccentric, alone in his cabin without a real job, yet famous among outsiders. Where had he been and what had he done before he joined the bank and came to the Yukon?

Whether his faltering romance with the stenographer—or the romance with Connie—was reflected in the lives of Athol and Berna in *The Trail of '98: A Northland Romance*, their relationship does portray conflicted stereotypes marked by exaggerated emotions. As an added complication in

105

developing his characters, Service would have felt his Methodist publisher, William Briggs, looking over his shoulder. As it was, the publisher objected to the novel's original ending—Berna was seduced by the hero's attractive brother—so Service rewrote the ending to make Berna "an inspiration to virtue." Dodd Mead in New York did the editorial work on the book and published it in the United States; Briggs published it in Canada.

The Berna–Athol relationship is not the strongest feature of the novel, nor is Service's character development memorable. It is the sweeping panoramic scenes of the Yukon that give the book its power. Robert's was a style of writing based on intimate knowledge and a wealth of detail, a style later made famous in Canada by the non-fiction work of Laura Berton's son, Pierre—who began, as Service did, by writing about his beloved Yukon. Geographically speaking, their points of view were almost identical, for Pierre Berton, born in 1920, grew up in a house across the road from Robert Service's by-then empty cabin.

Many first-person sources used by Robert for *The Trail of '98* also inspired Berton almost 50 years later when he researched his history of the gold rush, *Klondike Fever* (1958). One early source that Service likely found in the Carnegie library, and that certainly spoke to Pierre Berton, was *Two Years in the Klondike and Alaskan Goldfields* by William B. Haskell. It includes a vivid account of the White Pass in 1897 by men who struggled through what Haskell describes as a blockade of several thousand people:

> Horses, tents, feed, supplies and men were piled together in an apparently hopeless tangle. A drizzling rain was falling most of the time. Stubborn fires were smouldering and sputtering, and men were standing or wandering about as though they were dazed by the obstacles ahead.
>
> … When night came, they lay down on the damp ground … All along was strung a line of struggling horses and cursing men, picking their way over and around rocks, logs, and dead animals.[4]

Both Service and Berton used Tappan Adney's *Klondike Stampede*, one of the best first-hand accounts of the White Pass and Chilkoot trails. Adney's book was published in 1900 after *Harper's Weekly* sent him north in 1897 to report on the unfolding events. His description of horses suffering on the White Pass Trail lies like a blot on the North American psyche: "When the sun and rains of summer shall have melted the snow of the Chilkoots, the White Pass trail will be paved with the bones of horses." Adney remarked that "the history of this trail is yet to be written, and will only be heard by the firesides of old men."[5] A decade had passed and the best (and worst) stories were being heard and incorporated when Robert Service wrote his novel.

By putting Athol on the White Pass and Berna on the Chilkoot, Robert was able to include the whole picture in his book. Berna's father was given the distinction of dying in the avalanche that thundered down on the Chilkoot Trail in April 1898. Meanwhile Athol described the White Pass:

> The army before us and the army behind never faltered. Like a stream of black ants they were, between mountains that reared up swiftly to storm-smitten palisades of ice. In the darkness of night the army rested uneasily, yet at the first streak of dawn it was in motion. It was an endless procession, in which every man was for himself. I can see them now, bent under their burdens, straining at their hand-sleighs, flogging their horses and oxen, their faces crimped and puckered with fatigue, the air acrid with their curses and heavy with their moans. Now a horse stumbles and slips into one of the sump-holes by the trail side. No one can pass, the army is arrested. Frenzied fingers unhitch the poor frozen brute and drag it from the water. Men, frantic with rage, beat savagely at their beasts of burden to make up the precious time lost. There is no mercy, no humanity, no fellowship. All is blasphemy, fury and ruthless determination. It is the spirit of the gold-trail.[6]

Service later said that he finished his first draft in five months, making the most of the longer light as the days lengthened, and the creative energy it kindled. Sometimes he could write 3,000 words in a day, and sometimes he was biting his nails all day over his characters' lack of co-operation. Near the end it became a marathon of writing. When it was nearly done he headed downtown for a supper of beefsteak and onions, then came back and wrote all night and part of the next day until, 12,000 words later, he could write "The End" and sleep for 10 hours.

According to Service, it took another three months to revise, polish and test every word; he finished it in April 1910. But there is something wrong with his time frame. In his autobiography, he remembered his novel writing beginning in early spring (presumably of 1910) when in fact he must have begun well before he resigned in November 1909 if he were to write for five months, revise for three and have the book completed by the following April. Most of the book must therefore have been written in winter.

What he did remember vividly about that winter was the intense cold. He recalled walking on the Moosehide Trail with a bank friend when the temperature was –72 degrees F. In coonskin coats with the collars up, fur caps with ear flaps, hands in fur mittens hung on neck cords (to lose a mitt could be disastrous) and feet in moccasins, they experienced the kind of cold in which death lurks dangerously near. When his friend's face turned white with frostbite, he held snow on it for insulation until they made it back to a pub.

Facing the great cold without proper clothing could be fatal in the Yukon, and Service made an almost-fatal mistake one night when he got up to feed his Klondike stove. His indoor woodpile was gone, but more was stacked on the porch. Clad only in pyjamas and slippers, he dashed to the porch. To his horror, the door snapped shut and locked behind him.

The temperature was –60 degrees F, the lock a Yale, the door solid, the windows too high to reach. He had very little time to think. The back door was locked, but the bolt was old and worn. Desperately he plunged through the snow and charged the door. He felt it give, heaved his shoulder again and the bolt fell out. Once more he hit the door, and he fell headlong inside his cabin. As he later put it, he had frostbite on a portion of his anatomy that modesty forbade him to mention. It was some time before he could sit down comfortably, but he was extremely glad not to be a frozen corpse.

When his book was finished he had a sudden impulse to take the manuscript to New York himself. By the end of April 1910 he had reached Toronto, where he dropped in on his Canadian publisher, William Briggs, and then moved on, handing his manuscript in person to Frank C. Dodd at Dodd Mead in New York. As he ventured out of the North after six years there, he described himself as Yukonized, a bit brash, appalled by cities, but confident. This was a different Robert Service from the one who had wandered the west coast. Or was it?

He chose to travel to New York by train, via Chicago, and on the way a small disaster reminded him of tough times in his past. In a Pullman car he left his wallet on the seat, and when he came back it was gone. So there he was, with $20,000 in the bank but only loose change in his pocket. He used some of it to telegraph for $50 to be sent to him in Chicago. For four days he lived on 65 cents, saving a dollar for the Pullman porter. As if demanding penance from himself for his carelessness, he rejected the aid of fellow passengers and ate only apples and doughnuts. By the time he reached Chicago and had walked the many blocks to the First National Bank to pick up his $50, he was light-headed and faint from hunger.

In New York he stayed in the National Arts Club studio of a painter he had met by chance on the steamer *Casa* while coming up the Yukon River. Service had seen the man painting a scene just above Five Fingers Rapids, and fell into conversation with him. The man generously offered Service his New York apartment for his visit to the big city.

His editors at Dodd Mead were having trouble with Berna, a heroine not pure enough for the standards of 1910. Service reluctantly rewrote the ending, but even then the prudes of Boston refused to stock it, though it sold well in towns nearby. Like his books of verse, *The Trail of '98* was a big success, read and talked about all over North America. It was also popular in many other countries, and in 1928 was made into an epic silent movie. Although the *Dawson Weekly News* expressed some fear that the book painted all Dawson people as being tarnished by sin—at least at the turn of the century—it reported record-breaking local sales as Klondikers were "devouring" the book.

Meanwhile, its creator discovered he liked little about New York. He had been keyed up, excited to see this city of literary fame, but he found he didn't fit in with those he met at the arts club, including novelists Hamlin Garland and George Barr McCutcheon and poets Madison Cawein and Will Carleton. In his memoir, he mentioned that novelist David Graham Phillips was shot "by a madman" just outside the National Arts Club while he was there. If this is true, it means Robert spent close to a year in New York, since Phillips was shot on January 23, 1911, and died the next day. Service found that the literary men he met were "often contemptuous" and knew nothing about the Frozen North. He disliked their slick "city ways," the affectations of a society so far removed from the blunt, raw honesty of the Yukon. He was more interested in ethnic neighborhoods like Harlem, Chinatown and the Bowery, where he frequented the music halls and studied life as he had in San Francisco and Los Angeles. "All that was sordid delighted me," he later wrote, and on a visit to Greenwich Village his old need to escape took hold of him. He made a sudden decision to set out on foot for New Orleans, staying in cheap hotels along the way. He got to northern Pennsylvania before buying a first-class train ticket for the rest of the way.

Discouraged by the segregation and squalor of the French Quarter in New Orleans, he booked passage to Cuba, and when he tired of Havana he started to walk again—this time to Santiago. After three days he retreated to Havana, weary of the heat and the dirty accommodation. Reading in the Prado one day, he was reminded of his family, now living in Alberta. He decided to act out his own version of the prodigal son: he would go visit the "perfectly good mother" he had not seen in 13 years, pay off her mortgage and get to know his brothers and sisters.

In the Yukon he had been riding the wave of success on a cushion of financial security. He had got "high" on his book, happy as a small god creating his characters and portraying his beloved Yukon. Now, in the rest of the world, he was facing his own loneliness and looking at the rest of his life. Although his family had been in Canada since 1906, he had not yet attempted to see them. Now suddenly, he was going "home"—not to Scotland where he saw them last, but to the open prairie east of Edmonton.

chapter 11

Three weeks after setting out from Havana, in late winter of 1911, he found himself driving a hired team over the winter snow. Ahead, a tiny dot on the prairie, he could see what he'd been told was the Service home. This was Robert's version of his arrival but Stanley, in his memoir, says very clearly: "We met Willie and drove him down to the farm."

Robert's version says that when he knocked, a pretty girl opened the door. One of his sisters; but which one? So he announced that he was selling the Encyclopaedia Britannica.

His mother came to the door, drying her hands. There was no outpouring of emotion, just a brisk kiss and a pot of tea and piece of cake. But almost at once, he says, he felt at home. His sister was weaning a newborn calf by the stove, and Robert, the old Cowichan cowhand, held the animal and helped her rub it down. Two strapping lads came in: Stanley and Albert. They grinned and shook hands.

"The happiest of homes" was Robert's description of this farmhouse, which lay 10 miles south of Mannville and some 100 miles east of Edmonton. The household now comprised brothers Stanley and Albert, sisters Agnes, Beatrice and Isobel, and mother Emily, who was not the sickly, tired figure he remembered from Glasgow, but a bright little woman of intense activity. It made him feel good to see her so happy.

According to Stanley, the family had come to Toronto in 1906 (when he was 14), lived there two and a half years, then bought the Alberta farm.

Stanley's writing paints a vivid and sometimes tragic story of a turn-of-the-century family struggling with a father's depression and alcoholism, and it fills in a great deal that is missing in Robert's own account of his life. "Papa had depressions," Stanley wrote, "deep dark ones which he had to drink himself out of ... it was these sprees that not only caused some of my brothers to leave home, but also chased the Service family half way round the world."

Without Stanley's manuscript, the early life of the Service family would have remained a mystery; with it the family of seven boys and three girls comes into focus.

> Mama and papa were the sun and the moon around which revolved their constellation of 10 children. Mama was the sun who fought desperately to keep her little group of satellites in the light; while papa was the moon who cast a dreary and repetitious shadow over them all so that one by one they flew out of orbit. Sometimes as in the case of Willie [Robert] or Joe, they never reappeared during his lifetime ... Mama put up a losing fight in the case of her first five. They were all boys and they all left home, mostly for the same reason.[1]

In *Ploughman of the Moon*, Robert barely mentioned his brothers and sisters, although their struggles contained enough romance, drama and tragedy for the pen of any bard. Even John Alexander's Boer War adventure was ignored.

Peter left home when he was 17 and immigrated to Australia. When things didn't work out there he came home, and then immigrated to Canada. It was Peter who had the farming experience, and persuaded the family to follow him to Canada, and later, to move west to the prairies.

Joseph became a steward on a boat between Glasgow and Belfast, and according to Stanley, never came home again. Harry, the fifth son, became a bookie at the Glasgow racetrack, then moved with the family to Canada, but died tragically in Toronto.

In his autobiography, as he arrives in Mannville Robert says nothing of his father's recent death. Earlier in the book, he devotes a whole chapter to Robert Sr. and confesses that his father wrote many times begging his son to visit. In his last letter written from Mannville, he pleaded with his son to write and say he would come, even if he couldn't; but Robert was busy writing his novel and did not answer the letter. In retrospect he acknowledged his callousness, and consoled himself by rationalizing that *Songs of a Sourdough* had given pleasure to his father (who had helped find a publisher) and that he had lived long enough to see his son's success.

Stanley's manuscript expresses impatience with his brother for that chapter, which attempted to show their father in a sympathetic light. "Willie describes him as getting drunk once a year followed by a period of remorse, after which he was good for a year on the wagon. But Willie left home and never came back while papa still lived, so I don't see how he can claim to be an authority on the subject."

Things got worse as Robert Sr. got older. His drinking bouts "took on a regular manic depressive pattern which lasted for two weeks, during which time we would stay away from him as though he had the plague."[2]

The family's only defence from the embarrassment caused by their father was to move every few years. In Glasgow they went from Lansdowne Crescent to a terraced house in Kelvinside. In a January 1897 letter to Alick in Pretoria, Emily talks of emigrating: "I would go anywhere."[3] Harry favored going to London, she says. But their next move was to Hawkhurst in Kent.

Then Canada. Stanley writes: "Our three years were up and papa had disgraced us again, so Peter and Alick and mama came to the conclusion that we go someplace far away. They decided that we would go to Canada."[4]

Peter arrived in Canada first, in 1905, and went west, spending the winter in a sod hut on the Alberta prairie. The rest of the family immigrated in 1906, but stopped in Ontario. According to Stanley, they lived 4.5 miles outside Toronto, the boys attending Gladstone school in the city (Alexander Muir, author of "The Maple Leaf Forever," had been headmaster there, but died in 1906 just before the boys enrolled). In the Service family Bible, there is a note Robert Sr. wrote while living at Dufferin Terrace in Toronto (the note is reproduced in Appendix 1) that lists the birthdates of his children; he explains that the Clyde Shipping Co. had lost his "private letters, family treasures & certificates of birth of my children."[5]

Toronto was not a happy place for the Service family. Apart from their father's problems, the boys were in trouble. Stanley got beaten up by a group of boys, was unable to speak for some time and was out of school for a year. Harry, who had begun gambling at the Glasgow race track, now got into gambling in Toronto. He was found unconscious on a Toronto street and died of pneumonia in hospital the next day.

Stanley says that Peter had gone to Edmonton looking for a sanctuary for the family. He filed on a homestead south of Mannville, where there was a settlement of Scottish people, and built a one-room lean-to heated by a small Quebec heater. In late 1907 or early 1908 he returned to Toronto to persuade the family to move.[6]

Peter took Stanley with him and headed back west on a cut-price train ticket (a "harvest excursion") while their mother stayed behind to engineer the move for the family. Stanley, "advancing" his age to 18, filed homestead papers on land west of Buffalo Coulee on the edge of the Scottish settlement. After his troubles in Toronto, he thought he had arrived in paradise.

> It was heaven to me to smell that prairie air, the small wild roses and grass and the soft warmth of a cloudless blue sky was like a great free and lovely new world. And it was free too. All we had to do was to file on homesteaders rights and follow the rules of erecting a building, fencing the property and in the first three years plant forty acres on each quarter section."

The two brothers spent the winter on this new property rather than on Peter's original claim. There was an old sod hut already on the land. Here they cooked their meals of oatmeal porridge, beans, ducks and prairie chicken. They had canned milk, dried apricots, dried apples and prunes. They made "wads" by mixing flour, water, baking soda and cream of tartar, dropping these on a cooking dish and popping them in the oven.

While Peter went east to get the family, Stanley was left alone with an axe and a shotgun, with a garden of potatoes, turnips and parsnips to look after. Tired of hoeing, he could walk down to the slough and shoot a duck for dinner; years later he remembered it as "grand living."

"Of all the summers in the world an Alberta one can be the nicest. Just day after day of blue sky, and I drank it in. I grew to be a man at seventeen." His only regret was that his youngest brother, Albert, was not with him. "I guess everyone lives in terms of someone else and to me it was always Albert."[7]

Then Peter arrived with the badly battered family in tow. And it was here, on the open prairie at Mannville, that the family found their sanctuary. "When we reached the end of the pilgrimage there wasn't a sign of whisky for miles and miles around. And there were no roads. Papa gazed around him in wondering praise at the completeness of the wilderness: and in awed resignation as if calling down a curse, or offering a blessing, he raised his hands over his head and pronounced it 'The Sanctuary.'"[8]

Robert Sr. did not last long in his prairie sanctuary. At 74 he was worn out from depression, drinking, the shock of losing a son in Toronto, and possibly the

The grave of Robert Service Sr. at Mannville, Alberta. He died of a stroke in 1909, soon after the family moved from Ontario to Alberta.
PHOTO: ENID MALLORY

yearning for an eldest son who, according to Stanley, was "the apple of his eye," but never came home. He retired slowly to his bed, and died of a stroke on January 24, 1909. He is buried in the little cemetery at Mannville.

Emily Service was 53 when the family headed west in 1908, still the sun around which her family revolved. Of her five oldest wandering sons, only Peter was living nearby. Her daughters Agnes, Beatrice and Sibbie were with her, and her two youngest sons, Stanley and Albert.

Stanley had found Peter a hard taskmaster; he remembered back-breaking work from dawn to dusk. In his second winter he left the farm to go logging in the northern Saskatchewan bush. He came home in the spring "cocksure" and immediately quarreled with Peter. The result was that Peter moved back to his own section of land, leaving Stanley and Albert to work together under Emily's direction on the second claim.

With his father gone, and having matured himself, Robert was able to see what a staunch woman his mother was. Stanley and Albert did most of the farm work, but she was the glue holding the family together. Money was scarce—they still depended on her income from her father's estate, by now $1,200 a year—and they farmed at subsistence level. But what Robert remembered later was the great happiness in that house. His family had escaped into a sense of New World freedom. They told him their story of pioneering without complaint, almost as an adventure. They had lived in tents at first and worked extremely hard, but they were all healthy and part of a young, vibrant community. Stanley's well-hoed garden provided vegetables. The short curly buffalo grass fattened their livestock. Their house was large by prairie standards with "5 bedrooms, a dining room, kitchen and a big living room ideal for dances."[9] Emily Service had rosy cheeks and very blue eyes, and laughed easily. She played cards and read detective novels and liked her house to be full of young people.

There was no shortage of young bachelors on the rolling prairie, and at night they rode their horses to the Service home and swarmed around Robert's sisters. Robert found the crowd too young for him, and often escaped upstairs to read, recreating the pattern of his childhood in Glasgow. But music always drew him like a magnet. When he heard his sister Beatrice on the piano, he came down with an old guitar and joined her, contributing his own songs to the merriment.

In the settlement's little schoolhouse the Service family gave a dance for the entire community, for which Robert footed the bill. In *Ploughman* he remembered giving small checks to his sisters and the great joy they had in poring over the Eaton's catalogue deciding what to order. It is likely that he also helped his mother with the mortgage, as this had been part of his idea in coming home. Stanley eventually went off to medical school, possibly with help from his rich brother. Yet Robert says in *Ploughman* that he is sorry he did not do more for them.

By this time, the elderly aunts in Scotland who had loved and cared for him as a small boy could also have used some financial help, but it seems the thought didn't occur to him. Many years later, on a visit to Kilwinning, he stood by their graves and realized with regret that he could have helped them. All he could do then was to erect a granite stone to their memory.

In daily life Robert existed so much inside his own mind that he failed to reach out to family and friends. Stanley's assessment of him was quite blunt:

It is a sad commentary, but Willie was like an ostrich with his head stuck down into the sands of fiction so he could escape reality … We liked Willie immensely, but you had to accept him with more than the usual grain of salt, and allow for his sense of humour. This humour and disregard for the truth runs through all his books. He makes no pretense of adhering to fact. Most of his writing was pretense. He was full of sly fun. To ask him a serious question was to invite an irrelevant reply … For instance, he wore a ring on his finger with the initials J.C. carved on it. When my curious sisters asked who J.C. stood for he replied with a twinkle in his eye, "Jesus Christ."

Robert was not about to tell the family of his engagement to Jean Clark. Stanley remembered that Robert was "always good humoured and I never saw him angry. He was quite at home with the family and always chatty, but in a crowd or with strangers he would clam up. After his breakfast he would go for long walks until suppertime, and always with a book. I think I never saw that man without a book."[10]

Only musical evenings seemed to bring Robert close to the convivial prairie people, making him, briefly, a social being. The rest of the time, if not needed in the barn, he roamed the trails, reveling in being outdoors and alone, loving the sunlit snow, the first greens of springtime in Alberta and the "sapphire serenity of the sky." In the mornings he struck out with a gun to shoot prairie chickens until he discovered the family used only the breasts and discarded the rest; then he stopped sacrificing the birds and contented himself with hiking.

One day he felt a gloom come over the landscape, then a haze shut out the sun and he could see smoke moving like a wall rapidly toward him. The prairie was on fire. As he ran, flocks of birds streaked past him and small animals ran ahead of him. Waves of fire were now devouring the tall grass and trees were bursting into flame.

With the flames gaining on him, he made it to a slough, floundering and swimming across before the flames could encircle it. The house lay about a quarter-mile away, and he made a dash for it.

One of his brothers was ploughing a double furrow around the house and barns. His sisters were attaching sacks to brooms to use for beating out the flames. Robert got a shovel and helped them. When the fire arrived the five of them fought it desperately up and down the furrow, almost losing the stable to the flames. Then the canopy of smoke and flame passed by on either side. Exhausted and hysterical from their close call, they went into the house and drank tea.

Robert remembered how, after night fell, the prairie was lit up by living gems of fire still sparkling, and by the blazing houses of less lucky families on the distant horizon where the fire still traveled.

On spring days as the old wanderlust rose in Robert, his hikes began to get longer. On the prairie you could be a "stopper"—knock on any door and expect a bed and a bite, paying a dollar when you left. In this way, he visited settlements of many nationalities—Norwegian, Romanian, French, Slavic—covering about 200 miles all tolled.

The direction he hiked was usually north, and as he moved across the prairie he realized the significance of this. Feeling superbly strong and imbued with the energy of springtime, he yearned to keep moving north— all the way to the Land of the Midnight Sun. He knew he had to go back, and when he told them, his family was shocked and dismayed. Why would he want to go back there, to be alone and lonely?

Robert tried to explain his need for solitude. He told them about the little cabin with the moose antlers over the door and the hammock on the porch, and the wild roses that would bloom in June, and how it called him. His mother and the others shook their heads. Then he revealed the rest of the crazy plan evolving in his head. This time he would go in the hard way, via the Edmonton–Athabasca route—a circuitous, 2,000 miles using the great Mackenzie river system, then over the Richardson Mountains to the Yukon River watershed and down the Yukon to Dawson. Describing this route to the goldfields in 1898, Tappan Adney had used the word "insane." The word still applied in 1911.

chapter 12

On May 23, 1911, Service left Edmonton by stage, heading north for Athabasca Landing, where the river of that name makes its horseshoe bend to the south. Each spring the Athabasca Brigade departed from the Landing laden with supplies for the north.

The bad news—which Service and his fellow travelers received in Edmonton via telegram—was that the Hudson's Bay Company (HBC) brigade had already left Athabasca Landing. Service joined up with George and Lionel Douglas, who were heading north to the Coppermine River along with Dr. August Sandberg, a Swedish geologist. The quartet arranged to have a large canoe waiting for them at the Landing, which they would use alongside the one George Douglas was already transporting on one of the wagons. In this way the party, soon to number five when their HBC guide Henri met them at the Landing, would try to catch the HBC brigade at Grand Rapids, 130 miles downriver.

It took two days of overland travel to reach Athabasca Landing, stopping at settlers' homes for meals, and overnight at a farmhouse. Along the way Service got to know the Douglases and Dr. Sandberg. They were being sponsored by the Douglases' cousin, James Douglas of the American Phelps Dodge copper mining company, to search for the copper mentioned by Samuel Hearne during his epic trip northwest across the barren lands from Fort Prince of Wales on Hudson Bay to the Arctic Ocean 140 years earlier. For the best part of a year in 1770–71 Hearne's party had traveled in harsh

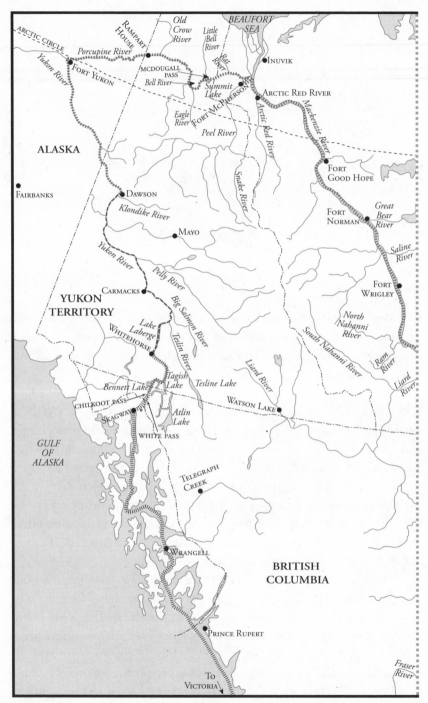

The Yukon Travels of Robert Service, 1904–09

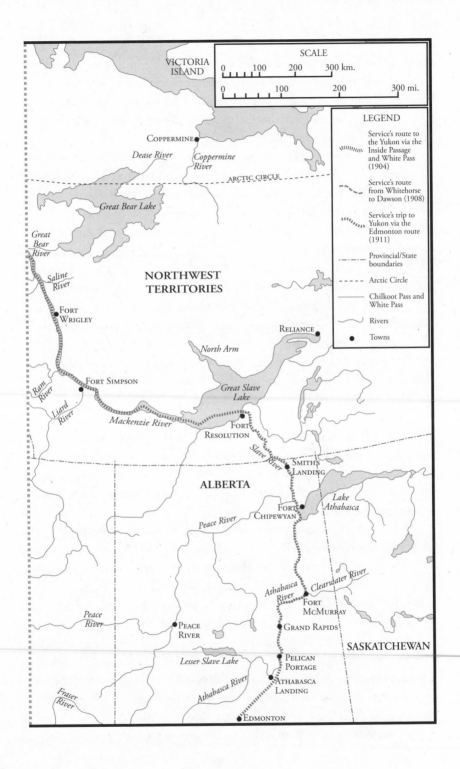

SCALE

0 100 200 300 km.

0 100 200 300 mi.

LEGEND

Service's route to the Yukon via the Inside Passage and White Pass (1904)

Service's route from Whitehorse to Dawson (1908)

Service's trip to Yukon via the Edmonton route (1911)

Provincial/State boundaries

Arctic Circle

Chilkoot Pass and White Pass

Rivers

Towns

VICTORIA ISLAND

COPPERMINE

Dease River

Coppermine River

ARCTIC CIRCLE

Great Bear Lake

Great Bear River

Saline River

NORTHWEST TERRITORIES

FORT WRIGLEY

RELIANCE

North Arm

Ram River

FORT SIMPSON

Liard River

Mackenzie River

Great Slave Lake

FORT RESOLUTION

SMITH'S LANDING

Slave River

ALBERTA

Lake Athabasca

Peace River

FORT CHIPEWYAN

Athabasca River

Clearwater River

FORT McMURRAY

Peace River

PEACE RIVER

GRAND RAPIDS

SASKATCHEWAN

Lesser Slave Lake

PELICAN PORTAGE

Athabasca River

ATHABASCA LANDING

Fraser River

EDMONTON

Arctic conditions to reach the river of copper. The trip is remembered not so much for the small amount of copper they found but for the massacre of a band of Inuit by the group of Copper and Chipewyan who were guiding Hearne, at a waterfall on the Coppermine River. A distraught Hearne named the place Bloody Falls.

The tiny community of Athabasca Landing was a jumping-off place for heading to the north, and it had attracted at least two land speculators in 1911. Service wrote of being offered a corner lot for $300. "At that time I think I had enough money to buy up the whole townsite ... I might have become a multimillionaire, and such a fate I would not wish anyone."[1]

One of the two men standing over a blueprint of a new townsite was Jim Cornwall, known as "Peace River Jim." Service described him as "Lord of the Athabasca" and compared him to Joe Boyle of the Klondike Mining Company, who was known as "King of the Yukon." He compared them to Roman emperors, stalwart and handsome, with strong frames and bold features. A few years later Service would know Jim Cornwall as the commander of a labor battalion in the trenches of the First World War, leading him on a tour of the battlefront in France and Belgium.

Service heard about Great Bear Lake and the Coppermine as he and his companions traveled downstream together for the 41 days it took to cover the 1,250 miles from Edmonton to Fort Norman; there the Douglas party would disembark to make its way east to the Coppermine, while Service would continue north.

Both Robert Service and George Douglas would write books that recounted this experience, thus giving us two distinct views of the same trip and of each other. Service's *Ploughman,* written more than three decades later, devoted five chapters to his 1911 odyssey. George Douglas, on the other hand, wrote *Lands Forlorn* soon after reaching his home at Lakefield, Ontario, 18 months later, while the trek was still fresh in his memory.

As they bumped along in the wagon en route to the Landing, the Douglas brothers ignored one fellow passenger, a garrulous drug salesman who consequently dubbed them "English nobs" and complained to Service that they considered themselves above the other travelers. Service stated that he himself, being Scottish, got along with everyone.

He later discovered that George and Lionel were Canadian born, but of

Scottish, not English, descent, while Service, the self-proclaimed Scot, had actually been born in England. George, a mining engineer, had worked in his cousin's copper operations in Arizona and New Mexico, while Lionel was a naval officer on leave from Canadian Pacific Steamships. "The engineer was tall and wiry, serenely confident, resourceful and without fear. He was a leader of men and would have made a splendid soldier. The brother was trim and well set, with a naval appreciation of discipline."[2] Dr. Sandberg, who had worked with George in Arizona, is described by Service as inclined toward melancholy.

In *Lands Forlorn* Douglas wrote: "Our own little party had been joined by Robert Service, who was making a journey to the North with the Hudson Bay Co.'s transport, and who like ourselves, had been surprised by the unexpectedly early departure of the brigade."[3] He did not explain who Service was, indicating that 1914 readers would be familiar with the name. Douglas lacks Service's penchant for character depiction; his comments on Service have more to do with his general competence—or lack of it—in practical tasks.

What Douglas remembered of Athabasca Landing was a frantically busy time sorting the small mountain of supplies and loading each of the two canoes with 1,000 pounds. The rest of their supplies would follow in a later brigade of scows under the famous riverman Captain Schott.

Service, writing in the 1940s, says they left Athabasca Landing the following morning, but Douglas says it was 6:30 in the evening. Taking advantage of the long bright evening, they paddled until 9:00 p.m., then made camp in a grove of spruce trees.

Service and the Douglas party had discovered that their guide, Henri, wasn't happy to be with them. The HBC agent had insisted that these newcomers have a guide until they joined up with the main brigade, and had held Henri back from the first flotilla of scows. Travel with the brigade was the high point of the year for the local Cree. Springtime, hard work, good food, maybe some smuggled alcohol and the merriment of a large band of men made an occasion no red-blooded young male wanted to miss. Here was Henri traveling instead with two "English nobs," a poet and a taciturn Swedish geologist.

Douglas says: "Our guide was a half-breed Cree; he didn't see any fun in paddling. He was worse than useless in camp and no good as a guide even if a guide's services had been necessary."[4] The Douglas brothers traveled in one canoe. The other canoe had Service in the bow, Henri in the stern and Sandberg in the middle.

The river had a good current, with turns every few yards. Drifting downstream that first full day was, to Service, "a joy hard to match." For many miles a family of ducks swam ahead of them. For lunch they lit a fire on the shore and dined on bread, butter, canned salmon, pineapple and a copious supply of tea. About 3:00 p.m. Douglas passed out chunks of chocolate, and they drifted, blissfully chewing.

Camp was made just before sunset. Service had a small mosquito tent, an oblong sheet of canvas with cords and a rope that he attached to trees or shrubs. Mosquito netting on the inside gave him a 7- by 4-foot space safe from insects and rain. Cold was another matter. While the Douglas party slept in warm sleeping bags, Service was heading north without one, using only a seven-point Hudson Bay blanket in which he shivered.

After nine hours of paddling on day one, Service remembered his muscles protesting painfully, while Douglas reported that the swift current made paddling unnecessary except for the pleasure of it. The Douglas brothers had grown up on the Kawartha Lakes (birthplace of the famous Peterborough canoe), their father had designed and built a unique folding canoe, and they had a paddle in their hands before they could swim. The Service canoe contained three very mismatched people. There was Henri doing nothing in the stern while two novices struggled to keep up with the lead canoe. "The Britannic Brothers surged ahead and for the honour of Scotland and Sweden we had to keep up."[5]

Under his breath Service called himself a damn fool for what he was doing. The Douglas party was on a business trip; what silly notion was taking *him*, a "phoney" explorer, on this improbable voyage, when he could afford to travel anywhere in the world in style and comfort?

But Service knew he would not turn back. He was young and strong, and this was something he felt he had to do even though he might be risking his life. With the hindsight of another 30-some years, he noted that he had not enough sense to be scared, for at that point in his life, even if the chance of survival was only 50–50, he was willing to take the odds.

Late on the second day they came to Pelican Portage. Here an oil well drilled by the government 15 years earlier had blown out its rigging, leaving a flaming jet of gas that was shooting 20 feet in the air. (It continued to do so until the well was eventually capped in 1918.)

Traveling down the Athabasca in an HBC scow. Robert Service is in the stern, writing on a paper on his knee.

The group pressed onward, Service exhausted and the others grumpy with fatigue. Henri suddenly decided to paddle—and he could certainly paddle. The canoe seemed to lift out of the water. Service and Sandberg joined in with their best efforts and swept past the brothers with shouts of derision. The brothers joined the race but could not catch up, and soon were shouting that it was time to camp.

On the afternoon of the third day they caught up with the 24 scows of the HBC brigade, camped on the island above Grand Rapids. They were made welcome and assigned a barge on which to put their canoe and gear. Service was surprised to see a grin on the face of Henri. He was home now, back with his friends and suddenly affable. Service recalled him saying: "You good canoe man. You work very good. Next time I let you take him steer."[6]

Service and the Douglas party set up their tents on the grassy bank and joined the others at tables and benches for a meal of mulligan stew, soup, fried hash, beans, hot biscuits, pie and coffee—followed by lively conversation.

Service was seeing the Athabasca scow brigade in a drama that had been enacted since 1885. Before that time the freight for Lake Athabasca and the Mackenzie River posts went north via Lake Winnipeg, the Saskatchewan, Sturgeon-weir and Churchill rivers, then over the divide in northwestern Saskatchewan at the famed 12.5-mile Methye Portage to the Clearwater River, thence to Fort McMurray, where that river joined the Athabasca. The reason for this long, difficult route was to

Crew and passengers of the brigade pose for the Douglas camera after a meal on shore.
PHOTO: GEORGE DOUGLAS/LIBRARY AND ARCHIVES CANADA/PA—145198

avoid the forbidding Grand Rapids, some 85 miles upstream from Fort McMurray on the Athabasca. But in about 1885 Louis Fousseneuve proved that he could run a scow through Grand Rapids. Athabasca Landing took on new importance. As a bison hunter with a steady aim, Fousseneuve had acquired the nickname "Sure Shot," so after becoming the acknowledged master of the Grand Rapids he was dubbed "Captain Shot." Still at it 25 years later, it was he who brought the Douglas outfit down the river.

Scows like the one Service was now riding were built new each year at Athabasca Landing. They were flat-bottomed boats, 50 feet long, 8 feet wide at their bottom and 12 feet wide at the gunwales, and manned by five or six men. A "sweep" (a large oar) 35 feet long was balanced on an iron rod at the stern to act as a rudder, and four other oars, each 22 feet long, were positioned on the sides. Most of the hundred-plus scows built each year were broken up for lumber downstream. Only the odd one carrying furs would make the difficult upriver trip.

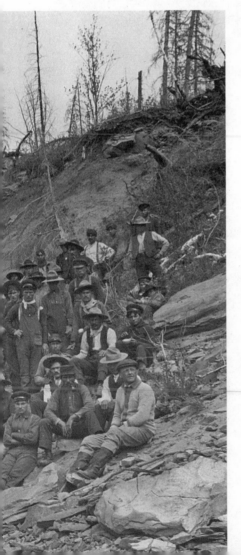

Next morning, Service watched empty scows run down the channel on the east side of the island, where the rapids were easiest to navigate. Meanwhile, the freight was carried to the other end of the island on a wooden tramway. It took two more days to get all the scows through the rapids, reload them and get the flotilla underway.

Robert found to his delight that he had nothing to do but watch the scenery slide by as they traveled the 85 miles from Grand Rapids to Fort McMurray. Douglas described the pleasant trip:

Nominally the brigade was under the

The scows of the brigade tied up on shore.

Nominally the brigade was under the charge of a captain, but its movements were in fact regulated by the whims of the Indian pilots, and we went ahead or stopped—mostly stopped—according to their inclination. Our voyage from Grand Rapids to McMurray took a week; this means that we were actually under way about two hours per day; it was a series of resting spells with short interludes of progress. But no-one worried, to-morrow was as good as today, the weather was fine and bright, the scenery beautiful, and grub plentiful.[7]

The picturesque journey was not lost on either Douglas or Service. Douglas was a superb photographer. His photos of the brigade tied along the island shore, or of a scow balanced precariously over the Cascade Rapids, are the best of this historic northern ritual that have survived. While Douglas recorded with his camera, Service made pictures using words. One of Douglas's photos shows the poet with a notebook on his knee. His poem "Athabaska Dick" later described the danger and drama of the Big Cascade, in the set of rapids some 19 miles before reaching Fort McMurray.

At one of the rapids, George Douglas—the man Service later called simply "the Engineer"—suggested that he and Service run the white water in one of the canoes. Service's account reflects the discord that had built up between him and Douglas. He considered it a foolish thing to do, but felt he had to take the dare. He unlaced his boots and slipped them off (in case they capsized and had to swim), for which he got a look of contempt from the Engineer—Douglas himself was wearing light moccasins. Douglas, seated in the back, warned his companion to sit still, but when a big boulder shot up in front of them Service poked at it and nearly upset the canoe. Meanwhile, one of the barges ran onto a rock and had to be rescued. The steersman said he had been distracted by the canoe escapade, so Douglas and Service were forbidden to pull any more silly stunts.

They were two very different people: Douglas the practical man, the careful planner, the no-time-for-fools person; and Service the poet, traveling without a clearly stated purpose, without proper provisions or a definite plan.

At Fort McMurray, the scow trip was over, and the quartet boarded the HBC steamer SS *Grahame*. By June 13 they had reached Fort Chipewyan on Lake Athabasca, and from there they traveled down the Slave River to Smith's Landing (now Fort Fitzgerald), where the *Grahame* unloaded

Robert bought a beautiful canoe from Chief Sun in the Mug on Great Slave Lake.
PHOTO: GEORGE DOUGLAS COLLECTION/LIBRARY AND ARCHIVES CANADA/PA–145189

passengers and goods. Here, 16 miles of wild rapids dropped the river 125 feet. Freight went by wagon to Fort Smith at the foot of the rapids, while the passengers walked there to take the HBC steamer SS *Mackenzie River* to Great Slave Lake.

On Great Slave, Service bought a beautiful birchbark canoe from an elderly Native said to be the best local canoe builder. He named her *Coquette*. The *Dawson Daily News* later said of his canoe: "There is not a nail in the craft. It is sealed at the joints with pitch and bound at other places with thongs of green spruce roots … Made by old Chief Sun in the Mug."[8] Douglas—who wrote later that Service knew nothing about canoes or paddling—probably gave him some lessons in handling his new bark. Service says he soon mastered it, and never once upset it in spite of riotous rapids on the rivers ahead.

From Great Slave Lake the SS *Mackenzie River* reached the great river after which it was named. Some 200 miles farther downstream, before the westward-flowing Mackenzie bends north and flows between the Mackenzie and Franklin mountains, it is met by the Liard River, where the HBC post of Fort Simpson is located. Douglas wrote that "the scenery below Fort Simpson is incomparably grand, a mighty river flowing among mighty mountains." A Yukon man like Service might be expected to take mighty mountains for granted, but he was enjoying every minute. The people he met were all fodder for his pen; he noted their demeanor and their eccentricities—the tough loneliness of the Hebridean men who manned the Hudson Bay posts, the obsessive grit of the explorers.

One explorer that Service remembered clearly 30 years later was "Handsome Harry" Radford—strikingly good-looking, rich and impressive. But there was something else: a callous streak and a lack of sensitivity were evident in even a brief meeting. In his cabin on the steamer, as he and Service shared a smoke, a field mouse ran across the floor, but instead of trying to get it out of his room, Harry wanted to play football with it.

Radford and his guide, George Street, set out from Fort Simpson to travel east across the barren lands to Hudson Bay. Douglas, who had bought a sheet-metal stove from Harry, photographed the pair as they left. Service accompanied them a short distance in his canoe and saw them off. Two years later he heard that Radford's kicking had got both him and his guide in trouble. Radford had booted an Inuit, who promptly killed him with his spear. Street died with Radford.

At Fort Wrigley, a Native man brought news to the *Mackenzie River* of trouble in a nearby trapper's cabin. A Royal North West Mounted Police inspector on board asked the Douglas brothers, Sandberg and Service to help him, and they set off together. Where the Salt River (now known as the Saline River) flows into the Mackenzie they found a well-built shack and a storehouse for furs.

Inside they found the remains of two men. The head of one had been blown shapeless by a bullet from a rifle. The other man had left a note and had apparently taken carbolic acid. The stench of the decaying bodies was overpowering. Service described the horror of seeing the caved-in faces and the long ashen hair of the men moving with armies of lice.

The last date marked off on the men's calendar was May 13; now it was the beginning of July. The men took turns going in to chop down the bunks, then rushing out, "driven gasping from the door. One brief visit and I was convinced that my physical end, if I can shape it, will be cremation."[9] Douglas photographed the remains as the other men dug the graves.

A grubby notebook told what had happened. Douglas transcribed what appears to be actual lines from the diary:

> Cruel treatment drove me to kill Peat. Everything is wrong he never paid one sent ship everything out pay George Walker [probably the man who staked them] $10 ... I have been sick a long time I am not Crasey, but sutnly goded to death he thot i had more money than i had and has been trying to find it.
>
> I tried to get him to go after medison but Cod not he wanted me to die first so good by.
>
> I have just killed the man that was killing me so good bye and may God bless you all I am ofle weak bin down since the last of March so there hant no but Death for me.[10]

Still sickened, the five men returned to the civilized comfort of the *Mackenzie River*, where a coroner's jury convened and concluded that the older man, Oliver, had been unwell, and had shot the younger man, then taken his own life by swallowing carbolic acid. It was a grim reminder about what can happen in the wild, and it left them wondering about their own long trips ahead.

At 2:30 the next morning the steamer reached Fort Norman. Service watched as the crew took ashore all of the Douglas gear. For the brothers and the Swedish geologist, any comfort now would be what they could make for themselves on their way up the Bear River and across Great Bear Lake en route to the Coppermine. More than a year would pass before they returned to Fort Norman.

As the *Mackenzie River* left the fort, Service turned his attention to three men huddled over a breakfast of fried bacon in the grey dawn. The one he remembered as an old Scottish guide was James MacKinley, an old HBC factor. Beside MacKinley was Cosmo Melville, a tall blue-eyed blond with the physique of a Viking. His traveling partner was a thin little man with a wiry beard, John Hornby. Writing about Hornby in the 1940s,

Where the Salt (Saline) River flows into the Mackenzie, two prospectors were found dead in their cabin, victims of isolation and illness that had caused one man to shoot his partner and drink carbolic acid himself. Robert Service is in the foreground, facing the camera.

PHOTO: GEORGE DOUGLAS/LIBRARY AND ARCHIVES CANADA/PA–145190

Service described his tragic fate in the winter of 1926–27 when he took his nephew and another young man to the Thelon River, where all three starved to death.

Looking back from the distance of the years, Service commented that the men he met in that broad Mackenzie valley nearly all met tragic deaths. "The Mackenzie was more murderous than the Yukon."[11]

Service must have been aware in 1911 that he might not survive. Many people warned of dire consequences if he continued. At Fort McMurray, the Indian agent—an ex-parson—had told Service upon hearing of his plan to cross the mountains alone that he was going to his doom. On board *Grahame*, a priest was appalled by Service's plans and told him that to travel alone was suicidal, that a single mistake would result in death.

For whatever reason, in spite of his success, his freedom from work and money worries, and his hard-won satisfaction with himself, Service was still careless with his life. Perhaps he really believed in a guardian angel. Or in predestination. Or there may have been moments when he didn't care. At a stop one day on the Mackenzie River—perhaps recalling earlier dips from his days on Vancouver Island—he was tempted to swim. He was urged not to do it: only a month before, he was told, a priest had been caught in the undertow and drowned. Service ignored the warning, dove in and was immediately caught in the current and swept away. He was sure he was done for, but he was a powerful swimmer, and by desperate effort he managed to haul himself out of the cold water and onto the shore about a mile downstream. Punished by hordes of mosquitoes on his bare skin, he made his way back to camp, amazed to be alive. "Why me?" he asked himself. "Why should a poor priest perish and a sinner like myself be saved?"[12]

Now, disembarked at Fort McPherson, 25 miles up the Peel River from the Mackenzie, Service faced a new dissuader: an old HBC man whom Service called John North (his real name was John Firth), who had spent almost 50 years on the Porcupine and Peel rivers and was post manager at McPherson in 1911. He lectured Service to be sensible and go back up the river.

The steamer *Mackenzie River* at Fort Norman.
PHOTO: GEORGE DOUGLAS/LIBRARY AND ARCHIVES CANADA/PA–145188

Fort McPherson, a fur-trading post since 1840, is on a flat-topped hill 24 miles upstream from the Mackenzie River. At St. Matthew's Anglican church, overlooking the Peel River, the Lost Patrol is buried.
PHOTO: GORD MALLORY

The local Mounted Police officer added his weight to the warning with a story already becoming a northern legend—the Lost Patrol. In the previous winter a four-man police party under a veteran Yukoner, Inspector Francis Fitzgerald, had set out from Fort McPherson to make the yearly patrol to the Yukon. They never arrived in Dawson City, and in March were found dead of starvation and cold only 25 miles from their starting point.

As the *Mackenzie River* prepared to head south again, it would have been easy for Service to step on board as everyone was urging him to do, but he seemed to fear a sense of failure more than he feared risking his life. He watched the boat come, and then go again. Either he would find some way to get over the mountain divide, or he would winter here in the long Arctic night.

chapter 13

It began to look like Service might have to spend the winter at Fort McPherson. None of the local Gwich'in people wanted to help a neophyte carry his canoe 100 miles to Yukon headwaters on the other side of the Richardson Mountains.

He camped on the shore with a party of Inuit, sketched the head man (who sketched him in return) and shared his canoe with the man's son, who showed him how to kayak. He tried to keep his mind off the nine months of Arctic winter that stretched dismally ahead of him.

Then one day, a party of three came up the Mackenzie sculling a scow named *Ophelia*. Captain McTosh and his lively woman were independent traders who hated the HBC. Jake Skilly, a trapper, was mate on their craft. As usual Service was not using real names—McTosh was A.A. Carroll, and Jake Skilly's real name was Frank Williams. Service never gave Mrs. McTosh a first name in his writings, referring to her as "the Lady." They were bound for Dawson and were aiming to make the *Ophelia* the first scow to cross the Rockies. McTosh managed to persuade a couple of Gwich'in to be their guides on the trip, and Service was invited to join their crew.

They set off on the Peel River through the muddy grey tundra, heading northwest to the mouth of the Rat River. Robert and Jake were in the Service canoe, the McTosh couple in the scow, and the two guides in their own canoe. On the second morning the land around them became hilly, the water became rough—and their work began.

Service had no idea how bad it could get. Day after day for three weeks they worked on the tow line, inching the unwieldy scow 80 miles to the higher altitude. At times they had to portage through willow brush, then hoist the scow over the boulders along the stream bed. There were days when they could only move the scow half a mile over the rock and rubble.

On the *Grahame* and the *Mackenzie River*, Service had reveled in the thought that he never had to work again. Money was rolling in from *The Trail of '98* and his two books of poetry. He had watched others unloading the cargo and knew that he was "a lucky stiff." Now, as he pulled and sweated knee-deep in the headwaters of the Rat River, he cursed himself for being a fool. He cursed the *Ophelia* and the stupidity of taking a scow over a mountain. In all his life he had never worked so hard.

The Rat River route leads to McDougall Pass, which, at only 1,050 feet above sea level, is the lowest pass in the Rocky Mountain chain. But it is nobody's idea of an easy trip. In essence you must climb a mountain on a river to reach Summit Lake before you can begin your descent on the other side. Modern canoeists have determined that the rise on the Rat River averages 29 feet per mile.

Every three hours the scow party threw themselves on the shore, where "the Lady" served grub. She cooked two strips of bacon for each person, then fried bannock in the bacon fat. That, with tea and sometimes blueberries, was the meal.

The times Service remembered afterward as good were the precious moments of rest, squatting on the sand and watching the woman cook supper, or smoking his pipe afterward, or pitching his tent by the river. At Fort Resolution he had traded his seven-point blanket for a loosely woven rabbit's-foot robe. It was perfect protection, and he blessed it every night.

On one rough stretch of the Rat River, between canyon walls, Service again came close to drowning. On the tow line the men were bent double, barely able to keep the scow from slipping back. Jake was poling, keeping *Ophelia's* head to the current, when his pole slipped and he lost control. Service, in harness at the end of the track-line, was jerked off his feet and dragged underwater downstream, his back bumping against every boulder.

A large rock at the mouth of the canyon saved him. It stopped the scow, letting Jake gain enough control to fish out the half-dead Service. At first he thought his back was broken, but a slug of brandy, hot tea and some nursing from the Lady brought him round. McTosh mused that the headline would have read: "YUKON BARD MEETS WATERY DOOM." Service, battered, weak and wild-headed, did not find the line all that funny.

While he recorded almost no details of the land or the wildlife on this journey, the people he traveled with were depicted sharp and clear, their singularities and peculiarities stored up for later use. The Lady was vivacious and attractive, and both Service and Jake envied McTosh his nights with her. By day she kept their spirits up with good grub and her good nature. McTosh was a big red-haired man who carried with him an edition of Shakespeare, which he and the Lady had read to each other in lonely trapping cabins to while away the Arctic nights.

But it was Jake Skilly whom Service painted in the sharpest colors. A little "rat-grey" trapper, he told Service harrowing tales of his northern life, of packing out hundreds of white fox furs from the Mackenzie Delta, of darkness and silence, of cold and starvation on the Arctic coast, all in a matter-of-fact voice. But when he spoke of his father, who had beaten him, his voice rang with rage and bitterness. He was going out now to collect the $2,000 his father had left him when he died, but the money would in no way lessen the hatred.

Jake was helplessly addicted to nicotine. He smoked all through meals and in his tent in the middle of the night. All day, every 15 minutes, he had to stop and cut a cigarette from his plug of tobacco, then roll it in a half-page of an old magazine. Without his cigarette he started to shake, and a wildness came into his eyes.

As the Richardson Mountains closed in around them, the river narrowed and became crystal clear. When it forked they had to guess which channel would lead them to the little lake at the summit of the divide. They had no map, and at this point the two Gwich'in guides quit. Without them the work was doubly hard, and there was a dark cloud of suspicion that the two Natives had turned back to McPherson because they had lost the trail.

Finally the day came when McTosh admitted that they probably were lost. Around them the mountains towered, bare and dark with jagged peaks and cones. Service felt he could not help lug that damned scow any farther if they weren't even sure they were on the right route. He resolved to turn back alone.

After a gloomy meal at which no one talked, Service walked upstream to get away from the others. He was to climb a pine tree, in hopes of getting a better view, when he saw a blaze on its bark. In great surprise he deciphered the name written there: Buffalo Jones.

C.J. "Buffalo" Jones was known to Service as the conservationist famous for his work to save the American bison. Jones had wintered in the Barren Lands in 1897–98 seeking musk oxen to take back and breed on his ranch in Kansas. On his return journey he had come down the Mackenzie to the Peel, crossed the Divide and traveled the Porcupine and Yukon to the sea. If Buffalo Jones had come this way, they must be on the trail to the Divide.

Returning to the others with this great news, Service became the hero of the expedition. They worked with renewed gusto for the next week as the stream narrowed to a rivulet. Finally they were pushing the scow through willows on a small prairie. The height of land! And in the distance, jewel-like, sat Summit Lake.

Using their poles as rails and skids, they painfully pushed their Noah's Ark across the final mile to the promised lake. As they got closer they worked in icy slime; at last solid ground gave way to swamp, which they poled through for 10 hours until the scow floated on the glacial water.

In the broad daylight of the Arctic night they went back for their cargo. Service made three trips carrying his bags of flour and bacon, sinking in the mud and struggling not to fall. On the fourth trip, as he carried his canoe, he was so tired that he had to throw it down and rest time after time.

> It was a weird camp at the height of the Divide, with the midnight sun shining like a great red ball. There were sudden squalls of pelting rain, and the loneliness had a sinister quality that struck fear in me. The little lake shuddered as it shone … As I looked at these iron mountains towering above the Pass I felt crushed with awe.[1]

Exhausted, they spent a whole day in that gloomy camp. There was no elation yet, for no one could see the stream that would lead to the Yukon River system. Service was unable to sleep for fear that this lake was somehow the wrong one and they were, after all, lost. But the next morning he found a fringe of green willows concealing a gully out of which poured a lusty stream. For the last time, they hoisted and hefted and pulled to let the scow down into the gully with ropes.

From Summit Lake they were now poised to ride the waters of the Bell and Porcupine rivers downhill for 500 miles to the confluence with

In sunshine, the Richardson Mountains present an unearthly landscape of austere beauty. In cold rain squalls, they cast a spell of gloom and desolation. The exhausted Service–McTosh party cowered beneath their oppressive power.
PHOTO: ENID MALLORY

the Yukon River at Fort Yukon, Alaska. From there, another 1,200 miles down the Yukon River would take a canoe all the way to the Pacific Ocean. But Service was planning to head upstream on the great river, to reach Dawson City.

Anxious to be alone and free of that cursed scow, Service saw Jake, McTosh and the Lady set out on the Little Bell River. He then followed in his canoe, singing "When You and I were Young, Maggie." His singing soon took on an edge as he and his *Coquette* were tossed around in rapids and swept over cascades, caught among boulders and precariously tilted. He knew what it would mean to lose all his grub now that he was alone.

For 12.5 miles the turbulent Little Bell gave Service the ride of his life, then smooth water ahead told him he had reached the Bell River. Here he found the McTosh party camped, their scow damaged from the wild water, their fur bales wet and spread out to dry. The *Coquette* was leaking too, and Service spent two hours chewing resin and patching every seam.

Jake and McTosh were fighting now, partly over Mrs. McTosh and partly over their trading. Worse, Jake had only three magazines left from which to roll his cigarettes and was having to cut down. Service knew by this point that accidents did happen—anything from a sprained ankle to a grizzly bear could spell disaster—but he chose to go on alone.

Day after day on the Bell River he moved along in idyllic bliss. He was literally on the top of the world, well above the Arctic Circle, resting his tired, battered muscles, wanting for nothing, and absorbing the stark, primitive beauty around him. He described a river 70 yards wide, smooth as a mirror and so clear that every pebble on the bottom was visible. A gentle current moved him past verdant banks where every few yards a mother ptarmigan in brown summer attire sat with her chicks. In the willows were snowshoe hares that had turned russet brown. Neither bird nor rabbit showed any fear of the figure slipping past in a quiet canoe.

The water was full of fish. The summer sky was cloudless, the air warm. When he made his camp he would swim, then cook his bannock and bacon, eat blueberries and make his tea. He could catch fish any time with a flick of his rod, but he preferred the bacon fat.

The Bell flowed through the mountains, then through tundra with spruce at the river's edge, but mostly moss and sparse bushes. There were 80 miles to cover before the river reached the Porcupine, and Service was in no hurry to get there. Once he saw his reflection in a pool and laughed out loud. The tanned, bearded creature in a sleeveless khaki shirt and pants hacked off at the knees, lean and fit, looked nothing like the bank clerk he had been.

Once, seeing movement, he loaded his Remington, thinking it might be a bear. Instead he came upon two men, prospectors heading up the Bell to trap during the winter. By the campfire the three men smoked together while the prospectors exchanged their tales of two years on the trail for news of the outside from Service.

As Service paddled on alone, the characters of the Mackenzie Valley and the Arctic coast were turning into poems in his head. He longed to be writing again. Finally, he reached the broad Porcupine, its water olive brown and its current stronger. Cloudbursts sent him scurrying to set up his tent.

One day he beached his canoe and made a trip inland to a dome-like hill that was colored with mosses and berries, rose and orange and red and gold, lemon and bronze and pomegranate. Nearby, a family of geese approached the water. The goslings were full-sized but unable to fly, and he killed four of them with his paddle. Leaving them on the riverbank with his canoe, he climbed the beautiful slope, feeling guilty at his deed; killing anything made him unhappy—and how could one person with only a small pan eat four geese?

From the top of the hill he looked down at the river moving through the tundra. He could see his canoe on the beach, the geese beside it. Walking on the moss was heavenly, the spongy, springy softness so inviting that he sank down in a hollow and went to sleep in the warm evening daylight.

When Service awoke, he sensed that he had slept a long time. He got to his feet and was immediately startled when he looked down at his canoe and saw a man standing beside it. Thoroughly alarmed he tore down the hill, sinking with every leap into the luxuriant moss.

The man was Jake, and just downstream was the *Ophelia*. Service's two weeks of solitude had been enough; he was delighted to see all three of them. The four geese suddenly made sense, with a big pot, a lady who knew how to cook them and four people to feed.

The birds were fat and delicious and made the reunion a celebration. There was trouble, however, between McTosh and Jake. His last magazine almost gone, Jake was down to one cigarette an hour, and he begged Service to take him in his canoe so he could get away from McTosh, whom he now referred to as "that carroty son-of-a-bitch." Then Mrs. McTosh also begged him to take Jake; she feared she could not keep the two men from coming to blows.

So Jake and his *Argosy* magazine settled in the stern. Service reckoned they could reach the little town of Rampart in three days and get all the paper Jake needed.

There could be no drifting now. In two and a half days the paper would run out, and Jake, already antsy from cigarette rationing, warned Service what might happen then. He began to goad him, remembering "them two stiffs" that Service had told him about in the cabin near Wrigley, "… wi' their head ablowed off? … I've jest been athinkin' that's what might happen to you an' me—if this here paper gives out."[2]

By the third morning Jake was down to his last pages, and Service felt they were both paddling for their lives. Not stopping for lunch, they made Rampart House late in the afternoon; it was the first settlement they had seen since leaving Fort McPherson. Rampart originated when the HBC's Fort Yukon, at the junction of the Porcupine and Yukon rivers, had to be abandoned in 1869 because it was now on American territory. The HBC moved first to the foot of the ramparts up the Porcupine River, then started a second post at the head of the ramparts—but these locations too, it turned out, were on the American side of the boundary. The third was established, finally on Canadian soil, at the current site. In 1893 the HBC abandoned the post, but by 1911 an independent trader named Dan Cadzow was doing business there with the Porcupine Natives.

As Service and Jake approached, they heard someone cry: "Smallpox!" This was followed by a warning not to come ashore. A man came running to the riverbank to tell them he was the doctor. He wrote them a note saying that since they had not landed they could avoid quarantine. He said a launch was coming upstream with vaccine, and when they met it they should urge the captain to hurry … or would they like to stay and help him?

Feeling ashamed of himself, Service said no. To risk death on the river doing something one loved was one thing, but death from smallpox was another, and he didn't have the stomach for it.

Behind him, however, he could feel Jake's rage. He offered to put him ashore but Jake refused, saying he'd take a chance on the launch coming with the vaccine. By now Service kept his rifle loaded, pretending it was for bear. Jake in the stern sneered and said, "I've got an axe here might be useful if we saw … a bear. I'm a good man at throwin' an axe."[3]

When Service tried to give him his pipe, Jake refused and demanded the slip of paper the doctor had given them. Service refused to give it up, and the tension built. There was no sleep for Service that night, and no cigarette glow from Jake's tent. In the morning Jake was beside himself, and he refused food and drink.

Finally Service made a deal with the devil that Jake had become. They would go on for half a day and if they didn't meet the boat by then, he would give Jake the doctor's note and they would turn back to Rampart.

Jake agreed, drank some tea, accepted Robert's pipe and they started out. About 11 the canoe started to leak and they had to stop while Robert patched it. Working on the canoe, he looked up and saw the tiny launch rounding a bend. Jake was on board in a split second—and smoking a cigarette a moment later.

The launch hurried on upstream with vaccine for Rampart while the canoeists—Jake now with an abundant supply of cigarette makings and in a benevolent mood—made their way downstream. Next morning, going around a bend, they came suddenly upon a sternwheeler tied up to a tree. It had struck a snag, and its crew was patching the hole by wedging flour sacks through it. From on board came shouts of admiration when the beautiful *Coquette* with Robert and Jake danced into view.

Service had a certain flare for the theatrical and could rise to the occasion when needed. He had determined to make his reunion with civilization "as dramatic as possible." But with his usual detachment he could also stand back and see how he appeared to others. Dirty, ragged, bronzed and bearded, he paddled to the steamer and strode proudly up the gangplank, met halfway by the captain, wearing white ducks.

In Service's account, when the man introduced himself as Captain Brown from Fairbanks, Robert replied that he had come from Edmonton and his partner from Baffin Land. The gasp from his audience was the approbation he wanted.

The captain's real name was Gray, and his steamer was the *Tanana*. In the summer of 1911 he was busy transporting supplies from Fort Yukon to the party marking the boundary line between Canada and the United States. Under Dr. D.D. Cairns, Dominion geologist, men were cutting a swath 20 feet wide through the timber and setting monuments along the line. They had worked their way north to the Black River near the Porcupine, but low water was making it impossible for Captain Gray to get his cargo to the survey party. So the horse feed, cement, monuments and food supplies had to be packed in along the boundary swath. Afterward, the *Tanana* had been heading up the Porcupine to Rampart before going back to the Yukon River and south to Dawson, but because of the epidemic raging at Rampart, the captain had decided to return downstream as soon as they could make repairs.

When Service told the captain he'd had enough paddling and wanted to take passage with him, there was hesitation. Service hurriedly added that he could write a check on the bank at Dawson both for himself and for Jake. But it was fear of smallpox that worried the captain. Service produced the doctor's note, which reassured the doctor. The McToshes arrived before the repairs were finished and also came on board.

On the long, lazy trip down to the Yukon River, then up to Dawson, Service said he borrowed a guitar and composed a song that the deckhands learned and continued to sing long after that journey. It was called "When the Ice Worm Nests Again" and was sung to the tune of "When the Roses Bloom Again." For many years its origin was unknown, although almost every Canadian could sing it. It became one of those songs so embedded in folklore that its origins seemed to be lost in mystery. Edith Fowke, in the

Encyclopedia of Music in Canada (1954), suggested it might date to 1898 and the Klondike gold rush, although she noted that Robert Service had published a version in his *Twenty Bath-Tub Ballads* (1939). The Service version differed considerably from what was then considered the traditional one. In 1938 the *Yellowknife Prospector* printed the song with a note saying it had been composed by four men on the Yukon River in about 1919, and that it was brought east across the mountains during the Fort Norman oil stampede by a man named Slim Behn, of the HBC.

Richard Finnie, a northern traveler and journalist, had heard a version sung on the schooner *Nigalik* at Cambridge Bay and quoted it in his first book, *Lure of the North* (1940). In his second, *Canada Moves North* (1942), he quoted the version published by the *Yellowknife Prospector* and credited it to "four chaps on the Yukon River about 1919."

Finally Finnie got to the bottom of the mystery. In an article in *Maclean's* magazine in 1945, he wrote about visiting Robert Service in France shortly after the end of the war, where he found the poet busy correcting galley proofs for *Ploughman of the Moon*. A couple of weeks later Finnie received a letter from Service. He had been reading *Canada Moves North*, and wrote: "By the way, it was I who wrote the ice-worm song. It was included in my *Bath-Tub Ballads* [Toronto, 1939] and I might have sung it to you with my guitar as I did to the steamboat crew who picked it up from my teaching. Only in the present version [the one in *Bath-Tub Ballads*] I composed my own melody."

The words of the song have changed with the singers over the years, but *Maclean's* printed the entire Robert Service original, which began:

> *There's a husky dusky maid in far Alaska*
> *On a slab of ice she sits and waits for me;*
> *And someday I'm going back to ask her,*
> *If my little Polar baby she will be.*

In another letter to Finnie, Service wrote that the original had been composed in his Dawson cabin before his long trip south, then went on to describe its dissemination:

> I had just come out of the Arctic and was paddling down the Yukon [he means the Porcupine], just below Rampart, in my birchbark, when on rounding a bend I came on a small river steamer tied up

to the bank. They were bound for Dawson from Fairbanks [though making a diversion up the Porcupine] but had struck a snag and were patching up the hole by wedging flour sacks through it. I thanked God for the snag and booked passage. The stewards and deck hands had a guitar, so I asked to be allowed to strum on it. I sang the ice-worm song, which seemed to make a hit with them. This was in 1911. It goes to show how something very humble may have a vitality that exceeds work of real artistic merit.[4]

Additional evidence supports Service's claim that he wrote the song in Dawson. In *The Trail of '98* (written there in 1909–10), he had his "pote" character quote a stanza of it. Although generally considered a myth, ice worms do exist in the Arctic, and Service would have heard the old-timers talk about them. They are related to the common earthworm, but are white, yellow, brown or black in color and are small, just 0.4–1.2 inches long. They live on the surface of temperate glaciers on a diet of pollen grains, fern spores and the red algae that grow on the glacier surface. Stroller White took the ice worm to new lengths when his *Weekly News* published reports of ice worms three feet long, with a head at each end of their bodies, appearing when temperatures fell below -75 degrees. His hoax may have inspired Service's "Ballad of the Ice-Worm Cocktail" as well as his ice-worm song.

chapter 14

Service reached Dawson on August 11, 1911. The next day, the *Dawson Daily News* reported his arrival in a story entitled "In From a Long Journey." The editor had interviewed Captain Gray as well as Service, and he liked Gray's description of the man he had picked up, "with face ambushed in an ebony thicket of three week's growth, nose lobster red, hands a Mongolian shade, trouser shredded ... done up in khaki with a sombrero over the cranium, while amidships the whole was held together with a belt drawn to the last notch ..."

It delighted Dawsonites to see their former well-dressed bank clerk and famous poet looking like Robinson Crusoe or a Frederick Remington sketch. "Although anxious to get the scent of salmon, bear's grease, whale blubber, bacon and bannocks removed, Service lingered a moment to greet friends on the street and it was apparent that he had experiences."

According to the *News*, Service was traveling on nothing but flour toward the end of his trip. Proud of his lean appearance, and running his fingers from chin to belt, he claimed he could count his vertebrae from the front. He had worn out six pairs of moccasins before finally going barefoot. "Back to nature pleased Robert wonderfully, and he is as red as a smoked moon, and happy as a candidate for parliament."[1]

The paper devoted a whole page to the news they gleaned from *Tanana*'s arrival. They discussed the boundary survey work and reported eight cases of smallpox on the Porcupine, and said two men under the direction of Dr. Smith were vaccinating the Native people. They reassured residents that the travelers from Fort McPherson had not stopped there. Along with Robert and Frank Williams (the man that Service named Jake) and the two Carrolls (the McToshes in the Service story) they reported a man named S. Phillips, a prospector. Robert's biography never mentions him; he may have been picked up by the Carrolls after Robert and Jake went ahead in the canoe.

Two days later they featured an article on the "Mackenzie Slayer" based on an interview with Service, who had "acted as one of the coroner's jury." He described the cabin on a terrace near the mouth of the Salt River overlooking the Mackenzie. "The builder of the place evidently was a master in construction of log cabins. The spot was the prettiest on the Mackenzie, and when our boat drew in the sun was shining brightly, the birds were singing and all nature was lovely. The surroundings were a sharp contrast to the horror inside that little cabin."[2] The *News* quoted Service at length and summed up their deaths as a typical frontier tragedy.

Meanwhile, Jake (Frank Williams) appeared to be headed for trouble. Just before they reached Dawson, he borrowed $100 from Service. Besides his nicotine addiction, Jake apparently had a gambling problem. He had lost $50 playing blackjack with the deckhands, and had pledged his furs in payment. He said he had made a bloody fool of himself—but he had his father's money to collect, so he would be okay.

The next time Service saw him, Jake had his inheritance. He had taken a bartending job and repaid Service. Six months later, however, Jake had gambled away all $2,000 of his inheritance; Service offered another loan, but this time Jake refused. He went away to trap, Service said, and, probably, to starve. A few years later, alone in a cabin on the Arctic Ocean, Jake's demons got the better of him, and he shot himself in the head.

Service swaggered around town as a celebrity for a week, but after that no one noticed him. He had shaved off his beard because "there were girls in the offing." This presumably refers to Jean Clark, since he was wearing her ring, but the romance apparently ended soon after. If Laura Berton's suggestion that Jean's parents disapproved of the vagabond life Service had led is true, they would not be reassured by his going off to New York, Cuba and Edmonton, then disappearing into the Arctic for three months. Whatever the reason, Jean and Robert went their separate ways.

He had returned to Dawson just in time for the annual Discovery Day celebrations on August 17. The Yukon Order of Pioneers marched from Pioneer Hall to Minto Park, headed by the Dawson Brass Band. Then, while a picture show entertained young Yukoners in the A.B. Hall, the adults got ready for the grand ball in the same building that evening. Service was delighted to be back. As soon as he had climbed the hill to his cabin, he was home. The moose antlers over the porch seemed to reach out to welcome him. He fixed up the place, put his rabbit's-foot robe on the bed and settled in for the winter.

Service knew he was considered eccentric, "morose and unsocial; but to be solitary was not uncommon in the North. And I was of the North, its lover, its living voice. Dawson was my home. I had no thought of ever deserting it."[3] He was also at peace with himself because he had faced his personal "Trail of '98" and conquered it. Thirteen years after the gold rush, he had made his way to the Yukon goldfields the hardest and longest way of all—over the Edmonton route.

As the snow came and darkness closed in, he beat out his snowshoe trails again and began to write, mentally shaping the poems as he hiked and putting them on paper when he got home. The book he was working on was the story of the Mackenzie basin and the land beyond the Arctic Circle. It was peopled by characters he had encountered there, and sometimes by glimpses of himself.

He later said that his first book of verse had been an accident, and the second had been hard work, but that this one, published as *Rhymes of a Rolling Stone*, was pure pleasure. The material came first-hand, from his own experiences, and flowed from his fingers. The language was fresh and evocative with phrases that have become catchwords of the North: the ragged edge of the world; the Land of Beyond; the white top-knot of the world; "the clover was in blossom, an' the year was at the June"; "granite-ribbed valleys, flooded with sunset wine"; Land of the Blizzard and Bear; the Hunger Plateaus; the stealthy silver moccasins of morn.

A poem entitled "The Great Divide of Thirty-Five" shows Service aware of a new stage of his life. For the men who don't fit in the towns and cities, who feel at home somewhere between Churchill and Nome (and possibly for himself), "I'm Scared of it All" ends:

To be forming good habits up there;
To be starving on rabbits up there;
In your hunger and woe,
Though it's sixty below,
Oh, I know that it's safer up there![4]

"Little Moccasins" sensitively evokes a father's loss of his child, who used to dance in the snow—and eerily presages his own grief as a father a few years later. "While the Bannock Bakes" is a story with a twist as two "irresponsibles" yarn together beyond the Arctic Circle and discover a link in their pasts. "Song of the Camp-Fire" evokes the solace and euphoria of fire, warmth, food, drink, a pipe and rest at the end of a grueling day.

When not writing, Service made a habit of climbing the Dome, even on the coldest days, then coming home to bathe in freezing water. He was determined not to lose the conditioning he had acquired crossing the Richardson Mountains.

Often he left his cabin for days and trekked to the gold creeks. The weather was bright and good when he set out on snowshoes for Gold Run one morning. It was almost 50 miles away, but Service was so fit that he made it easily by nightfall, put up at the roadhouse and went to visit some friends. Coming back the following day on a different trail, he took the wrong fork. The path petered out so he turned back, but then ran into another fork. This time the path ran up a mountainside, but he could see a roadhouse ahead and kept going. He found the building abandoned, and at that point should have turned back to Gold Run. Instead, he made the risky choice to go on, hoping to find a cabin.

By nightfall he was still out in the cold, higher on the mountain. He kept himself going by singing "The Bonnie Banks of Loch Lomond," remembering a day in his youth when he had hiked the length of that lake. Finally he could no longer sing. At one point he fell and had trouble talking himself into getting up.

He had come down into the trees now, and although the cold was eating into him, the drifts were not so deep. He wanted badly to lie down, but knew that would be disastrous. He chose a tree to walk around all night, to keep himself awake. Then a kind of delirium took over as the moon rose, and finally he sank to his knees in the snow, his legs giving out, thinking what a shame it was to finish like this.

In the moonlight across a small gully gleamed a cabin. Was it a cruel illusion, or had it been there all the hours while he tramped around the pine tree? Was it his special providence or his guardian angel? Or was he saved by the moon? Carefully, almost on hands and knees, he willed himself to reach that cabin. By the law of the Yukon a cabin in the bush had the latchstring on the outside of the door. He pulled it and fell inside.

No one was there, but beside the stove was a heap of kindling. Shaking with cold and weakness and joy he lit the fire and huddled beside it. Then, aware of his hunger, he hacked open a can of beans and heated it. He wanted tea but was too tired to make it, so he crawled into the bunk, under the heavy blankets, and slept.

In the morning he awoke to find a large man with snow-white hair, dirty and disheveled, cooking bacon and eggs. He seemed anxious for Service to stay. Although something about the man made Service uneasy, he agreed to stay one more night.

During the day the man, whose name was Joe Rich, took Service to see his mine. He jumped into the hole, then appeared to have trouble breathing. It was all Service could do to pull the huge man out. He lay gasping in the snow; he had forgotten that he'd made a fire in the hole before he went to town, and it had become filled with carbon monoxide gas.

They returned to the cabin, the prospector produced a bottle of Scotch and said that since each of them had saved the other's life, they had to celebrate. Whenever Service began to fall asleep Rich yanked him awake to tell him another tale of travel and adventure. Finally, he hauled Service up, hurled him into a chair and told him a story he had to get off his chest.

Waving a gun at Service, he made him promise not to tell his story. He said again that his name was Joe Rich, but maybe Service had heard of Cannibal Joe?

Service had. The man who struggled out from the Barren lands after his partner died of starvation … the man suspected of killing and eating his partner. Joe was in a wild state now, as he told Service how his partner Bob was the best pal he'd ever had, how each would have done anything for the other, how Bob died saying that his partner was welcome to use his body to survive. Then he shrieked at Service: "Not that. Not what you think. I never et Bob. I never et a single slice of him … What did I do? Listen—God curse me! I never et Bob, but *I fed him to the dogs and I et the bloody dogs.*"

His story told, Joe collapsed on the floor. After an uneasy night and more bacon and eggs, Service went on his way. His host's last words were: "... if ye had a bad dream last night ye jest wan to ferget it. Y'understand?"[5] Service did understand. He waited until 1945 and his autobiography before he told Joe's story.

There is so much drama packed into this whole adventure that a critical reader questions how much fiction is mixed with fact. But people did become lost and freeze to death. Miners were asphyxiated in their dug-out mines. And cannibalism was a horrid possibility when death by hunger stalked two or more travelers. Service may have juggled times and events and characters into place to create a dramatic sequence, but the stuff of which he wrote was real.

The question that everyone living in Dawson had to ask themselves was when to leave. Some who came over the Trail of '98 answered it as soon as they set foot on the Dawson sand. Met on the shore by disgruntled miners who told them the gold was all staked, they sold the outfits they had packed in with so much toil and pain, turned tail and went home.

But those who stayed and those who came later had to answer the same question. This year or next? Or never? There were those who got rich quick and headed out to brighter lights. There were those who planned to give it two years and—when they failed to hit pay dirt—gave it another year, and another, and ended their lives as old prospectors living alone, lonely, ill-fed, dirty, often ill or deranged, but still searching for gold.

The women also had to decide—the prostitutes seeing business slow down after 1900, the women who ran bakeries or laundries or boarding houses, who by now loved the Yukon but were watching the town dwindle and knew the future here looked bleak. Couples also had to weigh their chances—people like George and Martha Black, who stayed and made the Yukon their kingdom, and Frank and Laura Berton, who loved the Yukon too much and stayed until the Great Depression left Frank unemployed.

As people over the years decided to go, never could they leave in springtime, when the light was grand and the boats brought incoming crowds. Or in mid-summer, when fireweed flamed on the hills. Always it was the last boat before freeze-up—when the crowberries, bear berries and kinnikinnick on the tundra had turned to red and gold but the air was sharp with cold and the days darkening—that drew the crowd to the dock to leave.

When that last boat pulled out of Dawson in the fall of 1912, Robert Service was aboard. A year earlier he had been delighted to see Dawson again and had no thought of ever leaving it. He had finished *Rhymes of a Rolling Stone* in the spring, then lazed around all summer. Now that he had written his Yukon stories and poems and expanded his poetic domain as far as the Mackenzie and the Arctic Circle, he felt at loose ends. The cabin that had welcomed him home with its cozy warmth seemed suddenly lonely. His pen was still, his life seemingly without a purpose again. He was young, free and wealthy, with no need to work. So he talked himself into a trip to the South Seas.

But leaving was far from easy. A poem in *Rhymes of a Rolling Stone* shows how hard it was for him to go:

Good-bye Little Cabin
I hear the world-call and the clang of the fight,
I hear the hoarse cry of my kind;
Yet well do I know, as I quit you to-night,
It's youth that I'm leaving behind.[6]

As the boat moved into the river current, he looked up at the Dome, which he had climbed so often. Below the scar of the slide lay his little town where the Klondike joined the Yukon. His eyes sought out the cabin high on the hill, where he had been so happy for four of the best years of his life, and in a mental conversation with it, he promised to come back. But as he watched, the cabin door seemed to open, revealing a solitary figure "waving his pipe in farewell." A great sadness enveloped him, as if he knew he would never return.

Part 3

After the *Yukon*

"Never again would we see that eager, careless world; never exult in the golden present, thinking that the future would be equally serene. Never, never again."

Harper of Heaven

chapter 15

An era was ending as Robert Service left the north in 1912. The Douglas party, after wintering on Great Bear Lake and exploring the Coppermine, had also returned south. Adventure such as they'd had would not be possible again. Within two years, most of the northern men they knew would be caught up in the First World War. Out of that war would come the Canadian bush pilot; exploration by canoe and scow or by snowshoes and dog team would give way to air travel. Douglas would return to the North by plane. For Robert Service, the future lay in a different direction.

When he left Dawson, Robert carried with him the draft of his new collection of poems. He arrived in Vancouver also with a copy of *The Trail of '98*, a gift for Connie MacLean's mother. This copy of Service's first novel, inscribed not to Connie but to Mrs. MacLean, has been handed down to her granddaughter. In January Connie had married Leroy Grant, a surveyor and railroad engineer based in Prince Rupert, B.C. Mrs. MacLean or Connie's sister Isabel, who was a reporter with the Vancouver *Daily Province*, would have given Robert news of Connie's new life.

Before leaving Canada, Robert sent his small Bennett typewriter to his brother Peter. Ninety-three years later, in August 2005, Marguerite Service, wife of Peter's son Kelvin, in a ceremony outside Robert's cabin, returned the typewriter to Dawson City to join other Service memorabilia, now in the care of Parks Canada.

In 1912 when Robert left the Yukon, he gave his Bennett typewriter to his brother Peter. Peter left it to his son, Kelvin. In an August 2005 ceremony, Kelvin's widow, Marguerite Service, gave the machine on which Robert wrote his first four books back to Dawson City.

PHOTO: GORD MALLORY

One report says that Robert left Vancouver by ferry for Victoria, then took another ferry south across the Strait of Juan de Fuca to Port Angeles, Washington. He camped there on the Olympic Peninsula and polished *Rhymes of a Rolling Stone* before heading east to his publishers.

Rhymes of a Rolling Stone was published near the end of 1912 by both Dodd Mead in New York and William Briggs in Toronto (Fisher Unwin would publish the British edition in London in 1913). The *Toronto Star Weekly* was enthusiastic about Service and his latest book: "He missed some tackles and fumbled considerably with his story, *The Trail of '98*. But he's over the line for a Carlisle Indian touchdown with 'Rhymes of a Rolling Stone' ... They are the real 'Sourdough' stuff!"[1]

Critics recognized that this was a book inspired by experience and observation "on the trail." In the photo taken by George Douglas, Service is seen writing in the prow of a scow on the Athabasca. Probably these writing materials did not survive the trip over the Richardson Mountains—if they had, Jake Skilly would have rolled his sheets of notepaper into cigarettes and smoked them. But as Service had drifted on the Bell and Porcupine, the land and its cast of characters had played themselves into poems in his head. In his Dawson cabin they tumbled forth, as if writing themselves. The painstaking research required for *The Trail of '98* was replaced by something more immediate. When it was published, readers were quick to recognize "the real stuff."

The book covered a broader region than the Klondike. His trip from Edmonton had encompassed northern Alberta, Great Slave Lake and the Mackenzie River, the southern fringes of the Mackenzie delta, the Richardson Mountains and Alaska before the Yukon River had brought him "home" to Dawson. Vicariously, through the characters he met, he was able to expand his range. The Douglas party and his brief meeting with John Hornby and Cosmo Melville put Great Bear Lake and the Coppermine country on his map, and their place names too appear in his poems. The Inuit with whom he camped at Fort McPherson, and the traders—McTosh, the Lady and Jake Skilly—extended his canvas to the Arctic coast ("My partner's from Baffin Land," he had told the steamboat captain with theatrical flourish but a hazy grasp of geography).

While the public was enjoying his new northern book, Service found himself lured in a new direction. He shelved his idea of a South Seas holiday when the *Toronto Daily Star* offered him a job as a war correspondent in the Balkans, where fighting raged in 1912–13; "with curses in my heart I cabled acceptance."[2] Writing of those days in the 1940s, he still seemed unable to explain his motivation for doing it. He had no financial need to take the position, but perhaps his Calvinist roots made it hard to reject a regular paycheck. Or he may have been flattered by the offer, or seen the war zone as a new place to study humanity. Perhaps he had a need always to know the worst—whether it was a hanging in Dawson, the hardship of McDougall Pass or the Balkan War.

It had been 15 years since Robert first crossed the Atlantic on a "roach-ridden old tramp"; now he was returning to Europe in style aboard the 16,000-ton *Deutschland*. Surrounded by an excess of Teutonic arrogance, he was happy to disembark in Naples, cross overland to the Adriatic, then sail to Athens and on across the Aegean to start his new assignment.

Greece, Bulgaria, Serbia and Montenegro were attacking their former imperial master, Turkey, with the fighting centered close to Istanbul itself, on the November day when Service arrived. The Bulgarian army was stopped at the Chatalja defence line, some 25 miles from the walls of Istanbul, where both sides were battling an outbreak of cholera. Service said that although he could hear the guns at Chatalja (now Çatalca), he was not allowed anywhere near the action. To get closer to the front lines, he joined the Red Crescent, the Turkish equivalent of the Red Cross. He soon got a first-hand look at the terrible miseries of war: he was sent to the cholera camp at San Stefano (now Yeşilköy, on the outskirts of Istanbul) and found himself carrying out the corpses of the dead. That night, aghast at the filth and sickness he had worked in, he sought the sea. He swam and swam, until he began to feel clean again.

The next morning Service was dismissed from the Red Crescent because the colonel had discovered his Canadian newspaper connection. Back in Istanbul he was ordered to appear for questioning at the Commissariat of Police. Thoroughly alarmed that he might be branded a spy, he escaped by the first vessel leaving Istanbul. Later in life, in an interview with BBC and CBC radio, he said he "couldn't stick it" and deserted.

For four months he explored Europe, spending January 1913 in Bucharest, then moving on to Vienna and finally making his way toward Paris. In his autobiography, he said that this was not a happy time, but even so, he was practicing his craft, watching how people lived their lives, seeing color and movement and mood as a painter would.

One spring morning Robert arrived in Paris, visited Notre Dame and walked beside the Seine; he felt as if he had come home. Though he had never visited the city before, it had lived in his imagination as he read French literature in his youth. Just as Robert Louis Stevenson had welcomed him to San Francisco in 1897, Victor Hugo and Emile Zola now became his guides to Paris. Ready to play a new role, Robert adopted the bohemian life he had dreamed of as a teenager. He moved into a four-franc garret at 17 Quai Voltaire, purchased a sketchbook and began taking lessons at the studio of Colarossi, only to find that his modesty interfered with his painting of nudes.

Among the artists and writers who became his friends were a married couple from Canada, Frank and Caroline Armington, who were studying art in Paris. Spending time with them, Robert saw theirs as the "perfect partnership" and began to long for married life.

One day on the Place de la Madeleine he aided two sisters caught in a crushing parade crowd. To his surprise, the younger one thanked him in English. Germaine and her sister, Hélène, shared tea with Robert in a nearby café and invited him home to meet their mother. They were convent-educated daughters of a distiller whose business had failed; his wife had left, taken their three daughters and was raising them on her own in the city. On Sundays Germaine and Hélène showed Robert the outskirts of the city, and on a jaunt to Fontainebleau, he realized he was beginning to picture Germaine, the younger sister, as his wife.

Germaine Bourgoin and Robert Service were married on June 12, 1913, with publisher Frank Dodd as best man and the Armingtons in attendance. The newlyweds had a brief one-week honeymoon in London. At 25, Germaine was 13 years younger than Robert. As he introduced her in *Harper of Heaven*, the second volume of his autobiography, he served notice that she and their future family would not make many direct appearances in his story. "In these pages I will refer as little as possible to the problems of hearth and home, except to say that their joys far exceeded their sorrows."[3] We can nevertheless glimpse Germaine Service indirectly through Robert's immediate contentment, and by the admiration expressed by her descendants in later years. After Robert's death, Germaine recorded a few notes about their life that helped address some of the confusion contained in *Harper of Heaven*.

Six articles, serialized under the title "Zig-zags of a Vagabond," appeared in the *Toronto Star Weekly* in late 1913 and early 1914. This was a year of great happiness for Robert, and his writing reflected this as he wrote of Paris, of its Latin Quarter, of Montmartre, of Fontainebleau, of Brittany. The summer of 1913 was spent with Germaine, exploring the Brittany coast by bicycle, and at Lancieux near St. Malo he came upon the red-roofed house perched on a rock above the sea that would become their home. In name and in reality, it was his "Dream Haven."

He and Germaine returned for the winter to Paris, where they also kept an apartment, Robert's French steadily improving under his wife's tuition. *The Pretender*, his second novel, was published in 1914. Set mainly in the Latin Quarter of Paris, which Robert knew well by now, and with a writer as its main character, *The Pretender* also moves to London and New York, the Manhattan scenes allowing Service to take a swipe at the pompous, patronizing literary figures who had upset him badly in 1910 when he took *The Trail Of '98* there and was dismissed as a Yukon bumpkin.

While exploring the meaning of "pretender" through his protagonist—someone like himself who found the lines between reality and fantasy indistinct, but who is also a pretender in the sense of a claimant for the crown of literary fame—Service also gave a valuable picture of the Parisian Latin Quarter a decade before writers such as Ernest Hemingway and Morley Callaghan were making it popular.

While writing his novel and reveling in domestic bliss, Service said he first heard "the harps of heaven," an audible expression of his own great joy, which became the title, and subject, of his autobiography's second volume.

With his novel finished and published, he and Germaine spent an idyllic summer at their new Dream Haven until the ringing of church bells summoned the villagers and farmers to the town square for mobilization. War had begun! Service, watching it happen, felt in his bones words that would one day appear in *Harper of Heaven*: "... Never, never again."

chapter 16

Although Robert Service was now 40, he was confident that his physical fitness would let him pass for 35. He tried to enlist, but was turned down because of a varicose vein in his leg. Men he knew from northern Canada were now turning up in Europe to fight, and he was chafing to join them. Joe Boyle, whom Service and others dubbed "King of the Yukon," had put together the Boyle Yukon Motor Machine Gun Battery in the early days of the war. Jim Cornwall ("Peace River Jim") whose manly figure had so impressed Service on the Athabasca, was soon commanding a labor battalion camp in southern Belgium. Thousands of less famous men who had known the hardship and joy of the North now faced the hardship of the trenches, where there would be no joy, only horror. Miners mushed out of the bush with packs on their backs, ready to enlist. Martha Black tells of one man who walked 300 miles to enlist, only to be rejected because of his flat feet (he did eventually get to France).

Martha herself was not one to be left behind. George Black resigned as Commissioner of the Yukon in 1916 to organize a Yukon Infantry Company. When the company, under the command of Captain George Black, left Dawson on October 16, 1916, on the SS *Casca,* Martha was with him. Her youngest son Lyman, born in Dawson in January 1899, "who, like a dozen or more Yukon boys, was far too young to go," had enlisted and was aboard. Another son, Warren, was to command a troopship. Donald, at university in California, was in the process of enlisting.

As the *Casca* moved away from Dawson, the band struck up "Tramp, Tramp, Tramp the Boys are Marching" and sang a song that combined those lyrics with Service's song "When the Ice Worm Nests Again." Drifting over the water Martha heard the words of the parody:

> *There's a land of midnight sun,*
> *Where Boyle's dredges groan and hum,*
> *And the ptarmigan are warbling in the trees.*
> *And the whisky that they sell*
> *Makes you wish you were in—well,*
> *Our thoughts will float to you on every breeze.*[1]

After training in Victoria, the Yukon boys were to be sent overseas in January 1917. Martha hurried ahead to Ottawa to get permission to go with them. Finally the decision came down to General Bigger, the officer in charge of transportation at Halifax. Bigger tried to convince her that she would not want to be the only woman on a troopship of men. She reminded him that she had walked over the Chilkoot Trail with thousands of them. Martha won and sailed off on the SS *Canada* with her Yukon men.

Sadly remembering her elegant Government House in Dawson, Martha rented a bleak London apartment to be near her husband and sons while they trained. Then she threw herself into war work, visiting wounded Yukoners in the hospital, helping in the prisoners-of-war department, sewing for the Red Cross, giving lectures on "The Romance of the Klondike Gold Fields," acting as correspondent for the *Dawson News* and the *Whitehorse Star*, and administering the Yukon Comfort Fund. This fund had been collected by the citizens of Dawson and given to Martha to spend on "the boys" at her discretion. With her usual energy, she stretched the $50 per soldier to the maximum, providing them with care packages and special dinners when they came to London. She became a mother to all the Yukon soldiers in the war, and any who came to her door in London were sure of a hot meal and a sympathetic ear.

There is no record of Service visiting her in London, but his poems were often read to the homesick Yukon boys who did. One notable Yukoner who did visit Martha was Joe Boyle. Boyle, whose wartime efforts in eastern Europe made him a national hero in Romania and, if rumor be true, Queen Marie's lover, regaled Martha with the thrilling adventures that had become everyday fare for him. When Martha later met Queen Marie herself at a reception given by the Canadian High Commissioner in London, Marie told her how Boyle entertained them with wonderful stories of the Yukon and taught the royal family the rhymes of Robert Service. Then, to Martha's surprise, Queen Marie quoted a complete verse from "The Spell of the Yukon."

Service's role in the war was played out on the edge of the action, as a war correspondent for Canadian newspapers, then as an ambulance driver and finally as an intelligence officer. As in the Balkan War, he found it difficult as a reporter to get near enough to the action to report accurately. Journalists were hated by the top brass, and getting caught near the front without authorization meant serious trouble. Nevertheless, he made a reckless effort to reach the front at Dunkirk and came uncomfortably close to being shot as a spy. In December 1914 the *Toronto Star Weekly* ran the story under the title "R.W. Service Nearly Faced a French Firing Squad." The story was written by E.W. Walker, of W. Briggs publishers in Toronto, who had met with Service in London to discuss *The Pretender*. Service told Walker he was determined to go to the front to see what he could see.

He took the train from Calais to Dunkirk but got off at a village outside of town so that he could walk in unnoticed. He was soon within sound of the artillery; soldiers were everywhere. He spoke to weary French *poilus* (a slang term for "soldiers"), watched German prisoners march past, saw troops arriving in the port. He was delighted with his vantage points.

That evening, while watching ambulances load the wounded onto a train, he was apprehended by a gendarme, who demanded to see his papers. His passport, showing a record of his wanderings in early 1913, contained visas for travel all over Europe, including Germany; this did nothing to endear him to the French authorities. He was marched before a major, then a general, then locked in a small room where he spent a sleepless night well aware of the mess he was in. According to the *Star Weekly*, an officer told Service they liked to shoot spies in groups of three, and that they already had two, so he would complete the required party for a regulation execution.

The next morning Service begged to be taken to the British captain of the port, and this man believed his story. Mr. Walker, still in London a week later, was surprised to see Service reappear, and even more surprised to hear his story. The port captain had given him a sharp scolding for being where he had no right to be—there was a strict rule against correspondents following the army. The captain also told him that six men had been shot that morning as spies. He then ordered him to "take your papers and GET OUT," which Robert was glad to do. He took the train to Calais as fast as he could, and, according to the *Star*, "The Poet of the Yukon didn't stop till he got to London."[2]

Service saw a better opportunity to get to the front when he read of an American ambulance unit being formed in Paris. He met one of the leaders at the Hotel Meurice. The man told him that a bunch of the boys were whooping it up in the hotel bar, and someone had come up with the idea of an ambulance corps.

These were all well-to-do men, who owned their own cars and turned them into ambulances, volunteering themselves as drivers. They became part of the American Field Force, whose chief organizer was Richard Norton of Boston, a well-known archaeologist. This was a spontaneous organization of well-educated men, many with a literary or academic background. Among the first sponsors was the novelist Henry James, who wrote a 12-page pamphlet entitled "The American Volunteer Motor-Ambulance Corps in France" to explain its purpose. Before the end of 1914 they had 15 cars working in France, and the majority of Norton's men were young students from Harvard, Princeton, Stanford, Dartmouth and universities all across the country, all eager to serve although their country was not yet in the war. The unit's motive was humanitarian, to offer to the suffering wounded something better than the springless wagons drawn by the horses of the French Transport Corps. Cars in 1915 were not vehicles of comfort and were not always reliable, but they did offer greater speed. By the time Service joined, there were 60 of them in the field. The American Red Cross sent over 17 Ford cars donated by Yale and Harvard, and Service was asked if he could drive one. He named his vehicle *Dorothea*, and he coaxed and cajoled her along as best he could, while knowing nothing at all about her mechanics.

From the trenches, wounded soldiers were taken to emergency hospitals set up in town halls, churches or schools in nearby villages, often under cover of darkness. From here they were transported to railway stations to be taken to a larger hospital. Every day the drivers set out with their lists and maps, a cloud of dust following their long line of vehicles along the twisting roads of France. Each would branch off to some little village to collect their prostrate passengers.

Near the front lines they slept in rat-infested tents, dugouts or bombed-out houses, but headquarters—where they went in turn for respite—was a chateau. Here the French army provided their food, and the drivers—some of them millionaires—topped up the fare with bottles of their own vintage wine. Dinner every night was a raucous round of wine, song and hilarity reminiscent of the bank boys and their Mountie neighbors in Dawson.

Wanting to get closer to the action, Service volunteered for outpost duty, which took him into the trenches. He was like a moth drawn to the flames of war. "I loved those trips to the firing trench, or even into No Man's Land. We made them during the day when we had cover, but when we were exposed we took the wounded after dark. The danger enhanced the heartening feeling of saving life."[3]

His craving to see and feel and write about the action at the front was mirrored two years later by another writer, Ernest Hemingway, who served in Italy with the field force, which by that time was under the Red Cross umbrella. Both men were riding a wave of intense nationalism and altruism, and both were also driven by a reporter's intense curiosity. Hemingway's learning experience was shortened by the explosion of a trench mortar, which sent him to a field hospital with 28 shell fragments in his legs. Hemingway, like Service, would also work for the *Toronto Star*, though not until after the war.

From December 11, 1915, to January 19, 1916, Service's weekly dispatches appeared in the *Toronto Daily Star* under the heading "Records of a Red Cross Man." His article "The Valley of a Thousand Dead" was written from a village doctor's house:

> I am supposed to sleep, but how can one sleep if three batteries of 75's are blazing away in the next lot. The lurid flame of them lights up my room. Then there is the reply of the German batteries, a bursting marmite whose crash seems to jar the house to its foundations ... And all the time there is the wild tattoo of a thousand rifles. What do they think they are doing in this awful night of wind and rain? ... Desperate things are going on out there in the dark; horrible tragedies; jobs for me with the dawn. What a cursed place.[4]

Often his trips to pick up the wounded were in the middle of the night.

In another article for the *Star* he described a typical evening's shift: at nine o'clock the message comes and Service and his partner make their way to the line. Leaving the car they stumble through the darkness, passing other men who move like ghosts in the darkness, carrying food for the men in the trenches. Then, with the wounded men in the car, they strain their eyes peering into the darkness and drive the pitted roads while overhead they hear the scream of German *marmites*—French slang for the heavy shells named for their resemblance to ceramic cookery pots.

Then, after an hour's sleep, another knock on the door summons them to Hill 71. "Stupid, half-awake, we rise and crank the car." On the way back Robert's mate is falling asleep at the wheel as they drive the wounded to hospital. They throw themselves gratefully on their dirty mattresses, then are called out a second time. Hill 71 again, in the first light of dawn. They return and are allowed to sleep until nine. Then another call—always Hill 71.[5]

After an attack the roads are clogged with walking wounded, sometimes too weak to move out of the way. The desperate climb onto the footboards of his failing Ford. When he reaches the outpost hospital it is full and he is sent on to a farther post with *Dorothea* misfiring and a soldier close to death in the back of the car.

His *Toronto Daily Star* articles, with titles such as "'The Red Harvest' of the Trenches," "Where Grim Men Watch and Wait" and "On the Inferno's Edge," were not what military commanders wanted Canadians to read; the truth of war was too ugly. Sometimes the tragedy was laced with comedy, but not everyone was amused by Service's story of the little corporal at the Battle of the Marne:

> Wounded, lying in a marmite hole for a day and a half, he looks up to see a German with rifle and fixed bayonet standing above him. He shuts his eyes, expecting the bayonet to end his life, but nothing happens. He opens his eyes. The German has laid down his rifle and bayonet and has his hands in the air, and says in good French, "I am your prisoner, Kamerad."
>
> "You must be mad. I cannot stand up. How can I take you prisoner?"
>
> The German explains that he is quite sane; he is a professor of botany, he has never shot anyone and has no intention of doing so.

He has little physical courage and he hates this war. He has a wife and six children. He wants to become a prisoner so that he can return to his family when this cruel war is over.

The French corporal, who also has a wife and six children, begins to think the same thing: he could become a German prisoner and survive the war. They decide to flip a coin to see who will be whose prisoner. "So there in the marmite hole we toss, that Boche and I, with the bullets flying merrily overhead. He wins."

The German hoists the Frenchman on his back and they set out toward the French lines. German rifles crack from behind and a bullet goes through the corporal's hat. As they near the French trenches the professor rests his burden, then picks up his comrade again, this time prudently carrying him in front. Now the French rifles crack ahead of them and one rips through the corporal's sleeve. He is being used as a human shield. He yells out to his line and the rifles stop. In triumph he turns over his German prisoner.[6]

Such a story splashed across the *Toronto Daily Star* did not sit well with those who sought more recruits to win the war. Service's articles did not discuss the causes of the war or the ethics of the fight; they dealt with the day-to-day plight of the common man caught up in it. The bard of the Yukon never wrote tourist brochures while he was there, and he wasn't likely to write war recruitment leaflets from France. He would tell it like it was.

While he portrayed the rank desolation and his own fear with blunt honesty, Service sought to brighten the scene with glints of color and humor: a cheerful red-cheeked granny with chirpy voice and twinkling eyes in a bombarded village, yellow buttercups, the larks that sang above the fields of war, the red poppies in the morning mist, artillery horses "that first saw light on Canadian plains" in a cloud of golden dust cantering down to water, the comedy of trying to keep *Dorothea* running, the laughter of men at mealtime. He marveled at his own callousness and that of his comrades, who could cart in the wounded and dying, then drink wine and carouse together in the chateau. He guessed that it might be a mental defence mechanism that let them face it again the next day; the sadness would come later. "Once I had a soldier die in my car—but I prefer to forget that. There is so much I want to forget."

In *Harper of Heaven* Service often mentioned a sense of shame that he was not a fighting man in uniform himself. Sometimes he jumped out of a trench within sight of the Germans just to bolster his self-respect. "I was a show-off and a fool," he said later. But toward the end his nerve was failing him: he got jumpy, hating the crash and concussion of the shells. He had tried to avoid the boredom of war by courting danger, but concluded in his self-effacing style: "I had a yellow streak a yard wide."[7]

His ambulance service and his reporting ended abruptly, not with a battle wound, but a bad case of boils. He was invalided out of service and sent home to Paris, suffering from extreme fatigue and stomach trouble. Just before he left he heard that their ambulance corps had been mentioned in dispatches and cited to the order of the day. Their chief, Richard Norton, was to receive the Croix de Guerre (and would also receive the Grand Croix of the Légion d'honneur, the highest French decoration that could be awarded to a foreigner).

In June 1916 he and Germaine went to Dream Haven, where he began a long, slow recovery. Good things came out of that period. In January 1917 Germaine gave birth to twin girls, and Robert, making the most of his convalescence, gave birth to his fourth volume of poetry, this one a book about the war whose scenes of carnage, pathos and heroism had become so sharply etched in his head.

Drinking coffee so strong it made his heart thump, and listening to the waves under his window, he wrote 60 poems in five months to complete the collection. He felt they could not be very good, for they seemed to have cost him little effort, but as with *Rhymes of a Rolling Stone*, they were poems poured out from personal experience. He was healing himself by transferring the tragedies of war onto the pages in his typewriter.

The poems are not about the logistics or the generals or the grand movements of the war. They focus on the men in the trenches. Writing *Songs of a Sourdough*, Service had always regretted that he himself had not been on the *Trail of '98*. For *Rhymes of a Red Cross Man* he *had* been there. He had hauled wounded men to safety, seen men die, seen the padre pray over the bodies in the field, smelled the reeking mustard gas, dove for cover when shells were dropping. He had crawled along in his ramshackle car in pitch-black darkness with a load of wounded, sometimes hiding them in a ditch until darkness fell. "War does not improve on acquaintance," he wrote in *Harper of Heaven*. " It resolves itself into filth, confusion, boredom."[8]

There was a personal anguish to empty into his book, as his youngest brother, Albert, a lieutenant in the 52nd Batallion, Canadian Infantry (Manitoba Regiment), had died near Ypres in August 1916. In his autobiography Service made only brief mention of his brother, but *Rhymes of a Red Cross Man* was dedicated to him, and it contained poems that focused on the folks back home who must deal with lost sons. One of the poems was written for the women who mourn.

Stanley, in his memoirs, made it plain that it was not just the women who mourned. With Robert Sr. often out of commission, Stanley was like a father to Albert, his protector and teacher. "Albert was my whole life. He was the only thing in my whole life that I loved like that. He was my baby too. I brought him up."

Stanley, by this time, was a medical student at the University of Alberta in Edmonton. After Peter left in 1910, the farm had no longer prospered, though Stanley and Albert struggled to keep it going. In the fall of 1911, just a few months after Robert's visit to them had ended, early frost defeated them, leaving a frozen crop good only for chicken feed and fodder. "Albert and I took turns hauling wheat all winter for next to nothing ... twelve miles at twenty to forty degrees below zero."

"We decided this was a mug's game and in the spring held an auction."

They sold the farm and left their papa behind in the little Mannville cemetery. The three Service girls had married by this time, so it was Emily, Albert and Stanley who moved to a two-storey brick house at 10528 124 Street in Edmonton. For a time their brother Alick lived there too. In 1912 Peter married May Walker of Chailey, Alberta, in Edmonton. In the wedding portrait of the family it may be significant that Stanley and Albert do not appear. At some point during the following four years Stanley began medical studies at the University of Alberta, though his memoirs do not say exactly when.

When Albert joined the army he was given a commission in the 66th battalion but got himself transferred to the 52nd in order to get into the fighting sooner.

"It didn't take long—Hill 60 at the Somme. He was coming out of the trench and Lieut. L. Sherwood was on his way to take Albert's place. A shell burst and a piece of shrapnel knocked the back of Albert's head off."

When the news reached the brick house in Edmonton, Stanley tried to console his devastated mother, but he was in bad shape himself. "The numbing, crushing hurt of that telegram was beyond describing."[9] For years afterward he could not sleep soundly. He would wake up in the night sobbing.

In July 1917 Stanley tried to take Albert's place. He enlisted in the Army Service Corps and found himself in a training camp in Calgary, hating every minute of it. He did not take orders easily—not from Peter on the farm and not from sergeants in the army—and he had not recovered from the shock of Albert's death. In November Emily intervened and got him out of the army on compassionate grounds.

Stanley returned to his medical studies. As the war ended, and soldiers brought home the Spanish influenza, he helped fight the epidemic that ravaged Canada, along with the rest of the world. The University of Alberta was turned into emergency hospital rooms and the students became doctors. Stanley remembers everyone wearing "ridiculous gauze masks," a dozen deaths a day, and the sick being put into the unwashed beds from which the dead had just been carried out.

Rhymes of a Red Cross Man headed the bestseller list in the *Bookman* in 1917 and 1918. Critics could no longer ignore the significance of Robert Service's work. Witter Bynner, a poet himself, reviewing the book in the *Dial*, paid tribute to his "vast following" and suggested it was time to admit that the public was right. "We have been inquiring for the poetry of war. In my judgement, here it is."

The *Texas Review*, a literary quarterly, compared him to Kipling but suggested that, while Kipling had contributed nothing of poetic value to the Great War scene, the poetic genius of Service had got into the "trenches, the hospital, and the camp."

Service himself was fit for service again by April 1917, but by the time he tried to rejoin his ambulance corps it was being disbanded. The United States had entered the war, and the corps' young drivers were being absorbed into the regular fighting forces.

Robert, Germaine and their twin babies went to the Riviera during the winter of 1917–18. There, at Menton, 13-month-old Doris caught scarlet fever and died. Added to the shock of their loss was the fear that they would lose the other twin as well, but Iris survived. Five months later Robert confessed to a friend that he could not think of Doris without bursting into tears. In a poem that he never published he wrote about his sense of loss:

You've taught me Grief, wee piteous face!
And boundless pity too;
You're taking to your resting place
Part of my heart with you.[10]

The family returned north, but when the bombing became too frightening in Paris, Robert moved them to the relative peace of Dream Haven, though he could not feel easy about being so removed from the war. Then a letter arrived from the Canadian government offering him a job with the Canadian Expeditionary Force. He was to tour France and report on the activities of the force. He would have a Cadillac complete with driver, an officer guide, and freedom to choose his route.

Service was delighted with the assignment. He visited the Foresters in the beech woods of the Channel, in the pine forests of the Landes and the Vosges. He visited air fields, ordnance depots, hospitals and bakeries, taking notes and enjoying the trips. Then he was transferred to the Engineers, and his travels took him to the front lines and less joyous scenes. The Engineers were building light railways, connecting them to German rails wherever they could. They moved cautiously, always half-expecting to be blown up by a land mine.

He explored the Ypres area and visited the grave of his brother Albert at the Railway Dugouts Burial Ground, 1.2 miles southeast of Ypres. When he toured the camps of the labor battalion he spent time with an old friend, "Peace River Jim" Cornwall. With Jim, Service came upon scenes that were like chambers of horror, headless bodies, torsos like butchered meat. As they moved through hamlets there was a "sinister emptiness" where people had lived and played. Some villages were just heaps of rubble. Once they were shelled, and Robert, not wanting to appear timid in front of his hero, tried to disguise his fear by moving nonchalantly into a bomb shelter; once inside, he found Jim had got there well ahead of him.

This was a different Service from the cocky ambulance driver who relished his forays into danger. Now shell bursts made him "cower and cringe." Death had claimed his brother. It had also claimed baby Doris on the Riviera. Her "wee piteous face" had taught him the depths of grief and made him keenly aware of how precious life was. He wanted to survive this war, to get back to Germaine and Iris, to go to Dream Haven and begin to forget.

But Service was still at the front for the grand climax when British and

Canadian troops moved on the heels of the retreating Germans. One day in late October 1918, two officers of the 5th Battalion of the Canadian Railway Troops and a captain from headquarters staff were about to make a reconnaissance into an area being cleared of Germans, and at the last minute Service was invited to go along.

Through the debris of abandoned villages, the four men in the car pressed forward until they were ahead of the British forces, not knowing where the Germans were. The Canadian major wanted to reconnoitre a German light railway in the area so, not actually seeing any Germans, they kept going. Coming to a place where the road had been shelled, they left the car and started out on foot.

The three men with Service were Captain Ian A. MacKenzie (later Minister of National Defence), Captain G.E. Vaughan and Major Leroy Grant. An intriguing question here is how much Service knew of the names or history of the men he was with. In the heat of war and the haste of departure, introductions may have been brief. It is possible that he didn't know—and didn't find out until much later—that one of the men traveling with him was the husband of Constance MacLean. Leroy Grant, however, knew exactly who Service was.

Out of the charred destruction they began to move through green unspoiled countryside, and people came out of houses saying that the Germans had gone. In ominous tranquillity they hiked forward. Once a German aircraft swooped down, but they heard an anti-aircraft gun respond from the road, and the plane fled. Following the railway they found themselves on the edge of the city of Lille.

Suddenly women and children were everywhere mobbing them, "four strayed Canadians, the first of the British Army. It was ludicrous, touching, glorious. We were helpless. The crowd just hemmed us in, carried us along. Each of us had a bodyguard of about a hundred strong."[11]

By the time Service wrote his biography in the 1940s, he knew who Grant was, and in his rendition of the Lille story he gave Grant center stage, as the chief attraction to the French townswomen. In the 1970s, after Grant's daughter, Beatrice, discovered Robert's letters to her mother, she asked her father whether he had told Robert who he was when they met. He said, "Oh no, I couldn't do that!"[12]

Festooned with flowers, kissed and hugged, cheered and cried over, all four men were carried to the gate, where a huge crater had been blown by

Four Canadians unofficially liberating the town of Lille, France, on October 25, 1918.
From left: Captain Leroy Grant (husband of Connie MacLean), Major Ian MacKenzie,
Robert Service (making a speech) and Captain Vaughan.
PHOTO: QUEEN'S UNIVERSITY ARCHIVES

the retreating Germans. To get away from the crowd, the men scrambled
up the side of the crater. Service, as the French-speaking member of the
quartet, made a speech from atop the rubble. The actor in him leapt to
the forefront and he made the most of the occasion. He told them of the
victories won, of Germans taken prisoner, of towns already in the hands
of friendly forces, that the British army was coming behind them, that the
German Empire was finished.

The men were lauded, laughed over, offered precious wine and lifelong
friendships. It was such fun that the four of them felt they could have
stayed forever. In a newspaper article that appears to have been written soon
after the event and sent to a friend in Victoria, Service said:

> We were received by one of the civic dignitaries. We declined an
> official reception. We were wined and feted, asked to give countless
> autographs, made a host of friends and departed in an atmosphere of

joy that seemed almost hysterical. We left with intense regret. Gladly would we have stopped forever. It was glorious; it was wonderful, and yet it was deeply pathetic, an experience never to be dimmed by memory. When our grandchildren ask us what we did in the war we will say, "We delivered Lille."

When the men saw a staff car approaching with what looked like the real top brass, they decided to make a diplomatic retreat. With artillery, bands and Highland regiments, the British now made their triumphal entry into Lille. But the four Canadians speeding back to base "in a blaze of glory" would never forget that they had been the first to enter Lille. In his newspaper article Service quoted himself as saying to their new-found friends in Lille, "You have given us four Canadians, one of the sweetest and proudest days of our lives."[13] Leroy Grant, speaking to his daughter shortly before he died in 1976, echoed that sentiment: "It was one of the happiest days of my life."

During the last days of the war, Service was in Paris recording his war experiences. He started with a series of articles meant for the *Toronto Daily Star*. Then he began to see a book shaping itself. It would be called *War Winners*, its characters common fighting men like his dead brother Albert. It would move graphically across France as its author had moved, inspecting the military organization that provisioned the war. Then one morning the bells began to ring and he heard people shouting and singing and crying "Armistice!" He joined them in the street. When he returned to his apartment he could not stand to devote another moment to thoughts of war; he grabbed his manuscript, tore it up and went to join his family at Dream Haven.

We will never read that first-hand prose account of his war experiences— a sad loss for historians. Instead, Service began a new book of poems, interspersed with prose passages that included wartime scenes. When he had finished it he could not stand to reread it. *Ballads of a Bohemian* was published finally in 1921 and was, according to Service, the least successful of all his books in terms of sales. In the immediate aftermath of war, most of his readers, like Service himself, wanted to forget.

Critics continued to debate whether Robert's output was poetry or "only" verse. In Service's time, "poetry" implied the use of more sophisticated, high-flown language, more complex meters and more ambitious artistic goals, while "verse" referred to more straightforward rhyming and metrical structures, often intended to be recited aloud rather than read silently. There was a grey area—rhyming verse sometimes treated profound themes—and it was to this contested field that Service's work was designated, giving rise to the debate about its enduring value. Service's response was to deny that he had ever pretended to write "poetry" in this sense: "I would rather be a writer of first class verse than a third rate poet."[14]

Whether "verse" or "poetry," his best record of the war was *Rhymes of a Red Cross Man.* Critics compared its impact to *Songs of a Sourdough.* When men and women went over the White Pass and Chilkoot Pass they shucked off their pasts, left sweethearts and family, trading it all for the quest for gold. As Service poured his own loneliness and sense of emotional uncertainty into his early poems, he was expressing the parallel experience of a great many sourdoughs and cheechakos. The war had provided on a grand scale the same heartache and loneliness, and brought back the sense of excitement and desperate struggle that he had experienced in the North. The theater of war he had traveled in his reconnaissance job provided a canvas equivalent to the Yukon—devastating, stark with death, lit up by rare moments of human kindness and joy. Service caught all this in his *Rhymes,* and the public responded.

chapter 17

A new source of excitement for Robert in 1921 was the $5,000 check he received for movie rights to *The Shooting of Dan McGrew*. He announced that the family was going to blow it all on a trip to Hollywood.

Their boat docked in New York, and Robert, Germaine and four-year-old Iris then set off across the United States by train. As the train moved from desert to the brilliant green of California's orange groves, Robert's joy knew no bounds. He had loved this place when he was a homeless hobo, and he loved it now.

But how changed Los Angeles was, how bewildering. The movie industry had not existed when, as a down-and-outer, he had picked oranges there and lived in a mission—which was now replaced by a skyscraper. It was a strange experience for Robert, now flush with success, to walk where he had once searched for fruit in the gutter.

From the moment he arrived, Service fell in love with Hollywood. He visited all the studios, spent an hour talking to Louis B. Mayer, who had purchased the rights to his poem, and became friendly with several of the stars. He felt instantly a great affinity for movieland; illusion always seemed more relevant to him than reality.

Robert had rented a bungalow for six months, and from here he, Germaine and Iris sallied out to discover the wonders of this American paradise. They lived simply, having lunch in a cafeteria and cooking supper at home by a roaring fire fed with crates he scavenged from storekeepers.

Before Christmas, Robert and Germaine invited Robert's mother down from Edmonton. She arrived on the Oregon Express, and Robert saw descending from the train a little rosy-cheeked, blue-eyed lady with "a look of determination to make the best of being seventy."[1] Actually Emily was only 67, but Robert never could keep track of such facts regarding his birth family.

Germaine, an easygoing, sociable person herself, immediately liked Emily, who seemed to have grown younger in her 60s as the years, and financial help from Robert,[2] granted her increasing freedom from poverty and family burdens. In his wildest dreams Robert could not have imagined a happier family than the little group he saw in his Los Angeles bungalow.

Emily laughed a lot, still enjoyed the company of young people and, in addition to her fondness for detective novels, had developed a passion for solitaire, gangster films and banana ice cream. Robert described her as a "grand sport." At age 47, Robert was at last getting to know and appreciate his mother. Whatever the reason, the woman his autobiography describes in a Glasgow flat, in the Alberta farmhouse and now in the Hollywood bungalow, seems to be three different people. Was it Robert himself who changed, or Emily? Or both?

In studying his perfect little household, Robert stood so far back that he seemed to paint himself right out of the picture. What if he wasn't there? What if he was in Tahiti instead? It was an old dream, inspired by Robert Louis Stevenson—one he had brought to his sojourn on the American west coast in 1897 and kept alive in his wandering years. Now, as he lounged in his Morris chair reading *White Shadows in the South Seas* by Frederick O'Brien, Tahiti seemed close again, and certainly now more financially possible. Carefully he broached the subject. Germaine was silent, and it was his mother who joked about men thinking themselves indispensable and said the word: "Go!" If Germaine expressed her opinion of this in private, Robert never mentioned it.

In late January 1922, just after Iris's fifth birthday, Robert boarded the SS *Rarotonga,* bound for Papeete, the capital of Tahiti. Two weeks on the ship gave him time to read or reread Stevenson, O'Brien, James Hall and Charles Nordhoff, and Somerset Maugham.

Robert spent two months alone in a tiny rented cottage living Dawson-style, often reclining in a hammock on the porch. The nights were soft, the winds a caress, the air musical with crickets and the sensuous sound of mandolin and guitar.

"Bougainvillea wove purple tapestries and flamboyants flung their scarlet against the sky. Yellow, crimson, mauve gleamed the hibiscus blossoms, while the tiare—white and pure—loaded the air with perfume." He described the opulent, bare-breasted women with soft eyes and such rhythm in their movement that they seemed to sail past, and the amber-brown men who stalked majestically amid the palms. Robert's writing about Tahiti is magical, and his joy at this realization of a dream is tangible in the pages of *Harper of Heaven*.[3]

But there is always a serpent in paradise. A recurring theme in Service's writing is the dark undercurrent that exists in any paradise, in any magnificent city, and even in the pristine places of the Yukon or Tahiti—the crime, debauchery, poverty and sickness. Here it was filariasis, the result of a parasite in the blood causing painful, elephantine swelling of the legs and genitalia. As Robert met the men and women distorted by the disease he began to fear the streams he waded through, and the soil itself. Then on one of his tramps, he stumbled into the horror of a leper colony.

His new novel, already at the publisher's, was called *Poisoned Paradise*, and it explored the same theme in a different setting: the gambling life of Monte Carlo. He had spent some time exploring the slums and gambling dens of Paris, and in 1917–18, while living at Menton, he had explored nearby Monte Carlo. The detailed knowledge he displays in *Poisoned Paradise* suggests a good deal of study at the gaming tables, bringing to mind his early forays on the blackjack table at Whitehorse.

As usual Service studied people as closely as he did places and scenery. Along with cripples and wastrels, he studied the writers and artists he met in Tahiti, among them Charles Nordhoff and James Hall, destined for future fame as authors of *Mutiny on the Bounty* but already popular from their *Faery Lands of the South Seas*. Another friend offered him a cabin on the nearby island of Moorea. There Service felt he had come close to discovering Eden, feeling strongly the siren seduction that has held other writers and artists in thrall to these islands. How easy it would be to yield to the spell, to stay there forever.

This perhaps was a serious temptation for Service, the homeless loner of the west coast, the recluse of the Yukon cabin, the vagabond battling with the family man from France. Germaine may have feared when she let him go that Robert might not come back to Los Angeles. In his absence, unease may have crept into the family circle which had appeared so perfect to Robert.

But he did come back. Moorea was all beauty, but he found something cloying in that. The future for him was with Germaine and Iris and the real world. He would carry paradise home in his head, and inhabit it by writing about it.

In May 1922 Emily went back to Edmonton, then moved to Vancouver. Robert and his family made their way back to France, where his pleasant days included walking his little daughter to school, then writing until it was time to walk her home. During her stay in Los Angeles, Emily was always trying to persuade her son to write her a gangster novel. She told him she never read his poetry, but that a new Robert Service book always solved her Christmas-present problems (perhaps Robert got some of his penchant for "telling it like it is" from his mother). His latest book, *Ballads of a Bohemian*, had not been well received and was described as "flat" by some reviewers. Maybe it was time to take some advice from his mother and concentrate on thriller fiction.

Poisoned Paradise was published in 1922. His next book, *The Roughneck*, followed a year later and was the thriller Emily had asked for. In it, a series of lurid adventures took the hero and heroine to the idyllic settings Service had discovered on his travels in Tahiti. In 1924 Metro-Goldwyn-Mayer produced three movies based on Robert's writing. *The Shooting of Dan McGrew* had its world premiere in London, *Poisoned Paradise*, which won rave reviews and starred Clara Bow, followed, and in December *The Roughneck* opened in New York. It must have been a lot of fun for Emily Service to not only read a thriller written by her son, but go to a theatre in Vancouver and see it on screen.

Robert's writing career was put on hold in 1924, shortly after his 50th birthday, when a doctor told him his heart was enlarged and racing out of control, the result of drastic dieting and overzealous exercising. As a result he gave up alcohol, tobacco, red meat and coffee, and he felt so low that for a time he gave up writing too. In 1926, at the health resort of Royat in the Auvergne, he bathed in "rich, brown waters" under the care of the renowned Gabriel Perrin while his blood pressure returned to normal.

Never a writer to waste an experience, his cardiac trouble resulted in *Why Not Grow Young? Or Living for Longevity* (1928), a book about healthy living written by an enthusiast who felt he had come back from the grave. Although the book was literally dear to his heart, it had "only a sorry sale." His public wanted Yukon ballads or detective novels, and he had given them health advice.

There were two more thrillers in the 1920s: *Master of the Microbe* (1926) and *The House of Fear* (1927). In these books, both set on the Brittany coast near his own Dream Haven, gangsters, assassins, cutthroats, demons and werewolves romp through fishing and farming villages. The last movie to be based on one of his novels appeared in 1928, and was a fitting tribute to the roots of his success, for it took movie-goers to *The Trail of '98*.

chapter 18

In 1929 the Service family succumbed to the attractions of the Riviera and left Paris for an apartment at 4 rue Dante in Nice. For most of the 1930s, Service's pen was silent. The apparent reason for this was a libel suit brought against him in 1929 by an English peer, the 9th Baron Strabolgi. This man claimed that Service had slandered him by using the name Strathbogie (which, despite its spelling, is actually from the same root as Strabolgi) for a character in *The House of Fear*. Advisers believed the charge was flimsy, even ridiculous, and would not stand up in court. But for a man who valued privacy above all else, the horrors of a lawsuit paralyzed him, and he agreed to pay £10,000 in an out-of-court settlement. This came at a time when Robert had already lost a substantial part of his fortune in the Wall Street Crash, and for a time was short of money. Letters back and forth to family members show that he had to cut down on the financial help he was giving them.

H.G. Wells, who was then living in Nice, had become a friend, and Service sometimes had lunch at his home. He later recorded that Wells was very indignant that he would not fight the libel suit. At that time Wells was himself involved in a long battle with a Canadian woman named Florence Deeks, who claimed that his 1920 book *The Outline of History* had been plagiarized from her work, *The Web*. Her manuscript had been submitted to Macmillan in Toronto, then sent to their New York office and supposedly lost for a long time—the same period when Wells was writing his *Outline of History*, which he seemed to produce very quickly. A.B. McKillop, in *The Spinster and the Prophet* (2000), presents a strong case against Wells, but in 1932 the judgment went against Miss Deeks.

The Strabolgi affair about a similarity of name must have made Service remember his blatant use of a man's name in *Songs of a Sourdough* for the purpose of cremating him in a poem. In the Yukon a man might cuss another out or threaten to shoot him, but he wasn't likely to sue him about a personal offence. What Sam had done was simply march into the Canadian Bank of Commerce in Whitehorse and take out his money.

In the 1930s Service amused himself with a regime of moderate exercise, making music on his guitar, piano and ukulele, and then learning the accordion. He said later that during these years he would sometimes look at his row of published books on the shelf and feel they had been written by someone else.

During this time he also struggled to achieve an understanding of communism—which, from a humanitarian standpoint, appealed to him— so he decided to go to the Soviet Union to investigate it at first hand. He set off, unaccompanied, in July 1938 and traveled for two months, propelled by his curiosity and a writer's need for new material. He found that what appealed in theory appalled him on closer inspection, yet back home that winter, when he tried to write about the Soviet Union he realized how little he understood what he had seen and decided to take a second trip. He set off again in July 1939 as war clouds hovered over Europe, and almost left it too late to get back to Nice that fall. By then the border between Poland and Germany was closed, so with great difficulty and increasing fear he traveled via Latvia, Sweden and Norway, where he got a ship from Bergen to Newcastle, skirting far to the north to avoid German U-boat wolf packs already hunting the North Sea. In London it took another three weeks to get a visa so he could cross to France.

Back in Nice during the "phoney war" winter of 1939–40, he completed *Bar-Room Ballads*, his first book of verse in 19 years. Also that winter, his book of songs entitled *Twenty Bath-Tub Ballads* (including "When the Ice Worm Nests Again") was published.

Going back to poetry took Service back to the Yukon; for the first time in his writing career he was revisiting the past rather than tackling something new. Seven of his *Bar-Room Ballads* are set in the North and are full of Yukon gusto. It was almost inevitable that Jake of the Richardson

Mountains, with his nicotine addiction, would eventually appear in a Service poem—and here he was almost 30 years later in "The Ballad of Salvation Bill." Service gave him a happier ending than Jake (Frank Williams) had in real life. In the poem, the Jake character (Bill) was given a Bible to smoke on condition that he read each page before he used it. The Bible converted him and he became a preacher known as Salvation Bill.

> *And if a guy won't listen—why I sock him on the jaw,*
> *And preach the gospel sitting on his chest.*
> *So now I'm called Salvation Bill, I teach the Living Law,*
> *And Bally-hoo the Bible with the best ...*[1]

The collection included "The Ballad of Touch-the-Button Nell," the poem that W. Briggs had refused to publish as part of *Ballads of a Cheechako* in 1909. Thirty years later publishers had relaxed their morality margins, and Nell became one of the most popular characters in the new collection.

A Klondike event that lay like a dark shadow on Robert's mind all his life was the hanging he had witnessed in Dawson in 1908. In his new volume he sought to immortalize the unfortunate man in "The Ballad of Hank the Finn."

The "Ballad of the Ice-Worm Cocktail" deals with a Dawson icon already encountered in "When the Ice Worm Nests Again." Several sources credit W.C. Sime, one of Service's colleagues at the bank, with concocting the first ice-worm cocktail—a drink with a strand of spaghetti embedded in a chunk of ice.   In "The Ballad of the Leather Medal" Service extended the story of Sam McGee by writing about his two fictional children, orphaned when their pa was cremated. He also took a swipe at "The Shooting of Dan McGrew," which he had grown tired of hearing for the previous 30 years.

> *I reckon you've heard the opus, a ballad of guts and gore;*
> *Of a Yukon frail and a frozen trail and a fight in a drinking dive.*
> *It's on a par, I figger, with "The Face on the Bar-Room Floor."*
> *And the boys who wrote them pieces ought to be skinned alive.*[2]

Other poems in the collection were more serious and reflective musings about war, the purpose of life, and love. But a reviewer in the *Globe and*

Mail thought the "sourdough stuff" preferable, and predicted those poems would go over big in "this dark hour" when a bit of cheer was needed.

In "L'envoi" the author announced that he was 65 (the birthday was in January 1939) and vowed, as in the past, that these poems would be his last. But he could not and would not stop writing poetry as long as he lived.

The German Blitzkrieg began on May 10, 1940, and on May 20 the Service family fled Nice for Dream Haven on the Brittany coast. When they reached Rennes the train came to a stop and they found the town filled with British troops. By luck they found a taxi driver who knew them and agreed to drive them to Lancieux. The train, and now the roads, were crowded, at first with fleeing Belgians and then with people from northeastern France. Their own little town, when they arrived, was filled with refugees, and the sense of panic was contagious.

On the radio there was only bad news. Belgium had surrendered to the Germans. Then the first bomb fell on Lancieux, exploding in a nearby field. Robert's first "idiotic" notion, as he put it in *Harper of Heaven,* was to stay and fight: he could hide in the woods, he thought, and Germaine could bring him food at night. Germaine must have often been exasperated by the man she had married, with his flare for the dramatic and his flirtation with danger. However, Robert soon realized that a cave in the woods would be no place for an "old codger" such as himself.

Instead, on June 17 he set out on his motorbike to see how he could get the family out of France. At nearby St. Malo he found four cargo tramps evacuating the wounded, who were pouring toward every port. He was told there might be a chance of getting on one by being there when it sailed. While in St. Malo he heard that France had capitulated and that the British Expeditionary Force was being evacuated from Dunkirk. He went home and gave Germaine and Iris half an hour to pack, one suitcase each. Robert grabbed the papers he needed and destroyed the rest. Valise packed, he stood in his library of 2,000 books and touched his beloved volumes one last time. Then they left, Iris and Germaine wearing four dresses each.

At St. Malo they sought out the port captain and anxiously asked if they could get on a boat. A naval officer with "alcoholic heartiness" told them to get on *Hull Trader.* "And let me tell you, you're lucky. We have to stay and blow up the Port."[3]

Their ship was an old coal carrier. Another moored alongside was filled with khaki-clad infantrymen, and a third with blue-uniformed airmen. Friendly planes were swooping overhead to protect them from German bombers, as a steady stream of cars disgorged the wounded, then lined up to be dumped into the harbor by the port captain's men to make the port unusable by the Germans after the last ships had left.

The officers left behind waved a grim farewell, and *Hull Trader,* carrying 500 troops, several hundred wounded and 50 refugees, joined a motley array of vessels leaving France. In the hold was a cargo of high explosives that the crew had not been able to unload.

For once in his life Service cursed the full moon, a resplendent orb highlighting them on the sea, a target for enemy planes. But the planes they heard in the night must have been their own, and the U-boats failed to find them. In late afternoon the next day, they landed safely in Weymouth, and after being examined, deloused and interrogated, they took a night train, still under guard, to London. In the grey dawn, buses took them to a police station for another day of questions and examinations, but finally their passports were stamped and they were free to find a hotel. A few days later the Services rented a flat in Chelsea.

Near the end of July they sailed from Liverpool on the *Princess Helene,* bound for Montreal. In addition to a swarm of RAF cadets headed for pilot training in Alberta, there were 1,000 child evacuees aboard, fleeing the Battle of Britain. The first three days were the worst. Clad in life jackets at all times, with a lone destroyer as escort, they expected an attack by U-boats at any moment. As they neared Canadian waters and their naval guardian turned back, their worst fears subsided.

The boat that brought them to Canada was torpedoed on a later trip; the flat they had rented in Chelsea was bombed shortly after they left. But Robert Service's guardian angel had come through again, and he and his family reached safety in Canada.

chapter 19

Canada welcomed Robert Service in 1940 like a long-lost uncle. Reporters met him as he disembarked at Montreal on August 1. Here was a name all Canadians knew, and someone who could tell them what was happening in France and Britain. Service's arrival was splashed across the front pages of newspapers from Halifax to Victoria. On the day he arrived in Montreal, Vancouver's *Daily Province* ran the headline "Famed Northland Poet Returns."

The Collected Verse of Robert Service had been published in 1930 by Ernest Benn in London, and Dodd Mead in New York published *The Complete Poems of Robert Service* in 1933. Ever since *Songs of a Sourdough*, Service had been compared favorably to Rudyard Kipling, and by the 1930s his legacy in the English-speaking world was assured. A *New York Times* critic declared that the author of "Dan McGrew" and Edgar A. Guest were America's two leading folk poets.

By living in France he had escaped publicity and even recognition most of the time. His neighbors had some idea that he was rich and wrote poetry—but not in their language. In Canada the situation was different; every person on the street and every farmer and fisherman knew who Robert Service was, and identified with his verse. In giving them the North, he had given them a voice and a sense of national identity. A blizzard on the prairie was not much different from a blizzard in the Yukon. A night of fog on the Atlantic could be as cold and lonely as an Arctic night.

In early August, shortly after Robert had booked into Montreal's Windsor Hotel, a young, professional-looking man approached him in the lounge. When he asked Robert if he knew him, Robert said no. The man announced that he was his brother, Stanley.

Stanley was 17 years younger than Robert, and according to biographer James Mackay, it was Robert's money that put Stanley through medical school, although Robert never mentioned this in his autobiography. Robert had not seen Stanley since the three winter months of early 1911 that he had spent on their Mannville farm. In 1940 he still remembered Stanley as one of the strapping young farm lads; now here he was, 49 years old and attired in the dignified suit of a doctor.

Stanley and his wife drove Robert's family to their home in Ottawa. Stanley had moved to Ottawa in 1932 after 10 years at a clinic in Clifton Springs, New York, during which time he had also carried out research on liver extract at the University of Rochester. Now he was a specialist in internal medicine and the treatment of diabetes at Ottawa Civic Hospital.

After visiting Stanley's family, Robert, Germaine and Iris headed for Toronto, where they were ensconced in the Royal York Hotel. Here Robert's public descended on him. There were broadcasts and book-signing parties, and everywhere crowds of people wanting to see him. R. Saunders, the Canadian publishers of *Bar-Room Ballads,* were delighted to have the famous Robert Service captive in their city so soon after publishing his first book of verse in 19 years. Thus far in his life, Robert had managed to avoid book tours. Now he had two reactions to being a celebrity: first he would try to avoid it, but if that was unavoidable, he would enjoy it.

Among the large crowd of fans, there was one appearance Robert certainly enjoyed: Harold Tylor from his "bank family" in Whitehorse. Harold had been transferred to Dawson City for 1906, then, before Robert's arrival there, left for Vancouver in 1907 and finally got transferred back home to marry his girl in Toronto. In 1940 he lived nearby in Richmond Hill and was a traveling representative for the Bank of Commerce. During the war he would work with the Canadian Wartime Prices and Trade Board. He and Robert had kept in touch by mail sporadically since 1910. Now Harold whisked Robert and his family away to his cottage at Point Au Baril, north of Parry Sound on Lake Huron's Georgian Bay. This taste of Ontario cottage life would be long remembered with great pleasure. Robert signed the guest book there on August 10, 1940.

Reporters were quick to see the drama of these two—who were young when the Yukon was young—together again after their 30 years lived on different continents. Their reunion was featured in newspaper articles, and *Maclean's* magazine commissioned Robert to write a story. Service wrote a self-effacing humorous piece about his life and the expectations of his critics and his public entitled, "So I Have a Mild Face," and it was published in the January 15, 1941, issue.

Inevitably reporters quizzed him about the war in Europe. Here was someone who had reported a previous war for the *Toronto Star.* Their questions about the sad state of France, and Europe generally, made Service feel ashamed to be safely in Toronto.

Their stay in the city was brief. As in 1896, Robert was headed west. He, Germaine and Iris left Toronto on a Canadian National train bound for Jasper in the Canadian Rockies, with stops in Winnipeg and Edmonton along the way. East of Edmonton the train took them through the fields where Robert had hiked, hunted and once outrun a prairie fire. Robert's three sisters and his brother Peter had married in the Mannville area, then moved west to Edmonton or Vancouver.

In a letter to Harold Tylor, written from Jasper Park Lodge on August 23, Service revealed that he was still torn by his decision to leave Europe. He wrote that he was feeling good physically, but not mentally. In the First World War he had been in the thick of the action, driving ambulances under gunfire and enjoying the adrenalin rush while enduring the horrors. In St. Malo he had watched the ambulance drivers bring the casualties to the dock, but this time he himself had escaped with the wounded. In the secluded beauty and safety of Jasper National Park in Alberta, he felt a sense of guilt and separation. Although he was now 66, he wrote to Harold, "I wouldn't mind if I finished up shooting Huns from an English ruin."[1]

The Service family moved on to Vancouver, where they found the media waiting their arrival at the Pacific Central Railway Station on August 26. The reporters watched as his brother Peter greeted him with a whoop worthy of the Malamute Saloon. Robert and Peter grinned and shook hands. One reporter tried in vain to get him to talk about Dan McGrew, but Robert announced that his favorite was "The Cremation of Sam McGee." He preferred to talk about his lost 40,000-word manuscript about his travels to the Soviet Union, which he had been obliged to abandon in the Brittany cottage and which he expected never to see again.

Distinguished Canadian pilot
Sheldon Luck poses here with
Robert Service in front of the
aircraft *Yukon King* of Yukon
Southern Air Transport Ltd.,
ca. 1941.

PHOTO: LIBRARY AND ARCHIVES CANADA/
PA–124227

In a letter to Harold written on September 27, Robert reported that he and his family were settled in Vancouver at Sylvia Court and that he was in a better frame of mind, happy beside the sea and close to Stanley Park, where he walked every morning and felt the stress of the last months ebbing away.

His return to Vancouver brought back memories, and he soon sent a letter to Isabel MacLean, arranging to see her. In it, he spoke of expectation and suspense, saying "it will be like seeing two old sweethearts again." Connie was living in Kingston, where Leroy Grant, now a lieutenant-colonel, taught engineering at the Royal Military College. If Robert deduced that Connie's husband was the same major he had traveled with on the day in 1918 when they "liberated" Lille, he kept it to himself.

For years a report circulated that Robert Service flew to Whitehorse in 1940 with pilot Sheldon Luck of Yukon Southern Transport. A picture exists of Service and Luck on the tarmac the day before the flight was to take place. But Luck, interviewed years later, says Service did not show up next morning for the flight. In *Ploughman* Service said he never went back to the Yukon and mentioned an offer he received to fly to Dawson, presumably from Luck, which he refused. To see the crumbling town that once hummed with vitality would have been too sad.

In Vancouver another relative appeared. This time it was his sister Agnes. Again, he did not recognize his sibling. Agnes had married Andy Tod in Mannville during Robert's stay at the farm. Sibby (Isobel) married his brother Philip Tod. Alec (the spelling that Alick now used) and Peter Service also lived in Vancouver, Alec working as an electrician for B.C. Electric, and Peter operating the aptly named Sourdough Bookshop on West Pender Street.

Robert did not mention in his autobiography that his 85-year-old mother Emily had died here just a year before. Soon after her trip to California she had moved to Vancouver to live with Peter. *The History of the Vancouver Yukoners Association* noted that Emily Service "took a keen interest in our organization, attended the International Reunion in 1936 and was the first lady to be awarded the 'Friendship Bracelet' in honour of the oldest lady attending the Reunion."

The Vancouver Yukoners Association had been founded in 1928 at the Piccadilly Café on Granville Street. By this time Vancouver, Seattle and other Pacific Rim cities had become havens for Yukon men and women retiring to the south. "It was only natural that these Sourdoughs would get together from time to time at impromptu gatherings to enjoy each other's company, to reminisce and keep alive those friendships formed in a far off land, a harsh land, but a land of happy memories."[2]

In 1930 Yukon old-timers had filled the hotels and hailed each other on the Vancouver streets as they gathered for the Sourdough Stampede. By 1933 an International Sourdough Association had formed to encompass the clubs in various American cities.

A recurring theme of Robert Service's return to Canada was old acquaintances greeting him with the exclamation that they had thought him dead. Robert declared that he began to feel like a veritable ghost. In London, the *Times* had at one point published "Heritors of Unfulfilled Renown," an article about writers and artists killed in the First World War. It included his name, confusing him with his brother Albert or, more likely, with his brother Joseph's son Robert, who had been killed in the war. Another factor in the myth was perhaps his own seclusion in France, away from the attention of the English-speaking world.

On September 7, the *Vancouver Sun* published a piece entitled "Robert Service: Wallpaper Poet," in which Laura Berton recalled her memories of Robert Service in Dawson. The title referred to his habit of writing on sheets of wallpaper and then putting them on the wall so he could study and edit the lines.

While Service was living in Vancouver that fall, a death in Beiseker, Alberta, made headlines. The Vancouver *Daily Province* reported: "Sam McGee who was 'cremated' by the famed sourdough poet, Robert W. Service, now in Vancouver, died at Beiseker, Alberta …" The life that had unfolded for Sam was emblematic of that of many of the '98ers who, unlike Robert Service, had to go on struggling to make a living long after the brief moment of excitement in the Klondike had passed.

Sam McGee had left the Yukon in the spring of 1909, not because he wanted to but because his wife Ruth wanted to raise her children in the south. The demise of the Montana Mountain dream added to her argument. Before he left Whitehorse a group of 34 friends gave him a rousing send-off with an address that called him "a pioneer pathfinder" and "our leading road-builder here." They presented him with a gold-nugget watch chain and a letter of introduction to the premier of Alberta that described Sam as "the best [surveyor] the Yukon ever had and a genius at that kind of work."[3]

Sam tried his hand as a fruit grower at Summerland, B.C., but "didn't like playing nursemaid to fruit trees." The family then moved to a farm 60 miles from Vermilion, Alberta, in 1912—just as the Service family was selling its farm in nearby Mannville. In 1918 the McGees moved to Edmonton.

Sam's heart stayed in the Yukon and he kept trying to get back there, but he was dogged by tragedy. In July 1918, according to the *Whitehorse Star,* he made a short visit but was called home when his six-year-old daughter became ill with a burst appendix. Then Mrs. McGee became ill with cholera infantum, a dysentery that preceded the Spanish flu pandemic. A year later Sam tried again. Walter, his 17-year-old eldest son, was kicked by a horse and died while Sam was away. In 1921 Sam set out for the North a third time. This time Olive, his second youngest, got diphtheria and died.

In 1923 the family moved to Great Falls, Montana, where Sam helped build the road into Yellowstone National Park. Then he moved east to work on the Roosevelt highway in New York and Pennsylvania. In those years his family followed him, spending winters in Great Falls but summers in the mountains with the construction crews.

In Montana the American media discovered Sam McGee. Telegrams and letters went back and forth between Sam and Leonard Bass of Phillips H. Lord Inc. to arrange his appearance on a program in the series *We the People,*

Sam McGee had this picture taken in 1938, just before he went to New York City to be interviewed on the NBC program *We The People.*

PHOTO: COURTESY OF BEVERLY GRAMMS

to be broadcast nationally. No recording of Sam's radio debut has turned up but no doubt Sam set them straight on a number of misconceptions about him that Service's poem had engendered.

After Sam and Ruth moved back to Canada to live with their daughter, Ethel Gramms, at Beiseker near Calgary, the old Yukoner saw his chance to go north with Dick Coreless, a bush pilot he had met in Montana who had been flying north out of Prince George since 1928. The headwaters of the Liard River in the southern Yukon were inaccessible to a prospector on foot, since it took three months to get there and the same to get out, leaving no time for prospecting before freeze-up. With Dick's plane, Sam McGee and Dick's son could be flown in, dropped off and picked up months later.

Before flying into the bush, Sam made a sentimental visit to old friends in Whitehorse. "The Famous Old Sourdough Sam McGee Comes Back to Whitehorse After 30 Years," read a headline in the *Whitehorse Star.* If the Yukon could not entice Robert Service himself to come back, they at least had his best character in Sam. In Whitehorse he found that his original cabin had been moved and restored by the historical society and was now a tourist attraction.

McGee and young Coreless spent six months prospecting on the Liard River, and by August they had shifted to the Kluane district. They camped at Canyon City, where he and Skelly had run their roadhouse in 1904, then

Author Enid Mallory on Canyon Creek (Aishihik River) bridge. Sam McGee built the original bridge, and in 1904 he and a partner ran a roadhouse here.
PHOTO: GORD MALLORY

went to prospect on Burwash Creek. On August 28 McGee celebrated his 70th birthday there. But every morning he was a young prospector again, hoping to strike it rich that day.

His daughter says he came home with a small urn of ashes sold to him on a boat. The man claimed he was selling the ashes of Sam McGee. "Dad never told him that he *was* Sam McGee."[4]

With the exception of that Yukon trip, Sam's last years were hard. The losses of both a son and a daughter while he was absent had left a bitterness in the family that was never resolved; according to their grandchildren, Ruth suffered a nervous breakdown after the deaths, and never fully recovered. Yet her grandchildren remember her with respect as "one tough lady": they tell stories of her washing up dishes from a meal in a "tea-cup" of water, and how she would drag home several good-sized tree limbs when she went out for a walk—habits developed in the Yukon where water often had to be melted and wood could be scarce.

Sam, in his final years, became increasingly cantankerous. One grand-daughter described him as "more notorious than famous, I think—my grandfather was not anybody to mess with."

"Grandfather didn't relate particularly well with children," recalled another. "They were to be seen and not heard and if possible not seen too often!"

But there was still a twinkle in his eye when he talked about his beloved Yukon. Even the Service poem that had annoyed him in his youth became a symbol of his Yukon past of which he was proud. "I never minded the cold," he told a reporter who interviewed him in the Gowman Hotel in Seattle. "Service liked to twist things around."

Granddaughter-in-law Beverly Gramms said of Sam: "He was out for adventure, and wherever it was, he was." Just before he died he was trying to talk his daughter's husband into selling the Beiseker farm to go prospecting in the Yukon with him.

Sam died of a stroke on September 7, 1940. Having survived cremation by Robert Service, Sam must have thought himself immune to death; when the real thing came, he wasn't ready—he wanted to know what would happen afterward. He had no use for Ruth's Seventh Day Adventist religion and refused to let her into his room, but his son James was a Christian, and his father wanted to quiz him about God and the afterlife. James was the only person with him when he died.

Sam was not cremated, but was buried in the Levelland Cemetery near Beiseker. He was one of the 99 percent of those who went to the Klondike but never struck it rich. He would have been forgotten along with the others if a poet had not made him a legend. There was a report in Beiseker that Robert Service attended Sam's funeral, but this is so out of keeping with Robert's desire for privacy that it must fall into the category of local legend.

In Vancouver, where Robert heard the news, reporters swooped down on him, wanting to know how well he had known the real Sam McGee. Service said that he never knew Sam personally, only by reputation. He called him a decent chap, well known in northern circles, and confessed that he had taken Sam's name from the bank ledger because it provided the rhyme he needed. He only remembered seeing him once: when, shortly after *Songs of a Sourdough* was published, he came into the bank and told Service who he was. Robert was always embarrassed when questioned about his use of Sam's name and made no mention of a raft ride in Miles Canyon. Even if the tale of the raft ride isn't true, Robert would have appreciated Sam's joke in making up the story, just as he had made up the poem about Sam.

Shy of talking to reporters about it, Robert nevertheless knew very well how Sam McGee's name, borrowed for the miner cremated in the

Sam McGee was buried, not cremated, in Beiseker, Alberta. He died on September 7, 1940, soon after Robert Service and his family arrived in Vancouver, refugees from the war in Europe.
PHOTO: GORD MALLORY

firebox of the *Olive May* on Tagish Lake, contributed to his success. Like the Unknown Soldiers commemorated around the world, the miner from Tennessee immortalizes all the men who gave up their warm southern comfort to prospect or trap or operate a lonely telegraph station or cut cordwood for steamboats along the Yukon River—and who sometimes gave up their lives to the North. The man from Tennessee died of scurvy; there were others who froze on the trail or died hungry, sick and alone— and sometimes out of their minds—in remote cabins. And a few like Dan McGrew who died in barroom brawls.

Service told their stories, along with those of doctors like Sugden, the Mounties and the muscular Christians like Bishop Stringer, Cody and the Presbyterian Pringle brothers. In return his characters gave Robert Service lifelong freedom, fortune and fame.

Robert, Germaine and Iris celebrated Christmas that year with the Vancouver families of Agnes, Peter and Alec. Iris had a wonderful time meeting her cousins Sylvia, Shirley and Sheila. She especially liked Aunt Agnes. Shortly after Christmas they left the Vancouver rain for California, the place that always seemed like heaven on earth to Robert.

In 1976 Canada issued a commemorative Robert Service stamp on which David Bierk of Peterborough, Ontario, depicted "The Cremation of Sam McGee."

chapter 20

Robert, about to turn 67, wanted peace and quiet after the escape from France and all the attention he'd received in Canada, and he found it in Los Angeles at 1346 North Orange Drive. With days of sunshine, a little dog to look after, a daughter who liked to cook, a public library with thousands of books, and the Hollywood Hills overlooking the city of lights, he was almost able to forget what was happening to Europe. He borrowed books from the library 10 at a time, reading aloud to Germaine daily. At midday he went to local markets to shop for food. After a nap and tea, he hiked alone into the nearby hills and canyons as he had once done in the hills of the Yukon.

Robert portrayed the Service family in Hollywood as quite poor due to restrictions on money transfers from Britain. Service says with a dramatic flourish that in the first year they ate their pearls, in the second their diamonds, and after that the ladies' fur coats. The fact that his U.S. royalties were still strong and easily directed to California suggests that poverty was hardly an issue—but he could act the part. It made him feel like the wandering minstrel again. It also meant that he felt under no obligation to entertain guests, assuring the peace and isolation he loved so much.

How well this suited his more sociable wife and daughter he doesn't say. Germaine may have played the role of traditional wife in France, but the Second World War and her time in North America had broadened her horizon. She was busy working for the war effort at the Alliance Française, the American Red Cross and a Catholic center for black children, and studying English at the high school nearby. Iris ran the house.

From 1941 to 1945 the Service family migrated each fall to California, returning in the spring to enjoy the Canadian summer, with Vancouver as their base. In British Columbia, newspapers reported on their tours to Harrison Hot Springs and Vancouver Island. Soon after their arrival in Vancouver, Robert had written to Fred Corfield, replying to a letter sent care of his brother Peter. Robert said he would be delighted to accept Fred's invitation to visit the old place at Cowichan. He showed Germaine and Iris the Cowichan Valley and Eureka Farm, where he fed the pigs, herded cows and worked as a storekeeper for three years. The old store was still standing, though somewhat atilt, and was only a few years from being torn down in 1946. The Services stayed at the Empress Hotel, on Victoria's waterfront, while they explored the island. Money was apparently not a problem while on Canadian soil.

On October 8, 1941—a day before heading back south—he did an interview for CKWX radio in Vancouver; it may have been at this time that a wire recording of Robert reciting his poems was made. Marguerite Service, wife of Robert's nephew Kelvin, remembers hearing the recording and says it was "bone-chilling" to hear him recite "The Cremation of Sam McGee" (the British Columbia Archives has a tape apparently made from this wire recording). He also recorded a broadcast that was used for the inauguration of the new Whitehorse radio station on September 21, 1943. Robert was intrigued and delighted that he could sit in his living room in Vancouver and listen to himself speaking from the Frozen North.

On their return to Hollywood, Robert found himself in demand as a public speaker, a reciter of his own poems. His presence discovered by the Hollywood Authors group, he was soon a star attraction in its war effort after the United States entered the fray.

> I tried to put up a good show and give general satisfaction. It was an entirely new line, but my experience as a reciter helped me. I determined to develop any ability I had in this way, and memorized and studied some of my ballads. The McGrew and McGee pieces were my great stand-bys. I thought people would tire of them but they did not.[1]

As a teenager in Glasgow, as a young man on Vancouver Island, then as banker–poet in Whitehorse and Dawson City, Service had performed in

Robert's big moment with Marlene Dietrich, on the set of *The Spoilers*.
PHOTO: UNIVERSAL STUDIOS

skits and done recitations on stage, but never to a public so eager to hear him. Now, close to 70, he rose to the occasion by taking singing lessons to improve his voice. A Shakespearean actor who worked in a nearby ice-cream parlor became Service's coach, teaching him how to project his voice. Service found it difficult at first—several times he had attacks of dizziness while on stage—but he stuck with it, studied and became confident as a performer. Hollywood was giving him a new career.

After Pearl Harbor he toured army camps all over the southwest as part of the morale-raising USO concerts for the troops. He found that his heart condition weakened his stamina, and he could suddenly become very tired; prolonged contact with people, especially strangers, was also very tiring. The crowds that pressed upon him after recitations or during book signings were hard to handle. But he soldiered on.

The highlight of his Hollywood years came in 1942 when producer Frank Lloyd invited him to appear on the set of *The Spoilers*, a film depicting the Alaska gold rush of 1900 and based on the book by Rex Beach. The idea was to have Service sitting in a bar writing "The Shooting of Dan McGrew." Made up to look decades younger, he was dressed in a costume he chose himself, as romantic and foolish as the cowboy outfit he had worn on the train 50 years before. While he waited for his moment on stage, he wandered freely around the studio, secure in his disguise, taking in the fantasy land of glamorous women and he-men, where cowboys and Indians raced across the range just as he'd expected to see them when he was 22 and traveling across Canada on the train.

He watched Alfred Hitchcock direct a film and dance-hall girls do the cancan on the *Spoilers* set. Then came his part—a scene with Marlene Dietrich and her "ice-blue eyes"—after which he stayed on to see John Wayne, Randolph Scott and their stuntmen stage what he (and many others) considered to be the greatest saloon brawl Hollywood ever filmed.

The Spoilers was a big hit when it was released. Although Service later claimed that he agreed to appear in the movie because he was short of money, no doubt one of his tongue-in-cheek efforts to amuse himself, Canadian newspapers reported that his paycheck of $220 was donated to the Canadian Red Cross to launch its Dominion fund.

Robert apparently decided that the Hollywood set of *The Spoilers* was as close as he would ever get to Dawson's former glory days. In August 1942, when Germaine and Iris sailed up the Inside Passage, they were on their way to Dawson without him. When reporters questioned his decision not to join them, he made the excuse that he might be called back to Hollywood at any moment, presumably to entertain the troops. Perhaps expressing to his wife and daughter what the cabin on the hill had meant to him in his youth was beyond him.

Germaine and Iris traveled on the White Pass railway to Whitehorse, where they found themselves in the midst of the Yukon's most active period since the gold rush. From March to November 1942 army engineers and construction crews from Canada and the U.S. laid roadbed from Dawson Creek, British Columbia, to Delta Junction, Alaska—the precursor to the Alaska Highway, built to meet the threatened Japanese invasion of Alaska. In Whitehorse, about midpoint on the new road's route, the Service women felt the excitement of this enormous undertaking. Sam McGee's old house in Whitehorse was filled with construction workers. Germaine and Iris went on to Dawson City on the paddleboat *Klondike*, enjoying a pleasant and historic means of travel that would be made obsolete in 1955 by the North Klondike Highway. When Germaine finally stood inside the tiny cabin where her husband had lived, the loneliness of his existence there was palpable, and her reaction was reported to be "*ça m'a fait triste*"—"it made me sad."

When she and Iris returned to Vancouver, the whole family went south to attend the Sourdough Reunion in Seattle, a grand affair with parade, picnic, banquet and dance. Robert was the guest speaker, and he drew such a crowd that the guests had to be housed in two hotels, the New Washington and the Gowman, with a banquet in each, requiring Robert to do dual performances. Sourdoughs who had been young men on the Trail of '98 were in their sixties now. It was their time for looking back, and with the war hanging heavily over everyone's heads, it was a treat to remember a time and place were it was only cold, hunger and grizzlies—not your fellow man—that were feared.

The war years in North America gave Service a new lease on life—almost a second youth and certainly a new image. If the Second World War had not caused him to flee to Vancouver and Hollywood, he would likely have remained in obscurity in France, and those who thought him dead would not have been enlightened by his Canadian and American resurrection.

Coming back to Canada reconnected him to his past. Without the stimulus of Canadian scenes, the reappearance of forgotten faces and Hollywood's portrayal of the gold rush, there might have been no autobiography. But suddenly, along with public speaking, entertaining the troops, radio broadcasts, his film appearance and his musical aspirations, he was writing again. In 1941 when Frank Dodd, of Dodd Mead in New York, suggested Service write an autobiography, he declined. There would be a lot of baggage to carry if he wanted to make a journey into his past. He was not sure he could deal with it. But perhaps the challenge of confronting his past—the idea is summed up in the subtitle of his book, *An Adventure into Memory*—began to intrigue him. Whatever it was that triggered the need to do it, he began writing the memoir in the fall of 1943 and worked on it daily.

It was hard work to dredge up his early life. His compensation was that it freed him from the round of club meetings, radio rehearsals, lunches, lectures, visitors and fan mail that had taken over his life. His book became the ultimate excuse.

In his garage-cum-study he paced back and forth, stopping to tap out memories of his murky personal history on a typewriter perched atop an up-ended trunk. As he persevered the distant days came into focus. Again he tramped along the Pacific coast, hungry, broke and depressed. From the bank in Kamloops he rode his pony across the brown hills. East of Edmonton he explored the winter prairie. In Whitehorse and Dawson he felt the exhilarating cold and sunshine as short winter days lengthened into springtime.

By noon on an average day he had 2,000 words on paper. Then he would take his pup to the hills and let ideas percolate, much as he had done 30 years before, above Miles Canyon in Whitehorse or on the A.C. Trail to the Midnight Dome in Dawson.

Robert was in charge of this life story; he could edit and adapt it as he saw fit—and he did. He dealt with Connie by leaving her out entirely, drawing a veil over that period in his life. Along with Connie, his own family disappeared, to the chagrin of brother Stanley, who would try to set the record straight 30 years later. Almost any person of significance who did make it into the book was cloaked in disguise and contradiction.

In his writing, Service had found a way to escape the war, to forget the home, treasures and friends left behind in France, to live as a young man again.

By the time his recollections reached 1912, Robert realized he had a whole volume's worth of words, so he ended *Ploughman of the Moon* at his departure from the Yukon. Volume two could be written later—or not. The title for volume one came, according to Service, from the French poet Paul Verlaine:

Pedlar of dream-stuff, piping an empty tune;
Fisher of shadows, Ploughman of the moon.

With the book finished and the war still at hand, he resigned himself to the idea that if they could never go back to France, he would build a home in California, in the San Fernando Valley, and grow vines and fig trees. But gradually the news grew better, and in the summer of 1944, to the great joy of Robert and Germaine, France was liberated. Within a year the war was over and *Ploughman of the Moon* appeared in bookstores. "What a happy chappie I was—seventy odd and getting such a kick out of living! I was in such exultant health that just to breathe seemed joy." There was no more hiding in the garage. Once again he was plunged into social engagements, autographing sessions, hand-clasping, talking to student groups. "In the interest of my book I made a jolly good fellow of myself, which is not my line at all."[2]

Ploughman of the Moon received mixed reviews—critics were frustrated by the lack of dates and names, the vague and sometimes confused sequence of events, and his reluctance to mention his family. Regardless, the public gobbled it up, and the first 20,000 copies were gone by Christmas.

chapter 21

The Service family was also gone before Christmas. With the war over, they applied for a visa to return to France, waiting four months to get clearance. When they did, the train from California to New York took them from heat to slush, and they started an Atlantic crossing in a pre-winter gale. Their troopship, aptly named USS *Bardstown Victory*, had just brought home 1,500 American soldiers and was heading back for more. Empty, it was at the mercy of the waves, tossed about under a black sky, its decks awash and its 15 passengers seasick. The Services were quartered in the medical isolation ward, and by the time they reached France Robert had caught some residual germ and come down with flu. When they landed at Marseilles and got to the train station, they sat for four hours on their suitcases in a grizzly fog, cold and wet, and Robert sick with a wracking cough. Their dread of what they might find at their apartment in Nice added to their misery.

When they finally reached it, they found to their delight that, by some fortuitous oversight of Italian and German invaders, everything was as they had left it when they fled in 1940.

But life was not easy that winter in France. It was one of the coldest on record, and food was extremely hard to come by. In a letter to Harold Tylor on January 2, 1946, Service wrote that Christmas dinner was three potatoes and a sardine each. In a March letter, he thanked Harold for sending them a parcel—Red Cross parcels were available every two weeks through the British consul, but parcels from friends in Canada and the United States—and even some they had mailed to themselves before they left—brought great joy. Eventually they were able to order food through Eaton's department store in Canada.

In an April letter, Robert told Harold that he had not yet seen Dream Haven, but had news from there that the house had been occupied by the Germans and looted afterward; he did not go to see it until 1947, probably because of travel restrictions, the time-consuming move from Nice to Monte Carlo and his work on the second volume of his autobiography. The Services' winter residence for the rest of Robert's life would be the upper two floors of Villa Aurora on Rue d'Italie, beside the Mediterranean.

When Robert did make the trip to Lancieux he saw a still-standing wreck. According to his neighbors, the Germans had intended to blow up Dream Haven, but the arrival of American troops hastened their departure and saved the house. Inside, however, everything was destroyed: his library burned, his furniture gone, the woodwork ripped out. His first thought was that he was too old to restore it, but in the end he did, adding a conservatory across the front and going there each summer until he died.

In 1946 and early 1947 he completed his second memoir, *Harper of Heaven*. It was published by Ernest Benn in London, McClelland & Stewart in Canada and Dodd Mead in the United States. It lacked the intensity of *Ploughman*. To protect his family's privacy, he said little of his home life, so the main drama was his participation in the First World War, his visit to Tahiti and the exile from France during the Second World War. Unable to live at Dream Haven that summer, Robert visited his London publisher in July and then rode north to Scotland, for the first time in years.

In 1948 the Services visited Canada again. A letter from Bert Parker—his old Yukon friend and a leading force behind the Vancouver Yukoners Association—had asked if he would send a message and "be there in spirit" as they celebrated the golden jubilee of the Trail of '98 with a sourdough reunion in Vancouver. Robert cabled back: "In spirit be damned. Why not in the ruddy flesh."

Again the Service family set out by sea, then traveled across Canada by rail to reach Vancouver late in July. The conference began on August 12. Under the headline "Old Klondyke Sourdoughs Meeting Here," the *Vancouver Sun* could not resist stating that a bunch of the boys who had whooped it up in the Yukon were gathering to celebrate 50 years later in

While in Vancouver for the International Sourdough Convention, Robert Service launched the steamship *Prince George*.
PHOTO: HERITAGE HOUSE COLLECTION

Vancouver. The reporter singled out Klondyke Kate and Robert Service as the stars of the show.

Service was shocked to see his old friend Bert Parker down to 100 pounds from his usual 160 as a result of cancer of the esophagus. Bert had left the Yukon in 1918, and for 30 years his house in Vancouver had been a home away from home for any Yukoners arriving in the city. This reunion, which he helped to organize, would be his last.

For Bert's daughter, Liz Rowley, the week before the 1948 convention remains vivid in memory. With 18-month-old daughter Sue in tow, she drove her husband to work, then chauffeured Robert Service and her very sick but still enthusiastic father back and forth from convention affairs and St. Paul's Hospital, where Bert had a blood transfusion to keep him going. She remembers how Robert enjoyed the company of little Sue that day.

One day she drove Robert and her dad down to the Main Street pier, where Robert launched the steamship *Prince George,* destined to run on the Inside Passage route to Alaska. For years afterward, *Prince George* regaled passengers with a recording of Robert Service reciting his poems as the ship moved up the passage to Skagway.

In the 1960s, Alaska Airlines, flying from Seattle to points in Alaska, also entertained passengers with the rich baritone voice of Robert Service. Its brochure stated: "Mr. Service recorded these works in 1948 when he was a guest on the radio show of Mr. Bill Ward of Station CFUN in Vancouver, B.C." The poems were "The Shooting of Dan McGrew," "The Cremation of Sam McGee" and "The Spell of the Yukon." They were "not recited in their entirety," but the brochure offered a printed version as a souvenir and suggested you "read along as you wish."[1]

As the sourdoughs arrived in Vancouver for the convention, the *Sun* reported that 800 personal versions of the gold rush were being shared among the men who outfitted here. At the banquet Liz remembers her father sitting as president of the association, her mother, Helen, next at the table, then Robert Service. Helen, who arrived in the Yukon in 1916 after Robert had left, had kept in touch with Jean Clark, her Dawson roommate who had once been engaged to Robert. From Helen, Robert would have discovered that Jean had married another Yukoner, Jimmy Mason, and moved to a farm in Raymore, Saskatchewan. Liz and her sisters sang as part of the entertainment that night, and she remembers Robert writing a poem on his menu that he read to the gathering.

Four days later, after the conference had ended, the headline read: "Robert Service, 'Bard of the Yukon' Brings Tears." Robert had described his eight years in the Yukon as "some of the happiest" of his life. "All the things I am and have, I owe to the north." Then he recited his "Spell of the Yukon," and there wasn't a dry eye when he finished. Everyone there knew exactly what he was talking about, although Robert declaimed that he himself was just a piker: he had never carted a piano into the Yukon, had never seen anyone shoot Dan McGrew or cremate Sam McGee. No one cared. They loved the poem, and they loved Robert Service.

A letter to Harold Tylor from the Hotel Vancouver was less euphoric: he wrote that he was attending the sourdough convention because he owed them so much—but he would be glad to get home. He said the trip was hard on "an old Codger like me."

Although Robert kept his "conkey" heart ticking with careful diet and constant, moderate exercise, it was not always reliable, and sometimes it misbehaved when he was over-tired and socially pressured. Another note to Harold revealed that he had endured enough of the celebration, of having to glad-hand all the "seedy bums" who claimed to have been his bosom pals, though he didn't know who they were. He wished he could be fishing with Harold at his Muskoka cottage.

He was affected by another factor: the sadness of old friends passing or losing their hold on life. He told Harold he had seen their old boss, Leonard De Gex, partly paralyzed and not long for this world. Tylor would remember how warmly both he and Robert had been welcomed into the "family" by De Gex and his kindly wife at the Whitehorse bank.

Then he added that he had just heard of the recent death of Hiram Cody, who preached at Christ Church and shared with Robert a love of the English language and the need to write about the grand North they shared. Robert's last memory of him was when Cody, with his young wife and baby, came to Dawson in August 1909 for the Governor General's visit. Although they never saw each other again, they kept track of each other's literary output. Cody had been a prolific writer: along with his biography of Bishop Bompas and his poetry and magazine articles, he wrote 24 novels. He left the Yukon in 1909 to serve in his native New Brunswick until his death.

On August 25 a story in the Vancouver *Daily Province* shocked and saddened Service: "A Klondike Sourdough who made the Yukon his life died here Monday just a few days after he helped organize the 50th anniversary reunion of men and women who trekked the famous Trail of 98."[2] Bert was gone.

Bert had spent 20 years in the Yukon and had staked, then abandoned, a claim on Hunker Creek that later sold for $20,000. In Dawson he sold newspapers and worked as a surveyor and engineer before moving to Vancouver. Just before the reunion Bert had written a two-page article in the weekend section of the paper; his opening paragraph seemed to presage his death, which he knew was imminent: "The other day, thinking about sourdoughs who have gone over the great divide and others who will be meeting in Vancouver next month, it struck me that, if there was one thing that made for success on the Trail of '98, it was resourcefulness."

Parker went on to point out what the Klondike gold rush meant to the city of Vancouver.

> I outfitted in Vancouver, the same as thousands of others did and as other thousands in other coast cities. Vancouver was small and pretty primitive ... the men and women who hit the Trail of '98 had a lot to

do with putting Vancouver and Victoria on the map in a big way ... they bought mountains of stuff in these towns when they outfitted. And they brought millions of dollars back and put them into the building of B.C.[3]

Bert's article was part of a manuscript he was writing for his grandchildren; he wanted to set down his memories of the gold rush before he died.[4] Ill as he was, he kept at it while he helped organize the 50th reunion. When the reunion was over and the manuscript done, he died.

Robert knew it was time to pack up and go home to France. To a reporter, he said that he was now living on borrowed time—there was no time now for anything but work. A strange remark for a man who had achieved fame and fortune long before and had often shirked work. But in fact, he spent the next 10 years working as hard as he ever had.

With Germaine and Iris, he left on the *Empress of Canada* from Montreal on September 4, 1948. It was 52 years since he had first disembarked in Montreal. He would not return to Canada again.

Service kept up a prodigious output of poetry from then on: *Songs of a Sun Lover* was published in 1949, *Rhymes of a Roughneck* in 1950, *Lyrics of a Lowbrow* in 1951, *Rhymes of a Rebel* in 1952, *Songs For My Supper* in 1953, *Carols of an Old Codger* in 1954, *Rhymes For My Rags* in 1956 and *Cosmic Carols* in 1957—amazing for a man in his seventies and then eighties. The press reported on his work habits: at eight o'clock he did his exercises for an hour, then had his coffee. He worked until noon, had lunch and a sleep, then a three-hour hike on the hills above his villa in Monte Carlo or along the coast at Dream Haven, and finally dinner. Sometimes he could not resist going over his work in the afternoon. From May until November he swam every day in the sea.

Although literary tastes changed with time, and his later poems were never as popular as his early ones, there are some gems among them, evidence of a wider understanding of the world, a sharpening of early ideas and a willingness of the old agnostic to deal with God and eternity. "God is not outside and apart from Nature, but her very heart ..."[5]

Iris married in 1952, at age 35, to James Davies, manager of Lloyd's Bank in Monte Carlo. Robert became a grandfather at the age of 78. Writing to Harold Tylor in 1953 he said, "I never thought I would wheel a

Robert Service with his wife
Germaine on right and daughter
Iris on left, pictured here in
Canada during the war years.
PHOTO: LIBRARY AND ARCHIVES CANADA/
PA—178390

kid in a pram but watch my smoke."[6] He was a devoted grandfather to little Annette and her sister, Armelle, born two years later.

His sense of fun was apparent in another letter: "After a romp with Nanette I feel all in. Besides she is a little devil, full of original sin. She steals, bites, throws things around, and is a strip teaser. Whatever will become of her."[7]

To Harold, he wrote that most of his old friends were now dead and that he missed them a great deal. After the death of Harold's wife, Clarisse, in 1954, Robert began urging Harold—six years younger than him—to travel. By this time, Robert himself no longer wanted to: his family, his home and his work were enough for him. The need for adventure, or to prove himself by courting danger, were passed—he was "dug in" at home.

Harold Tylor did travel, and Robert enjoyed his trips vicariously. In a 1956 letter, Robert mentioned how he envied Harold's having seen Hong Kong and how he wished he had seen Australia, New Zealand and China.

In 1954 Pierre Berton wrote an article for *Mayfair Magazine* that brought back a flood of Yukon memories for Robert; a letter to Harold noted how impressed he was by the material Berton had found. He reminisced about taking Laura Berton to dances in Dawson and said he was going to write a preface for her new book, *I Married the Klondike.*

Harold remained Robert's closest link with their Yukon past. In 1956 when he came to France for a visit, he planned a surprise . He walked along the Rue d'Italie in Monte Carlo toward Villa Aurora, bumped into Robert and gave him the Arctic Brotherhood salute.

"Who are you?" Robert asked. "Did I ever meet you?"

Harold said, "Several times, since we lived together for a year." This was followed by much pounding of backs and the exchange of old Yukon expressions like "you so-and-so old Sourdough" and "my old Tillicum." Then the two of them went up to Dream Haven and relived old times, walking by the sea or sitting in Robert's conservatory.

W.C. Sime—the inventor of the ice-worm cocktail—said in a letter to Harold from Keno Hill in the Yukon Territories in the early 1950s that he and Service had also exchanged letters. Sime was one of the gang in the Dawson bank bunkhouse, under D.A. Cameron. He recalled what a fine bunch they were, mentioning Gibbs, Jack Bell, Jimmy Rothwell, Cameron and Bun Maynard, then added that Bob Service wrote him once in a while from France. Since Service himself rarely used names in his autobiography, letters written by friends such as Harold Tylor and W.C. Sime help to put names and faces on some of the characters he described. Sime ended by remembering how they used to head for the dance halls, he with his bagpipes, and the gang all following.

Grace Kelly's wedding to Prince Rainier of Monaco in 1956 brought the world press to Monte Carlo and also focused new attention on Robert Service. The Kelly parents visited Robert and Germaine at the Villa Aurora, and reporters kept coming to Robert for interviews. In a *Daily Mail* article in April 1956 Robert was quoted as saying that the "rhyming racket" was not what it was, but the old ones still sold. To Harold he wrote of the busy time they had entertaining the Kelly family at Villa Aurora and dealing with reporters knocking on their door.

Often the letters to Harold talked of health problems and his need for exercise and rest. Germaine became concerned about his swimming in the cold sea, and the climb up from the beach afterward, so from about age 82 he began to swim less often. Taking periodic rests and avoiding social situations helped to keep his heartbeat under control.

Sometimes in these later letters to Harold a little crotchetiness crept in. He said he no longer bothered with people who didn't know his work, complained that people were not interested in his later, more "philosophical" poems and confessed if anyone mentioned McGrew, he felt like spitting at them. As he grew older and more aware of his mortality, he wanted his public too to deal with the more serious issues. He wrote:

> *Of panicked peoples, dark with dread,*
> *Of flame and famine near and far,*
> *Of revolution, pest and war ...* [8]

Two simple lines in *Rhymes of a Rebel* express his unshaken belief that all men have potential, that the few who succeed do not do so through merit, only luck:

> *God help the guys as good as I*
> *Who never—get a—break.* [9]

His public never deserted him. In 1955 he told Harold of a new volume coming out (*More Collected Verse,* published by Ernest Benn in London) of over a thousand pages.

Although he was considered the bard of the common man, the high and mighty—kings and queens, presidents and prime ministers—loved his verse too. About the time Service was threatening to spit if he heard the word "McGrew" again, Prince Philip was quoting from "The Shooting of Dan McGrew" and "The Cremation of Sam McGee" at an Institute of Mining and Metallurgy banquet at Grosvenor House in London. He was about to start a Canadian and Australian tour and told the group of prospectors, geologists and mining engineers that everything he knew of their work was based on what he had read of Service.

Ronald Reagan was a fan of Robert Service, had his verses committed to memory and used them instead of sheep when he couldn't sleep. He would start with Dan McGrew, then, if still awake, switch to Sam McGee, "... and that usually did it." Reagan wrote in his autobiography of a state dinner he'd attended, with the Queen Mother seated between him and Pierre Trudeau. Trudeau suggested Reagan recite Dan McGrew, and the Queen Mother, who professed to be a great fan of "the lady that's known as Lou," urged him on. Reagan, with help from the Queen Mother, recited the whole poem.

Queen Marie of Romania was one of the many Europeans who found pleasure in the poetry of Service during the dark years of the First World War. When her beloved Joe Boyle died in London in 1923, she had an old stone cross from Romania erected on his burial site, and the granite slab covering his grave was inscribed with two lines adapted from Service's "Law of the Yukon."

Man with the heart of a Viking
And the simple faith of a child.

Les McLaughlin, writing in the *Whitehorse Star,* told a vivid story about U.S. Senator John McCain, who could quote the entire 701 words of "The Cremation of Sam McGee." In 1968 he was a prisoner-of-war in North Vietnam's "Hanoi Hilton" prison camp. In a neighboring cell a man he could not see—and never met—tapped out "Sam McGee" in Morse code through the cement wall of their cells. McCain had no way to write down the poem, but its words brought color and drama to the solitude of his cell and imprinted themselves on his mind.

By the 1950s Robert could no longer attend the international sourdough reunions. In 1955 he wrote that he would not cross the sea again. Instead, he sent a poem that expressed the peace he found in later life.

A child-wise calm will come to you
The pain and passion overpast.
Ah, you will see my say is true
The best of living is the last.[10]

In May 1958, however, the calm of old age was briefly interrupted by an event that took an old man back to his remarkable youth. Pierre Berton arrived in Monte Carlo with a Canadian Broadcasting Corporation crew to make a film about Robert Service for the series *Close-Up.* Berton was not just any reporter; he was the lad who had grown up in Dawson City on 8th Avenue, across the street from the cabin where Robert had lived.

Service had prepared for his special moment on stage. To Berton's surprise, the elderly poet handed him a script, told him that he, Service,

When Pierre Berton interviewed Robert in Monaco in 1958, Robert told him their talk about Dawson took "... ten years off my life; I've enjoyed every minute of it."
PHOTO: COURTESY OF THE BERTON FAMILY

was "the big shot" in this interview, that since this was likely to be his last appearance before the public, he wanted it to be a good one. Berton and crew were sent away to learn their lines and come back the next day.

In a *Toronto Daily Star* column, Berton described the visit. His first impression was of "a small, wiry man with a shock of white hair and the sharp features of a Scots dominie." When they returned the second day, Service wanted to get a recitation of "McGrew" out of the way first, in case he wasn't up for it the next day. "And so, in a thick miner's dialect, not untinged with his native Scots lilt, he recited once again the old, old tale of the man from the creeks who spins out his song of woe on a honky-tonk piano in the Malamute saloon."

Berton said that Service was genuinely sad when the filming was over. For him, it was Hollywood again, and his spirit was back in the Klondike. "Is it over? Is it really over? Well! I'm sorry. I should have liked to go on forever. You know, this has taken 10 years off my life; I've loved every minute of it."[11]

Berton compared him to an old telegraph operator he and his parents had met on the Yukon river as they poled and drifted down it in 1926. The old man kept running after them, pleading with them to stop and stay over with him. Service, in his doorway with the wind blowing his hair, dramatically brought to mind that lonely man, who could have been a character from *Songs of a Sourdough*.

In an August 1958 letter to Harold, Robert said that Berton put him on the spot by asking if he believed in the afterlife, and expressed the opinion that no one did these days. On a more hopeful note, he said in *Carols of an Old Codger*:

> *Aye, though a godless way I go*
> *And sceptic is my trend*
> *A faith in something I don't know*
> *Might save me in the end.*[12]

Robert spent most of the summer of 1958 at Lancieux, enjoying Dream Haven, with family visits, walks on the beach, his books and his pen. In a 1956 interview for the *Daily Telegraph* he had remarked that he would probably die with his pen in hand while trying to describe death. In the last year of his life his pen was certainly often in his hand. As Alaska moved closer to statehood that summer, Acting Governor Waino Hendrickson requested an ode from Service for the inauguration. The poem, "Sourdough Star," appeared in *Newsweek* on July 14, 1958.

In the 1960s Alaska would acclaim Service their Poet Laureate, and Canadians newspapers would decry this "act of piracy" and defend the Canadian legacy of their favorite poet. The *Colonist* in Victoria ran a piece entitled "Conspiracy Afoot to Steal Service."[13]

As sourdoughs continued to meet on the American west coast each year, Service's lyric encouragement and the laughter his poems engendered meant a lot to Yukoners walking the trail of old age. The Yukon experience was—and still is—one of youth. It revels in those long days of June light and brags about surviving the winter. It is full of hope and joy, adrenalin, immortality and impossible dreams. When it is over, it's what an old man remembers.

The poem Service sent for the 1956 reunion was entitled "Old Sourdough"; the one written for 1957 was "Mush On." For the 1958 August celebration in Vancouver, he sent a message to rally the aging troopers: "I wish I could hail the old gang with a cheer, but the best I can do is to wish them well for another year. So bless us all and once again with guts and grit MUSH ON!" The accompanying poem, "Sourdough's Lament," began with this verse:

When I was a Klondike high-roller
I titled my poke with the best
And though the climate might be polar,
I'd plenty of hair on my chest.
Now while I've no trace of rheumatic,
And maybe I shouldn't complain,
I'm worried because I just ain't what I was,
And I wish I was 80 again.[14]

Toward the end of his life Service admitted to three ambitions: to write 1,000 poems, make a million dollars and live to be 100. It was generally reported that he achieved the thousandth poem (some of his later verses were published after his death). His poetry made him richer than he ever hoped or wanted to be. Salesman Russell Bond, writing in 1958, quoted a letter from Service that said *Songs of a Sourdough* alone had sold more than a million copies and that "if I had never written another line the *Sourdough* would have kept me in comfort for the rest of my life …"[15] When he died later that year, *Life* magazine estimated that the public had bought 2 million copies of Service's work, while *Time* magazine reported that 3 million copies of his poems had been sold and 20,000 copies per year were still being sold. Service was serious about the third ambition; this was what the health book, the fitness regime and the special diet were all about. Learning how to live, both physically and emotionally, had been a year-by-year trial-and-error process for Service. In his first 30 years, as he confessed, there were a lot of errors, but he had trusted his guardian angel and believed that what he did was what he had to do. By his 40s he was beginning to get it right, and by the time he was 80 he thought he had the hang of it. His mind was humming along nicely, letting him compose a poem a day as he aimed for the 1,000 mark. When Pierre Berton interviewed him in May

1958, living was still a radiant experience for him; he could cheerfully have gone on to 100.

It was not to be. It would be Germaine, who lived quietly and unobtrusively with him, who would go on to the age of 102. Service would have seen the irony in this, and no doubt put it in a poem.

His last public poem was the one he sent to the 1958 Yukon reunion— a fitting finale to his life. "The Yukon made me," he often said, and he gave the Yukon his last poetic words.

Robert Service died on September 11, 1958. It was widely reported that he had passed away after an attack of influenza, but Germaine, in a letter afterward to Robert's brother Peter, said there had been no illness except the state of his heart. He was his usual cheerful self when he had lunch with her that day, then went off for his daily rest. Germaine was talking to their maid, Henriette Pezeron, in the room below Robert's when his window opened and he called out to Henriette for help. Germaine and Henriette found him slumped in a chair and got a doctor within 10 minutes, but it was too late. His heart, which had been a chancy thing since 1924, had finally given out. He was 84.

When he was gone, critics renewed in literary journals, magazines and newspapers the argument as to whether he was a poet of merit or merely a versifier. Bruce Meyer, in volume 7 of *Profiles in Canadian Literature* (1991), said this debate "suggests a narrowness on the part of critics ... Without a recognition and reappraisal of Service's place within the Canadian literary context, two major events in the country's culture, the Klondike and the First World War, are deprived of an important chronicler and spokesperson."[16]

In a short newspaper article, Service himself had attempted to answer the question of verse *v.* poetry, saying he had always disavowed any claim to be a "poet" in the conventional sense in which the term was then understood.

> Then what is pure poetry? I should call it vision—imaginative voltage—evocation. It is the magic formula that gives you a thrill of revealment, the word or phrases or lines that give you a flash of insight, the picture projected on the mind whose imprint stays fresh forever. It is an illumination that lights up the whole page, the revealing phrase that tells you something you knew and did not know you knew.

For many readers, that definition of poetry immediately calls to mind some of his own lines. But he ends by saying he is "content to be a humble verse writer in the company of Bret Harte and Eugene Field, bless their dear hearts!"[17]

Only once in his surviving writings—in a 1958 letter to Stanley—did he reveal that he might have liked some recognition in literary circles. He mentioned that *Life Magazine* was devoting a spread to him in July, so it seemed he was finally being "discovered." But why, he asked, did literary critics in Canada continue to ignore him?

Since his death, biographers have searched for the real Robert Service. Carl Klinck, in 1976, attempted to find Service the man by combining evidence from his autobiography with "that which is subjective or subliminal in his novels, ballads, and songs." But the review of that book in the *Globe and Mail* had the headline "The Real Robert Service Remains Elusive as Ever."

G. Wallace Lockhart, while writing *On The Trail of Robert Service* (1991), often found that Service had covered his tracks. James Mackay, who did a prodigious amount of research for *Vagabond of Verse* (1995), called Service's two-volume autobiography "a masterpiece of obfuscation" and described Service himself as "one of the literary enigmas of our time." Robert's old friend Hiram Cody—a man not usually at a loss for words—tried twice to write articles about Service as he had known him, but both times gave up. Pierre Berton began his chapter on Service in *Prisoners of the North* (2005): "Robert Service is a hard man to define." When Service handed him a script to memorize for their 1958 interview, Berton must have realized that here was a man who would tell a reporter only what he wanted him to know. His brother Stanley described him as "brazenly unconcerned with facts. He was strictly fiction and if we pointed out to him that this or that of his writing was not fact, he would probably look at us pityingly as though to say, 'Poor thing—so what?'"

Service never told anyone the whole truth. His need to cover up probably stemmed at first from insecurity; in a 1951 letter to Stanley he speaks of an inferiority complex, caused by his early failures, that would stay with him all his life. But as the years went by he came to enjoy more and more the game he played with his public. It tickled his humor that he was thought to be dead while he was actually soaking up sun on the Riviera, as far away from the Yukon cold as one could get. It amused him to write an autobiography by selectively choosing or actually improvising facts, confusing any would-be biographers by the absence of dates, the few actual names, the omission of the young woman to whom he dedicated *Songs of a Sourdough*, the siblings he pretended not to remember, the father whose drinking problem he chose to whitewash, and a wife and daughter he never mentioned by name—though in their case this must largely have been due to an understandable wish to protect the privacy of his cherished family.

The controlled reticence also hid kindness and generosity. Robert's financial support of family members, noted earlier, goes unmentioned in the autobiographies. An Ottawa woman, Hetra Bertuleit, spoke to the *Ottawa Citizen* (October 19, 1974) about the wonderful help she had from the Service family in Monte Carlo when her first employer died and she had no place to stay. She became part of the Service staff in the early 1950s and had a sense of being part of the family. Robert Service never forgot how it felt to be down and out.

Robert's introversion often puzzled his more outgoing brother; Stanley described him as having a "self-confessed neurosis. He had to live with it or overcome it, and I do not think he ever licked it. To the last he was still an introvert and antisocial. His medium of expression was his pen. Anytime he stayed at my home he requested us not to have friends in, and friends he knew in Ottawa he made no effort to see."[18]

The relationship between Robert and Stanley is interesting. Growing up on separate continents, 17 years apart in age so that Stanley was still an infant when Robert left home, they had little chance to get to know each other apart from the winter that Robert spent with the family on their Alberta farm. Yet after that they kept in touch and provided support for one another. They were reverse images of each other: Robert the famous poet who had wanted to become a doctor when he enrolled at McGill, Stanley the respected doctor who wrote poetry as a hobby (several of his poems appeared in the *Ottawa Journal*) and tried to publish a western novel and a book about his family's experiences in Scotland and Canada. His wife, Helen, who gave his notes to the National Archives, said he left his attempted writing career too late. His unpublished memoir reveals that Stanley too had a way with words; it also adds an important new dimension to his brother's life story. Helen told the *Ottawa Journal* that Robert always seemed proud of Stanley's accomplishments; and Stanley's fond, if sometimes exasperated, admiration for Robert is evident in his memoir, as

On a stone bench on the banks of the Koksilah River, a memorial plaque to Robert Service quotes these lines from "Heart o' the North":

I who have been life's rover
This is all I would ask my friend
A little space on a stony hill ...
Eternity passing over.

PHOTO: GORD MALLORY

he summed up Robert's life by saying: "If any man enjoyed fame, fortune and freedom while he was still alive more than our Willie, he would be a rare creature."[19]

In the first part of his life Robert was passionate, distraught, sometimes desperate, often enthusiastic, even ecstatic, moving quickly from delight to the depth of despair. In the second part he became calm, confident, even debonair. His early feelings for Constance MacLean were part of the intensity of his youth, and his early poems ring with the passion of youth. It was Connie MacLean who, in 1903, told him to make a success of his life first, then come back to her. In 1908 he took her advice to the limit, leaving her for the spell of the North, for Dawson and all the promise it held in his mind. He was going back to write *The Trail of '98* because he felt chosen to "arise and sing" and write the definitive novel of the Klondike gold rush, to take the part only he could play on the dramatic stage of the Yukon All the years of frustration, of learning to write, of studying Burns and Kipling and Stevenson, Thoreau and Borrow, had led to this place.

Although written only a few years later, *Rhymes of a Red Cross Man* (1916) was produced by an older, wiser man performing in a different space; here the romantic heroism of the Yukon is tempered by an awful awareness of humanity's capacity for evil. There is a great deal of compassion, personal knowledge of grief and, in spite of wry soldier humor and even laughter, a sense of deep suffering. Like *Songs of a Sourdough*, this was a book exactly right for its time and place.

Robert's two volumes of autobiography define the two parts of his life. *Ploughman of the Moon* begins with his childhood in Scotland and ends when he leaves Dawson in 1912. *Harper of Heaven* begins with the horror of the Balkan War and ends with the radiant contentment of his family life in France. His life with Germaine, in contrast to the emotional turmoil of his early years, was like sailing on calm waters, and it defined the last 45 years of his life. There is no dedication in volume one, but the second volume is dedicated:

To my Wife and Daughter
Who have helped me to a
Heap of Happiness

Robert's granddaughter recalls that her grandfather deeply loved her grandmother for 45 years and that they lived in perfect harmony with one another.[20] Germaine's tribute to Robert is contained in a letter to Stanley in 1958 after Robert's death: "... it is for his great kindness more than his work that I admired him most."[21]

In the article he wrote for *Maclean's* magazine in 1941, Service said that in his younger years he seemed out of touch with the world and reality; his need then was to be alone and to be traveling. These, he remembered, were not happy years. But at some point he discovered that life could be fun. The light he kept glimpsing in the bleak, lonely, hungry years burst forth in the sunshine of success. The shadows would always be there, and he still felt compelled to probe the darkness—whether of war, poverty or depravity—so that he could understand it and write about it. But his enormous success let him live his life mainly in the light.

To the end, Service remained the trickster, using words to hide behind, to laugh or sometimes cry, but never to reveal himself. Words were his lifelong passion, his joy and his love. He could make them dance, shiver with cold or choke with loneliness and despair. He set his words on the stage of many parts of the world—Tahiti, Monte Carlo, Paris, the fields of war—but they danced their best on the wide white stage of the Canadian North.

Family of Robert Service Sr. and Emily Parker

A note in the front of the family Bible, written by Robert Service Sr. at 709 Dufferin Terrace, Toronto, says that his private letters, family treasures and certificates of birth of his children were lost by the Clyde Shipping Co. when the family immigrated to Canada, so "registration of said births in my own handwriting is to be found on page."

Robert & Sarah Emily Service: Married at Churchtown, Parish Church, North Meols, Lancashire, 21st October 1872.

Robert William: 16th January 1874; Preston, Lancashire, England

John Alexander: 22nd January 1875; Preston

Thomas Henry (Harry): 6th January 1877; Preston

Joseph Whitehead: 16th February 1879; Lansdowne Cres., Glasgow

Peter Halstead Whitehead: 12th March 1881; Glasgow

Agnes Anne: 2nd April 1883; 8 Roclea Terrace, Hillhead, Glasgow

Jane Emily Beatrice: 16th July 1885; Glasgow

Janet Isobel: 22nd November 1888; Glasgow

Frederick Stanley: 20th April 1891; Glasgow

Albert Niven Parker: 2nd October 1893: Glasgow

Books by Robert Service (first publication only)

Songs of a Sourdough. Toronto: William Briggs, 1907.

The Spell of the Yukon and Other Verses. New York: Barse and Hopkins, 1907 and Philadelphia, E. Stern & Company, 1907.

Ballads of a Cheechako. Toronto: William Briggs, 1909.

The Trail of '98: A Northland Romance. Toronto: William Briggs, 1910.

Rhymes of a Rolling Stone. Toronto: William Briggs, 1912.

The Pretender: A Story of the Latin Quarter. New York: Dodd Mead, 1914.

Rhymes of a Red Cross Man. Toronto: William Briggs, 1916.

Ballads of a Bohemian. New York and Toronto: Barse and Hopkins, 1921.

The Poisoned Paradise: A Romance of Monte Carlo. New York: Dodd Mead, 1922.

The Roughneck: A Tale of Tahiti. New York: Barse and Hopkins, 1923.

The Master of the Microbe: A Fantastic Romance. New York: Barse and Hopkins, 1926.

The House of Fear: A Novel. New York: Dodd Mead, 1927.

Why Not Grow Young? Or, Living for Longevity. New York: Barse and Hopkins, 1928.

The Collected Verse of Robert Service. London: Ernest Benn, 1930.

The Complete Poems of Robert Service. New York: Dodd Mead, 1933.

Twenty Bath-Tub Ballads. London: Francis, Day and Hunter, 1939.

Bar-Room Ballads: A Book of Verse. Toronto: R. Saunders, 1940.

Ploughman of the Moon: An Adventure into Memory. New York: Dodd Mead, 1945.

Harper of Heaven: A Record of Radiant Living. New York: Dodd Mead, 1948.

Songs of a Sun-Lover: A Book of Light Verse. New York: Dodd Mead, 1949.

Rhymes of a Roughneck: A Book of Verse. New York: Dodd Mead, 1950.

Lyrics of a Lowbrow: A Book of Verse. New York: Dodd Mead, 1951.

Rhymes of a Rebel: A Book of Verse. New York: Dodd Mead, 1952.

Songs For My Supper. New York: Dodd Mead, 1953.

Carols of an Old Codger. New York: Dodd Mead, 1954.

More Collected Verse. New York: Dodd Mead, 1955.

Rhymes For My Rags. New York: Dodd Mead, 1956.

Cosmic Carols. London: Ernest Benn, 1957.

Songs of the High North. London: Ernest Benn, 1958.

Later Collected Verse. New York: Dodd Mead, 1965.

The Best of Robert Service. London: Ernest Benn, 1978.

Endnotes

Part 1

Robert Service, *Ploughman of the Moon: An Adventure into Memory* (New York: Dodd, Mead, 1945), 142.

Chapter 1

1. Robert Service, *Ploughman of the Moon: An Adventure into Memory* (New York: Dodd, Mead, 1945), 142.
2. Ibid., 145.
3. Stanley Service, *Autobiography*, 13, Stanley Service papers (Ottawa: National Archives of Canada).
4. Robert Service, *Ploughman*, 158.

Chapter 2

1. Robert Service, *Ploughman*, 191.
2. Ibid., 198.
3. Ibid., 215.
4. Ibid., 225.
5. Ibid., 248.
6. Ibid., 249.
7. Ibid., 260.

Chapter 3

1. Robert Service, *Ploughman*, 267–69.
2. Aileen Campbell, "Hundred Years of Service," *Vancouver Daily Province* (May 4, 1974), quoting Norman Corfield.
3. Reby MacDonald, "Robert W. Service's Pre-Klondike Days at Koksilah," *Daily Colonist* (1939).
4. Vivian Purney, "Beneath Their Boughs," *Daily Colonist* (June 12, 1969); article includes poem reprinted from the *Duncan Enterprise* (December 5, 1903).
5. Charles Harrison Gibbons, "When Robert Service, Bard of Yukon, was Verse-Writing Store Clerk at Cowichan," unidentified newspaper clipping, Yukon Archives.
6. *Daily Colonist* (1902).
7. Stanley Service, *Autobiography*, 3 Stanley Service papers.
8. "Memories of Robert Service," *Cowichan Leader*, (January 24, 1946).
9. *Daily Colonist* (June 1902).
10. John Spears, "Memories of Service's Days at Cowichan Bay," *Cowichan Leader* (December 17, 1931).
11. Elizabeth Norcross, February 25, 1959. Notes in Cowichan Valley Archives.
12. Leslie Drew, "Islanders Recall Service," *Daily Colonist* (July 11, 1976).

Chapter 4

1. Robert Service, letter to "Miss McLean c/o Dr. Perry, Duncans Station, E&N Rail," December 9, 1902, Beatrice Corbett papers (Kingston, ON: Queen's University Archives).
2. McGill University Calendar, 1903–04. "Service, Robert William" is listed under "Partial Students" (part-time students).
3. Robert Service, letter to Constance MacLean, September 15, 1903 (Beatrice Corbett papers).
4. Ibid., September 29, 1903.
5. Robert Service, *Ploughman*, 292.
6. Robert Service, letter to Constance MacLean, Sunday Evening, [October] 1903 (Beatrice Corbett papers).
7. Robert Service, *Ploughman*, 296.

Chapter 5

1. S.B. Steele, *Forty Years in Canada* (New York: Dodd, Mead, 1915), 306.
2. Victor Ross, *A History of the Canadian Bank of Commerce*, vol. 2 (Toronto: Oxford University Press, 1922), 145.
3. Ibid., 150.
4. Ibid., 137–51.

Part 2

Robert Service, "The Cremation of Sam McGee," in *The Spell of the Yukon* (New York: Barse and Hopkins, 1907).

Chapter 6

1. Robert Service, *Ploughman*, 315.
2. Ibid., 314.
3. Ibid., 312.
4. "Lionel Cadogan Cowper died yesterday ... " *Weekly Star* (October 12, 1906).
5. Robert Service, *Ploughman*, 313–14.

Chapter 7

1. "Memories of Capt. T.V. Fleming, M.C.," (Whitehorse: Yukon Archives).
2. Robert Service, *Ploughman*, 323.
3. Ibid., 324.
4. Ibid., 325.
5. Dr. Leonard Sugden, "Chief John House—Siwash Dipsomaniac," in "A Yukon Episode," from *Reminiscences of a Surgeon of Fortune*, 7 (unpublished manuscript, courtesy of Dorothy Sugden).
6. Stanley Service, *Autobiography*, 43 (Stanley Service papers).
7. R.B. Bond, "I Sold Service to the Public," *Globe* (June 28, 1958), 7–8.
8. Robert Service, *Ploughman*, 326.
9. All poetry extracts from Robert Service, *The Spell of the Yukon* (New York: Barse and Hopkins, 1907).
10. Sam McGee, letter to Leonard L. Bass of Phillips H. Lord, Inc., New York, February 3, 1938.

11. *Weekly Star* (June 29, 1906).

12. Interview with Sam McGee in the Gowman Hotel, Seattle, *Seattle Daily Times,* n.d.

Chapter 8

1. Robert Service, *Ploughman*, 337.
2. Ibid., 338.
3. Robert Service, letters to Connie MacLean, March 25, 26 and April 3, 1908.
4. Carl F. Klinck, *Robert Service* (1976); G.W. Lockhart, *On the Trail of Robert Service* (1991); and James Mackay, *Vagabond of Verse* (1995); Mackay added a note about Connie in the second edition of his book (1996), published after the CBC interview.
5. Beatrice Corbett, interview with author, 2004.
6. Robert Service, "Quatrains," in *The Spell of the Yukon*, 72.
7. *Weekly Star* (April 3, 1908). In his autobiography, however, there is no mention of any contact regarding his writing while in Vancouver. "Contrary to my expectation I found my book was little known, and I was a small frog in a big puddle." (*Ploughman*, 337.)
8. Robert Service, *Ploughman*, 333.

Chapter 9

1. Robert Service, *Ploughman*, 342.
2. Victor Ross, *A History of the Canadian Bank of Commerce*, vol. 2, 158.
3. Tappan Adney, *The Klondike Stampede* (New York and London: Harper, 1900), 417.
4. "Poke Bags & Gold," *Current Account* 4/8 (December 1954), 5 (reprinted from the *Klondike Nugget*).
5. Ibid., 5.
6. Victor Ross, *A History of the Canadian Bank of Commerce*, vol. 2, 165.
7. Ibid., 171.
8. Robert Service, *Ploughman*, 347.
9. Ibid., 353.
10. Laura Beatrice Berton, *I Married the Klondike* (Toronto: McClelland and Stewart, 1972), 68–69.
11. Martha Black, *My Ninety Years: Martha Black*, edited and updated by Flo Whyard (Anchorage: Alaska Northwest Books, 1976), 87 (first published as *My Seventy Years*, London: Thomas Nelson, 1938).
12. Laura Berton, *I Married the Klondike*, 69–70.
13. Clayton Betts fonds #9412, Yukon Archives. An explanatory note attached to this photograph in the Yukon Archives says "The original 'Solomon boots' fashioned from a pair of grizzly feet by Solomon Albert, after losing his own toes to frostbite."
14. Laura Berton, *I Married the Klondike*, 69–70.

Chapter 10

1. R.J. Latshaw, "Robert Service, As I Knew Him," *Alaska Magazine* (May 1971), 20, 56–57.
2. Robert Service, *Ploughman*, 88.
3. Ibid., 365.
4. William B. Haskell, *Two Years in the Klondike and Alaskan Gold-fields, 1896–1898* (Hartford, CT: Hartford, 1898), 460, 466.

5. Adney, *The Klondike Stampede*, 83.
6. Robert Service, *The Trail of '98: A Northland Romance* (New York: Dodd, Mead, 1910), 87–88.

Chapter 11

1. Stanley Service papers, 3.
2. Ibid, 15.
3. Letter from Emily Service to John Alexander Service, "Dear Alick," January 1897 (Stanley Service papers).
4. Stanley Service, *Autobiography*, 36–37.
5. Service family Bible (Ottawa: National Archives); see Appendix 1.
6. Marguerite Service, interview with the author, June 2005.
7. Stanley Service, *Autobiography*, 57 (Stanley Service papers).
8. Ibid., 4.
9. Ibid., 59.
10. Ibid., 66.

Chapter 12

1. Robert Service, *Harper of Heaven*, 71.
2. Robert Service, *Ploughman*, 408.
3. George. M. Douglas, *Lands Forlorn* (New York: Knickerbocker Press, 1914), 13.
4. Ibid., 18.
5. Robert Service, *Ploughman*, 41.
6. Ibid., 412.
7. George Douglas, *Lands Forlorn*, 23–24.
8. "In From a Long Journey," *Dawson Daily News* (August 12, 1911).
9. Ibid.
10. George Douglas, *Lands Forlorn*, 45–46.
11. Robert Service, *Ploughman*, 425.
12. Ibid., 417.

Chapter 13

1. Robert Service, *Ploughman*, 440.
2. Ibid., 450.
3. Ibid., 452.
4. Richard Finnie, "Ice Worm," *Maclean's* (November 1, 1945).

Chapter 14

1. "In From a Long Journey," *Dawson Daily News* (August 12, 1911).
2. "Confessions of Mackenzie Slayer," *Dawson Daily News* (August 14, 1911).
3. Robert Service, *Ploughman*, 457.
4. Robert Service, "I'm Scared of It All," in *Rhymes of a Rolling Stone* (New York: Dodd, Mead, 1912), 160.
5. Robert Service, *Ploughman*, 466–67.
6. Robert Service, "Good-bye Little Cabin," in *Rhymes of a Rolling Stone*, 191.

Part 3

Robert Service, *Harper of Heaven*, 71.

Chapter 15

1. "R.W. Service's New Verses Are Real 'Sourdough Stuff,'" *Toronto Star Weekly* (November 9, 1912), 1.
2. Robert Service, *Ploughman*, 468.
3. Robert Service, *Harper of Heaven*, 54.

Chapter 16

1. Martha Black, *My Ninety Years*, 108.
2. "R.W. Service Nearly Faced a French Firing Squad," *Toronto Star Weekly* (December 26, 1914), 13.
3. Robert Service, *Harper of Heaven*, 80.
4. Robert Service, "The Valley of a Thousand Dead" ("Records of a Red Cross Man"), *Toronto Daily Star* (June 8, 1916).
5. Robert Service, "'The Red Harvest of the Trenches" ("Records of a Red Cross Man"), *Toronto Daily Star*, (December 18, 1915).
6. Robert Service, "Service Visits the Front Trenches Where Grim Men Watch and Wait" ("Records of a Red Cross Man"), *Toronto Daily Star* (January 15, 1916).
7. Robert Service, *Harper of Heaven*, 80.
8. Ibid., 80.
9. Stanley Service, *Autobiography*, 85 (Stanley Service papers).
10. Robert Service, Gillis family collection (folder 3), Yukon Archives.
11. Robert Service, "Canadians Kept on Huns' Heels," unidentified and undated newspaper clipping, Kingston: Queen's University Archives.
12. Beatrice Corbett, interview with author (March 2004).
13. Robert Service, "Canadians Kept on Huns' Heels."
14. Robert Service, "Service Rates Himself as Verse Writer," unidentified clipping, probably from a Chicago newspaper from the second half of the 1940s, author's collection.

Chapter 17

1. Robert Service, *Harper of Heaven*, 107.
2. Robert Service letter to Stanley Service, February 22, 1934, mentions an allowance he had been paying their mother for a number of years (Stanley Service papers).
3. Robert Service, *Harper of Heaven*, 110.

Chapter 18

1. Robert Service, "The Ballad of Salvation Bill," in *Bar-Room Ballads* (Toronto: R. Saunders, 1940).
2. Robert Service, "The Ballad of the Leather Medal," in *Bar-Room Ballads*.
3. Robert Service, *Harper of Heaven*, 397.

Chapter 19

1. Robert Service, letter to Harold Tylor, August 23, 1940 (Peterborough, Ontario: Trent University Archives).

2. "History of the Vancouver Yukoners' Association" (Victoria: British Columbia Museum, 1974), 1.
3. Russ Peters, "The Real Story of Sam McGee," *Rural Times* (July 24, 1995).
4. Jim Butler, "McGee's Daughter Refreshes Old Memories," *Whitehorse Star* (July 29, 1983) quoting Ethel Gramms.

Chapter 20

1. Robert Service, *Harper of Heaven*, 407–8.
2. Robert Service, *Harper of Heaven*, 423.

Chapter 21

1. Alaska Airlines brochure, "a souvenir of your flight on the Golden Nugget Jet featuring Gay Nineties-Gold Rush décor," Peter Service collection (Ottawa: National Archives of Canada).
2. "A Klondike Sourdough who ..." *Vancouver Daily Province* (August 25, 1948).
3. Bert Parker, "Sourdoughs of '98 Trek to Vancouver," *Vancouver Daily Province* (July 1948).
4. This was published posthumously as "Kid in the Klondike," *Maclean's Magazine*, November 1953. In 1977 it was reprinted privately for Helen Parker on the occasion of her 90th birthday.
5. Robert Service, "Rosy-Kins," in *Songs of a Sun-Lover: A Book of Light Verse* (New York: Dodd, Mead, 1949), 145.
6. Robert Service, letter to Harold Tylor, November 15, 1953 (Trent University Archives).
7. Robert Service, letter to Harold Tylor, September 30, 1954 (Trent University Archives).
8. Robert Service, "Tranquillity," in *Songs of a Sun-Lover*, 52–53.
9. Robert Service, "Opportunity," in *Rhymes of a Rebel: A Book of Verse* (New York: Dodd, Mead, 1952), 25.
10. Robert Service, letter and poem to the Vancouver Yukoners Association, February 17, 1955 (Victoria: British Columbia Archives).
11. Pierre Berton, "Robert Service Reads McGrew for Close-up," *Toronto Daily Star* (July 5, 1958).
12. Robert Service, "Agnostic," in *Carols of an Old Codger* (New York: Dodd, Mead, 1954); reprinted in *Later Collected Verse* (New York: Dodd, Mead, 1960), 137.
13. "Conspiracy Afoot to Steal Service," *Daily Colonist* (June 14, 1967), 2.
14. Robert Service, letter and poem to the Vancouver Yukoners Association, February 15, 1958.
15. R.B. Bond, "I Sold Service to the Public," 7.
16. Bruce Meyer, "Robert Service," in *Profiles in Canadian Literature*, vol. 7, edited by Jeffrey M. Heath (Toronto: Dundurn Press, 1991), 52.
17. Robert Service, "Service Rates Himself as Verse Writer."
18. Stanley Service, *Autobiography*, 68 (Stanley Service papers).
19. Ibid.
20. Anne Longepe, letter to author, March 21, 2005.
21. Germaine Service, letter to Stanley Service, 1958 (Stanley Service papers).

Bibliography and Sources

Newspapers and Periodicals

Alaska Magazine

Cowichan Leader

Daily Colonist (Victoria)

Dawson Daily News

Duncan Enterprise

Glasgow Weekly Herald

Globe Magazine

Maclean's Magazine

Rural Times (Calgary)

Seattle Times

Times Colonist (Victoria)

Toronto Daily Star

Toronto Star Weekly

Vancouver Daily Province

Vancouver Sun

Weekly Star, Daily Star (Whitehorse)

Archival and Family Sources

Beatrice Corbett papers (Kingston, ON: Queen's University Archives)

Memories of Captain T.V. Fleming (Whitehorse: Yukon Archives)

Sam McGee papers (private collection, courtesy of Beverly Gramms)

McGill University (Montreal)

Peter Service collection (Ottawa: National Archives)

Stanley Service papers (Ottawa: National Archives)

Leonard Sugden papers (private collection, courtesy of Dorothy Sugden)

Harold Tylor papers (Peterborough, ON: Trent University)

Books

Adney, Tappan. *The Klondike Stampede*. New York and London: Harper, 1900. Reprinted as *The Klondike Stampede of 1897–98*. Fairfield, WA: Galleon Press, 1968.

Bennett, Gordon. *Yukon Transportation: A History* (Canadian Historic Sites 19). Ottawa: National Historic Parks and Sites Branch, Parks Canada, Indian and Northern Affairs, 1978.

Berton, Laura Beatrice. *I Married the Klondike*. Toronto: McClelland and Stewart, and Boston: Little, Brown, 1954.

Berton, Pierre. *The Klondike Fever: The Life and Death of the Last Great Gold Rush*. Toronto: McClelland and Stewart, and New York: Alfred A. Knopf, 1958. Revised edition, as *Klondike: The Last Great Gold Rush, 1896–1899*. Toronto: McClelland and Stewart, 1972; reprinted, Toronto: Anchor Canada, 2001.

Black, Martha Louise. *My Seventy Years*, by Mrs. George Black ... as told to Elizabeth Bailey Price. London and Toronto: Thomas Nelson, 1938. Revised edition, as *My Ninety Years* (ed. Flo Whyard). Anchorage: Alaska Northwest, 1976. Third edition, as *Martha Black: Her Story from the Dawson Gold Fields to the Halls of Parliament* (ed. Flo Whyard). Anchorage: Alaska Northwest, 1998.

Cody, H.A. *An Apostle of the North: Memoirs of the Right Reverend William Carpenter Bompas*. Toronto: Musson, and New York: Dutton, 1908.

Douglas, George M. *Lands Forlorn: A Story of an Expedition to Hearne's Coppermine River*. New York: G.P. Putnam, 1914.

Fenton, Charles A. *The Apprenticeship of Ernest Hemingway: The Early Years*. New York: Farrar, Straus and Young, and London: Vision Press and Peter Owen, 1954. Reprinted, New York: Octagon Books, 1975.

Finnie, Richard. *Canada Moves North*. New York: Macmillan, 1942.

Haskell, William B. *Two Years in the Klondike and Alaskan Gold-fields*. Hartford, CT: Hartford, 1898. Reprinted as *Two Years in the Klondike and Alaskan Gold-fields, 1896–1898: A Thrilling Narrative of Life in the Gold Mines and Camps*. Fairbanks: University of Alaska Press, 1998.

Heath, Jeffrey M. (ed.). *Profiles in Canadian Literature*, vol. 7. Toronto: Dundurn Press, 1991 (chapter on Robert Service by Bruce Meyer).

Hodgins, Bruce W. and Gwyneth Hoyle. *Canoeing North Into the Unknown: A Record of River Travel, 1874 to 1974*. Toronto: Natural Heritage/Natural History, 1994.

James, Henry. *The American Volunteer Motor-Ambulance Corps in France*. London: Macmillan, 1914.

Jennings, John. *Bark Canoes: The Art and Obsession of Tappan Adney*. Richmond Hill, ON: Firefly, 2004.

Jones, Ted. *All the Days of His Life: A Biography of Archdeacon H.A. Cody*. Saint John: New Brunswick Museum, 1981.

Klinck, Carl F. *Robert Service: A Biography*. Toronto: McGraw-Hill Ryerson, and New York: Dodd, Mead, 1976.

Lockhart, G.W. *On the Trail of Robert Service*. Edinburgh: Luath Press, 1991.

Lundberg, Murray. *Fractured Veins & Broken Dreams: Montana Mountain and the Windy Arm Stampede.* Whitehorse: Pathfinder, 1996.

Mackay, James. *Vagabond of Verse: Robert Service, A Biography.* Edinburgh: Mainstream, 1995; second edition, 1996.

Mallory, Enid. *Coppermine: The Far North of George M. Douglas.* Peterborough, ON: Broadview Press, 1989.

McKillop, A.B. *The Spinster and The Prophet.* Toronto: Macfarlane, Walter and Ross, 2000.

Morrison, David R. *The Politics of the Yukon Territory, 1898–1909.* Toronto: University of Toronto Press, 1968.

Morrison, William R. *True North: The Yukon and Northwest Territories.* Toronto: Oxford University Press, 1998.

Ogilvie, William. *Early Days on the Yukon and the Story of its Gold Finds.* New York: John Lane, 1913.

Olive, William Henry Trewolla (ed. Allan Safarik). *The Olive Diary: The Gripping Tale of W.H.T. Olive's Adventures in the Klondyke of 1898.* Surrey, B.C.: Timberholme, 1998.

Porter, Cyril R. *Klondike Paradise: Culture in the Wilderness.* Surrey, B.C.: Hancock House, 1997.

Pringle, George C.F. *Tillicums of the Trail: Being Klondike Yarns Told to Canadian Soldiers Overseas by a Sourdough Padre.* Toronto: McClelland and Stewart, 1922.

Pringle, George C.F. *Adventures in Service.* Toronto: McClelland and Stewart, 1929.

Reagan, Ronald. *An American Life.* New York: Simon and Schuster, 1990.

Ross, Victor. *A History of the Canadian Bank of Commerce,* Vol. 2. Toronto: Oxford University Press, 1922.

Seymour, James William Davenport (ed.). *History of the American Field Service in France, "Friends of France," 1914–1917,* 3 vols. Boston: Houghton Mifflin, 1920.

Steele, Sir Samuel Benfield. *Forty Years in Canada: Reminiscences of the Great Northwest, with Some Account of his Service in South Africa.* New York: Dodd, Mead, and London: H. Jenkins, 1915. Reprinted, New York and Toronto: McGraw-Hill Ryerson, 1972.

Stewart, Robert. *Sam Steele: Lion of the Frontier.* Toronto: Doubleday Canada, 1979.

Vancouver Yukoners Association, Sourdough Committee. *History of the Vancouver Yukoners Association.* Vancouver: n.p., 1974.

White, Elmer J. (ed. R.N. De Armond). *"Stroller" White: Tales of a Klondike Newsman.* Vancouver: Mitchell Press, 1969. Reprinted as *Klondike Newsman.* Skagway: Lynn Canal, 1990.

Index